Marketing in action ●

. . . Jon Sutherland and Nigel Gross

Pitman

Pitman Publishing

128 Long Acre, London WC2E 9AN

A Division of Longman Group UK Limited

© J Sutherland and N Gross 1991

First published in Great Britain 1991

British Library Cataloguing in Publication Data
Sutherland, Jon
  Marketing in action.
  1. Marketing
  I. Title II. Gross, Nigel
  658.8

  ISBN 0–273–03459–6

Printed and bound in Great Britain

Dedication to
Vera and John, Audrey and Sid,
we gratefully acknowledge that we are
what they made us!

Contents

Preface

Before we try to say anything worthy about this book, may we first acknowledge our debt to Paula Sutherland, who substantially wrote Chapters 15 and 16 and without whom the book would not be what it is.

We have attempted to make this book as comprehensive as possible. The structure should logically flow and follow through the various marketing considerations, in addition to looking at the business environment in general. Each chapter starts with its own summary 'overview'.

The book contains a wealth of practical and, above all, *real* case studies, rather than using fake companies. We are indebted to all those who have given their approval. The problems set in the case studies should provide a basis for interesting and useful assignments covering all aspects of marketing. Students will also find a very handy set of short, revision-type 'test yourself' questions at the end of each chapter.

The book should prove useful for BTEC National Certificate and Diploma students, as well as for the marketing section of the A level in Business Studies. BTEC Higher students and those studying for either CIM or CAM Certificates will find it invaluable as a basic reader.

Now read on!

Jon Sutherland and Nigel Gross

Acknowledgements

May we thank all those below for their interest and help in this project and for their permission to feature some of their work and thought. We are very much indebted to them all.

Manjeet Kangura, Mike and Stella of Electric Echo, independent design studios

Steve McIvor and Clare Lothian of the British Union Against Vivisection (BUAV)

Sue Rorstad of Poppies UK Ltd

Gary Sankey of Harbour Designs

John Weatherley of Re-An Products

Stephen Webb of European Precision Mouldings

John Jewsbury for hints and tips

Matt Kelly for help and understanding

Diane Canwell for help and support

Tony Nicholson of Border Television

Paul Boughton, Editor of *GamesMaster International* magazine, published by Newsfield

Jane Wightwick of The One That Got Away Ltd

The Citizens Advice Bureau

Liz Hartley for the personal touch and Liz Tarrant for her understanding and patience.

Our thanks also for the use of photographs to Barclaycard, Cadbury's, Elan International, InterCity, Isuzu, the National Westminster Bank and Wimpy International.

1 What is marketing ?

SO WHAT IS MARKETING? . . . .

Marketing is based on the concept that the most important consideration is the customer. This is not a very new idea, neither is it a complex one. For a company to be successful, it must attempt to reach ever more customers in order to generate sales and thus, hopefully, profit. Satisfaction is the key to this, matching the customer's needs with the perceived requirements. Successful companies are those which most closely match customers' needs.

Just what is marketing, exactly? Let us start by ruling out what it is not. Marketing is not advertising: it is far broader than that. It is not sales technique: marketing encompasses far more that just sales. Neither is it product promotion. Marketing is not market research, although market research is a useful tool of marketing. Marketing is all about serving customers and keeping them happy and satisfied. Basically, marketing is a philosophy that sets out to make sure that whatever the organisation produces is what people want to buy. Marketing differs from selling in the sense that selling concentrates on trying to persuade potential customers to buy what the organisation has to sell. Some people would go as far as to say that the aim of marketing is to make the process of selling unnecessary. The argument goes like this:

1 What do people want?
2 How many do they want?
3 How much will they pay?
4 Can we make a profit?
5 If we can, we'll make what they want.

This is the approach of a market-orientated organisation. The organisation is geared to the needs of customers – it notes and acts on quality, reliability and price. In other words, the organisation is customer-orientated and looks to the market to give it vital information about what it should produce.

The alternative view, and sadly a very common one, is the complete opposite to the market-orientated approach. A product-orientated, or sales-orientated organisation would change the five points to the following:

1 We think people need this product.
2 Why don't we produce it?
3 We'll make 10 000 then.
4 We'll charge, what ... £10 each?
5 OK, let's sell them. ...

This approach does not take into consideration what the customer wants. The organisation thinks only in terms of what it makes and what it wants to do. These organisations tend to be very sales-orientated, indeed they have to be. If you have produced something and do not have a buyer, then you have to sell it to someone. Selling aims to persuade people to buy products that the organisation offers. Having said all of this, some organisations are extraordinarily successful at selling and gear their entire business operation to selling, and may even produce products that their sales force feels 'comfortable' trying to sell.

Marketing is many things to many people. Let us try to identify all the main elements of marketing and see how they relate to the way people do see marketing:

1 Marketing aims to focus the attention of the organisation on what its customers expect and need.
2 By defining specific targets, marketing can seek to satisfy the specific wants and demands of customers.
3 Marketing tries to establish the concept of making decisions in relation to the 'user' of the product or service.
4 The concept of customer satisfaction should be seen as going alongside that of business success.
5 It is no good having a marketing idea, if you do not make a plan and do something with the idea to make it work.
6 Marketing needs analysis; it also demands good planning and tight controls.
7 Marketing is, basically, a business philosophy. As such it should encompass all business decisions and considerations.

8 Organisations may very well have to reorganise themselves in order to allow the new marketing approach to work for them.

9 Finally, to summarise, marketing is made up of two things: firstly it is the recognition of the customer as the central consideration; secondly, it involves the adoption of new management techniques.

MARKETING IN HISTORY . . . .

Now for the history lesson! Yes, we know, but don't turn this page over yet! Believe it or not, you might just learn something from this brief (and we promise it is brief) history, which shows how marketing has developed.

Early years – the beginning

The British economy changed beyond recognition in the fifty or so years from the end of the eighteenth to the beginning of the nineteenth century. An agricultural-based economy gave way to the beginnings of an industrial-based one. Britain was the first country to make this momentous move and for many years was the most successful.

Britain was politically stable (unlike France, for example, which had just beheaded most of its royalty and ruling classes). Britain had good coal and iron resources (countries like Holland needed to import the bulk of their raw materials), and people had already begun moving into the towns as the old feudal system had collapsed – France, for example, was still very feudal. (The feudal system was a land-based economic and social system which had tied most people down and prevented them from moving). Added to this was Britain's geographical location – ideally placed to do trade with Europe and the New World – its seafaring tradition and near dominance at sea, and finally Britain's sheer inventiveness which produced many new machines and processes.

For all Britons this was a time of change. Some changes were obviously for the better, but change also brought misery as families were uprooted and fell into poverty with appalling living conditions. Many towns expanded too fast and simply could not cope with the sudden influx of thousands of new workers. Despite all of this, many things happened, very quickly, for the better. Output in almost every aspect of production was up; heavy industry suddenly emerged, producing new products from the abundant iron and coal. Steam was adopted as the main source of energy for these new industries, itself made possible by coal as a primary fuel, and iron which made the machines that the steam powered. Machinery revolutionised the textile industry, transport, communications and even agriculture. Particularly important for marketing were the changes in communications – the coming of paved roads, railways and the penny post.

What were the people like that were behind all these amazing changes? Why did all this happen so suddenly? This period is known by some historians and economists as the Age of Individualism. People's ambitions were limitless – they wanted to be successful, more efficient, create a larger profit. In effect they were driven by self-interest. The argument goes something like this:

1 This new process or invention is designed to make things faster and just as well as if they were being made by hand.
2 If we make more, can we still sell them?
3 Of course – they will be cheaper. More people will be able to afford them.
4 Right, we'll need to retrain the workforce.
5 I suppose we'll have to take on more staff.
6 True, and pay more.
7 We'll generate more money, pass more on to our workforce, and they'll be able to afford to buy more, and there'll be more of them buying, which means that industry will have a bigger market.
8 It all comes back to us, the industrialists, in the end – just think of the profits.
9 And all the benefits to society as a whole.
10 Being a capitalist is just being public spirited, isn't it?

The view above is very similar to that of an extremely influential writer called Adam Smith. Indeed, there is still an Adam Smith Institute which offers social, economic and political ideas in line with Smith's writings. Incidently, a considerable number of the ideas put forward by the Conservative Party since 1979 have been inspired by Adam Smith and his present-day admirers.

TALKING POINT AND ACTIVITY

Can you think of any products that are still produced in the 'old ways' and are handmade or crafted? Do these producers of crafts just make what they can and then hope to sell them?

Research into craft manufacturers and try to find out whether they have a marketing strategy, and how this affects both their rate of production and what they produce.

The big step – industrialisation to the Second World War

Craft industries were based around the producer: the scale, scope and speed of production were determined by the skills of the individual craftsman. With the advent of machines, the production could be split up into simple, repetitive tasks. Each worker on the production line would be able to increase speed and skill by doing one particular task. Greater output was assured. This meant cheaper, more plentiful goods, and profits with which to market them, and buy more.

The old agricultural system had never been very efficient, not even self-sufficient. People relied on bartering their surpluses to obtain those goods that they could not produce themselves. By the end of the eighteenth century a complex, interwoven system had developed that linked production, distribution and finance. It had been a long time in changing but there could be no turning back. The fundamental basis of the modern industrial economy had arrived and Britain was ideally placed to make the most of the changes and lead from the front.

Virtually from the middle of the nineteenth century to the beginning of the twentieth century, Britain was *the* dominant industrial force in the world. The population (in England and Wales) had increased from around $6\frac{1}{2}$ million in the mid-eighteenth century to almost 20 million in the mid-nineteenth century, in less than a hundred years. Britain produced half of the world's iron and cotton, nearly two-thirds of its coal and almost three-quarters of its steel.

This is not the entire picture. Britain's position was based on two other factors. First, despite Britain's fast-growing prosperity, the majority of the population lived in appalling conditions, often unable to enjoy the fruits of their own labour. They could afford the basics of life and very little else. The second major factor was Britain and her Empire. In the colonies Britain found a ready market for her finished goods, along with the raw materials with which to make them in the first place. Production was firmly rooted in Britain, while the market was largely in the countries of the underdeveloped world.

By the end of the nineteenth century Britain had two rivals, coming up fast and threatening to leave Britain behind. The United States and Germany overtook Britain's steel production. Coal and textiles too were being threatened by many rivals. Until the outbreak of the First World War, however, Britain's economy was still expanding. Coal, cotton and steel remained the backbone of the economy,

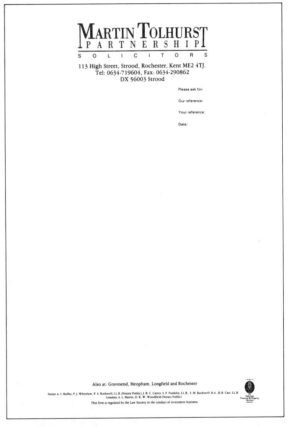

A very good 'before and after' of a redesigned letterhead. This example needs little explanation as the results speak for themselves. Letterheads help to market the organisation's image.

with engineering products, such as railway equipment, selling well. New products had arrived on the scene and promised good returns for the future, for example cars and electrical goods.

The war led to Britain's decline, forcing the disposal of many overseas assets to pay off war debts and, with trade nearly frozen by the actions of the German navy, Britain had been replaced. Japan, amongst others, had stepped in to provide goods to Britain's old markets. There followed The Great Depression of the 1930s, with incredibly high unemployment, and Britain had to face another sad truth. Old markets for Britain's raw materials were fast disappearing as countries began to exploit their own resources.

The slow recovery from the depression was assisted by new industries, such as telephones and radio. Car production was in full swing, and was teaching the workforce the arts of mass production. As the economy lurched towards efficiency, adapting to the new demands placed upon it, another catastrophe hit Britain and the world – the Second World War.

In a war as total and all-consuming as the Second World War, the entire population had to be mobilised to meet the continuous demands for tanks, guns, ships, aircraft and ammunition. Consumer products, which had been the mainstay of the burgeoning British economy, gave way to the materials of war. More of the population was sucked into war production, even in the depressed areas of Britain. There were some benefits in terms of retraining and almost total employment, but the cash to pay for it all had to come from somewhere when the last bullet had been fired and the ink on the surrender document was dry. Inevitably it came from the sale of more of Britain's overseas assets.

The second Industrial Revolution – muscle v micro chip

After the Second World War, Britain was forced into economic change. The Empire was almost gone and the early advantages had been lost. After a period of adjustment and rationing which extended into the 1950s, the British economy was back on the rails. Until the 1970s there was almost total employment, better health provision, and cheaper basic commodities left more disposable income, allowing greater spending on consumer durables (like fridges), cars and furniture. As transport and communications became more efficient and sophisticated, the world became 'a smaller place'. This market accessibility allowed international corporations to flourish and by the 1970s multinational organisations accounted for between 10 per cent and 15 per cent of Britain's total output, and around a fifth of exports.

Production efficiency continued to improve as changes took place in social, economic and political attitudes. New markets were formed as the computer extended people's ability to work out problems, and the new communications systems allowed greater and more flexible contact between people. Television and radio relayed complex messages to their audiences. The technology to build all these machines improved and robots were developed which could cut people out of the process almost completely. In most factories the need to do repetitive and boring tasks was at an end. People had more leisure time. Employment patterns and working conditions were changed utterly by the new industrial methods.

Britain now needed to find new markets for her products. The old Empire and new Commonwealth which replaced it had been the traditional markets. These markets were now in serious decline. Britain began to look, rather belatedly, at Europe and at the United States. Rather than exporting 'finished goods' and importing raw materials, as had been done in the past, Britain now exchanged its 'finished goods' for those of another country.

Mass production is one thing, but no use on its own. Without mass consumption there is no market for the mass-produced goods. The mass consumption relies on consumers having the wherewithal to purchase what is on offer. If a country has a head-start, like Britain had, it can export mass-produced goods and sell them at a good profit. After all, at one time Britain had all the cards in selling in the Empire and Commonwealth: the English language was almost universal; things were sold in pounds, shillings and pence like the English money; they were weighed in English pounds and ounces; and always the countries came under British law or, at worst, the military occupation.

What then happens when the position is lost? How does one country improve its position relative to another? Answer: it sells more. But is that the real answer? In other words, do you think that if you make more of something than anyone else then it automatically means you will sell more? No, of course not. Does it mean that if you make something you will be able to sell it? No. You cannot just advertise or promote and so sell without any problem. The two things do not go together.

Take Sir Clive Sinclair as an example. His ability to produce new and innovative products is amazing, and his vision of the future relies on technology taking the grind out of life. His computers have sold in their millions. So why did he fail? Why was he forced to sell his company after two spectacular failures? The QL (Quantum Leap) Computer and the Sinclair C5 (a plastic, battery-charged, one-seater vehicle), although very advanced, were not what the market wanted. They both failed, and so helped to bring about the fall of Sir Clive.

TALKING POINT

Do you think that certain countries are better at supporting their manufacturers than others? Most countries have organisations that assist in the promotion of their country's products. How would you find out about such an organisation? Where would you go to get the information?

Technology itself has brought about great increases in risk. More money has to be invested simply to get something on to the market. Whilst the research and development is being done, changes in taste, attitude and needs are happening. The consumer has become far more discerning and, above all, now has much greater choice. Success in the market depends very much on having the best product and not on 'being British'. That concept does not have much influence any more.

So how do manufacturers known what to make? How can they gear their mass-production facilities to achieve the best results? Market research, which we will look at in greater detail later, is a vital key in deciding the direction an organisation should take before it initiates mass production. Risk reduction is the central core to this way of thinking. The marketing approach is a difficult concept for many organisations to fathom, but in the end it is their only means to guarantee survival in this highly competitive and cut-throat world.

TEST YOURSELF

1 Give your own definition of marketing.

2 What is the difference between marketing-orientated and sales-orientated approaches to business?

3 Indicate at least five main elements of marketing.

4 Who was Adam Smith and what influence does he still wield, long after his death?

5 How did people market basic goods made by craftsmen?

6 How did war production change the way in which products were marketed after the war was over?

7 What brought about Britain's decline as an industrial force in the world, and why?

8 List some of the main changes that have made the concept of 'British made' no longer a major consideration in the buyer's choice of product.

9 How does marketing relate to risk reduction?

10 Briefly chart the changes in production over the years since the age of the craftsman and look at the gradual change in marketing over those years.

A WORKING
CASE STUDY

Softix

Softix is a company which specialises in database software.

Designing letterheads is one of the most frequent jobs encountered when it comes to marketing, since even the smallest of companies nearly always wants its own unique letterheading. It is also a field where the client often has very strong views on what is required.

The letterheads reproduced are for a small and relatively young company, and were designed to make them appear larger and perhaps a little more established than they actually were. Getting this across is very important for fledgling companies, as you can imagine!

Activities and tasks

1 What do you think of the image that has been created for Softix?

2 What do you think their logo conveys?

3 Your next task is to turn the Softix problem on its head. Imagine a massive international company has decided to set up a subsidiary company to sell upmarket, luxury cars. It wants to portray an image of a small, craftsman-type enterprise whilst still letting people know that the firm is part of a much larger group. The first thing required is the letterhead. Budget is no problem, so get on with it!

4 Imagine you have your own small business. Design your logo and letterhead. Write down what image or message you want to put over with your design, and then ask what other people in your group think of it.

FURTHER READING

Wealth of Nations, Adam Smith, Rawdon House
Introducing Marketing, Christopher, McDonald and Wills, Pan
Principles of Marketing, P Kotler, Prentice-Hall

2 The market itself

UNDERSTANDING THE WORLD . . . . .

The world is an ever-changing place. Products and their marketing methods must change, too, if producers are to survive. Except in times of crisis, organisations adapt gradually to a succession of events which have an influence on them. These events fall into four main categories: political, economic, social and technological (known as PEST):

Political effects Such as changes in government, legislative change, pressure from interest groups and the implementation of government policy.

Economic effects Such as changes in the interest rate, inflation, balance of trade, value of the pound and pressure from external markets.

Social effects Such as the changes in the proportion of age bands, e.g. the aging population, greater employment or unemployment, changes in leisure pursuits and changes in taste or buying habits.

Technological effects Such as new computer software and hardware, new manufacturing techniques and improved production through improved machinery.

The political system of a country very largely determines the business climate. The differences between Western Europe and Eastern Europe are much less marked than they used to be. However, comparisons between Western Europe and much of the third world show more favourable conditions in the former. Not only does an organisation have to be aware of what is going on within itself; it must also keep a close eye on the political environment and attempt to forecast any political changes which may affect its business.

The government's attitude can be a fundamental factor in the business commu-

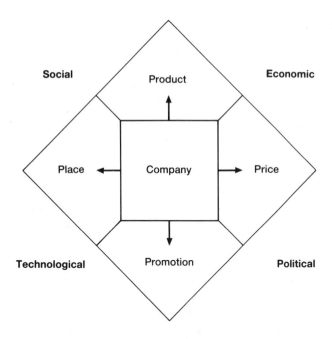

Marketing mix and the environment.

nity's success. Governments who reduce taxation, relax controls and offer other benefits to the business community can be seen as having a favourable attitude to business.

Some countries protect their own industries by making it difficult for other countries to trade there. The Japanese have been accused of this and, while they do not prevent foreign companies from trading in Japan, they do not exactly make it easy. Political instability is another problem to contend with. Some countries will abruptly change regime or policy, playing havoc with business connections and deals.

Law and changes in law can also affect business. Opportunities or constraints may arise, affecting the business environment to a greater or lesser extent. On the constraints side, for example, cigarette manufacturers cannot advertise as freely as they used to do; Sunday trading laws have made it difficult for certain retailers to open on that day; and legislation necessitated the fitting of car seat belts to all new cars.

In the consumer protection field, laws state the liability of a company in relation to its products. Companies must also be aware of the differences in law from country to country. Consumer protection is not the only area of law where companies must keep abreast of changes and differences. One of the positive benefits of the single European market (the European Community) is that many of these different laws will be swept aside and replaced with a single set of regulations.

Many pressure groups constantly work to influence the government to create tougher laws controlling businesses. On the ecological side, groups attempt to convince the government to legislate against businesses which endanger the planet: this may cover anything from petrol fumes to aerosols and nuclear power. An aware organisation should monitor relevant pressure groups as well as proposed government legislation to be well placed and ready for any change. In fact, some organisations form their own pressure groups to protect their interests.

The economic strengths and weaknesses of a country are directly linked to the political stance and attitudes of its government. Analysing the potential future of a particular market must include a number of obvious, and not so obvious, economic factors. It is increasingly more important for a researcher to think about world trends in economic fortunes, rather than just the economic factors that relate to the country with which their organisation is particularly concerned.

A good start is to have a look at the overall wealth of a country: in other words, how big is the economy and is it growing or not? There are two key figures to consider. The first is the country's gross domestic product (GDP), which tells you the value of the goods and services that are produced within the country. The other is the gross national product (GNP), which is a broader category covering both the GDP and all of the country's overseas earnings. Simple conclusions may be drawn from these two figures.

You would expect that the bigger these two figures are, the more chance you would have to thrive in that economy, but not necessarily so. The main factor that neither of these figures takes into consideration is the population of the country. A high GNP in a highly populated country could mean that individually the people living there are not that well off. An example of this would be India, which has a high GNP but a population so large that it makes the country not very rich in real terms. On the other side of the coin there are countries with a modest GNP but which have good overall levels of wealth, such as the small populations of the oil-rich states in the Middle East.

What we are doing then is calculating a very crude figure. Roughly speaking, we are dividing the GNP by the population and arriving at a 'per capita' (per head) income for each individual. At the top of the standard-of-living chart are the Middle Eastern oil states with a per capita income in excess of £10 000 per year; Europe comes in at about £5000 per year; and some third world countries (like Ethiopia and Sudan) with as little as £50 per year.

There are several other major indicators on the economic front that look at the overall prosperity of the country. The first is the growth rate of the economy, which means how much is the GNP increasing (or for that matter decreasing) from year to year. Great Britain, for example, has a modest rate of growth (usually around 3–5 per cent), whereas other countries have huge growth rates (particularly developing countries).

The next two indicators are closely linked. They are the purchasing power of the individuals in the country, and the country's inflation rate. The latter affects the former since inflation erodes the strength of purchasing power in real terms. Purchasing power itself is of vital concern. The amount of money spent by an average member of the market at which the product or service is aimed will largely determine the success of that product or service. Purchasing power can be affected by a whole series of factors:

1 **Wage levels**   Comparing these to price levels you can roughly figure out what the average person has in his or her pocket.

2 **Price levels**   If prices are high relative to wage levels, then products and services are expensive and there will be greater competition for the money that is available to spend. If prices are low relative to wages, then there is more scope for entering the market and successfully seizing a portion of it.

3 **Taxation**   Again this affects the money available to the potential purchaser. In highly taxed countries (such as Great Britain) the level of purchasing power is diminished and in lower-taxed countries (like the United States) the tax factor is not such a great drain on people's purchasing power.

TALKING POINT AND ACTIVITY

What factors can cause inflation? Try to find out what sort of reasons have caused inflation. Which countries are more prone to high inflation than others?

Have a look at Germany in the 1920s and see how high inflation was then and what caused it.

4 **Inflation**   Inflation directly erodes the purchasing power by driving up prices in relation to the increases elsewhere in the economy. Countries all suffer to a greater or lesser extent from inflation. In the worst extremes inflation is a continual spiral which drives up prices, then wages to compensate for the increases in prices, then prices go up again to pay for the increases in wages, and so on. A great many things can trigger off an inflation spiral and they may not necessarily be the fault of the country's government.

Germany in the 1920s had arguably the worst rate of inflation in modern times. So bad was the rate that workers insisted on being paid in cash hourly! Here is a rough guide to the falling German mark (DM) over the early part of the 1920s:

July 1918	£1	=	20DM
January 1919	£1	=	43DM
January 1920	£1	=	314DM
January 1921	£1	=	315DM
September 1921	£1	=	500DM

October 1921	£1	=	720DM
November 1921	£1	=	1200DM
January 1922	£1	=	32000DM
January 1923	£1	=	112000DM
February 1923	£1	=	220000DM
June 1923	£1	=	622000DM
August 1923	£1	=	15000000DM
September 1923	£1	=	22000000DM
October 1923	£1	=	183000000000DM

When the mark reached its bottom value, a loaf of bread was a staggering 200 000 million DM! When Germany revalued the mark the exchange rate was one new DM to a trillion old marks.

TALKING POINT AND ACTIVITY

Can you identify at least ten countries with 'more than acceptable or manageable' levels of inflation?

We have talked about purchasing power in its most general terms. In reality, though, purchasing power is a little more complex than this. How do we determine what the purchasing power of an individual actually is? After all, what someone has to spend is what they earn, isn't it? No. Then it's what they've got left after tax? No, not quite. How about what they've got left after they've paid their bills?

The money which people have left after paying tax and national insurance (and now, of course, community charge) is known as disposable income. But, as we have seen, this does not tell us what people really have to spend. It is what is known as the discretionary income in which we are particularly interested, and so is everyone that is trying to sell somebody something! This discretionary income is what is left after you have paid all your bills, such as gas, electricity, telephone, rent or mortgage, food and clothing. Deducting the costs of all these basic requirements leaves the discretionary income – if there's any left, of course! This is a much better indicator of the true purchasing power of an individual or family.

So far we've talked mainly about what an average person has in terms of purchasing power, but is there such a thing as Mr, Mrs or Ms Average? Averages hide a multitude of different incomes. What the market analyst is interested in finding out is the distribution of that wealth. After all, you could have a hundred people with an income of £20 000 and a thousand with an income of £10 000. The first thousand earn a total of £2m, the other thousand earn £10m. That gives an average per capita of £10 909. This average is not that useful, particularly since the target market may be those with an income of over £15 000 per year.

Britain has more poorer people than rich ones, which brings the national average down. Sweden, for example, has a much more evenly spread distribution of income, making the average more useful. Other countries, like Nigeria, have a low average but a small, rich minority who are avid consumers of expensive products. A closer look, therefore, at the distribution is always worth while as it may reveal very interesting and useful information that is hidden in the averaging process.

TALKING POINT AND
ACTIVITY

Can you think of anything that is
more commonly bought in the UK
than in other similar countries in
Europe? Here's one for free – try to
find out the reasons for it: the British
buy and rent more videos than any
other country in Europe. Why?

Consumption patterns differ from country to country. The demand for various things often depends on the cultural make-up or background of the country itself. You cannot automatically assume just because people have a higher level of discretionary income that it will automatically mean they will spend more on luxury goods. Tradition and habits play a large part in the relative consumption patterns and sometimes are hard to identify.

You may have come across the word 'demography' in other subjects, and in marketing, too, it can play an important role. Demography is the study of population. It looks at all the factors that determine how many people there are, how fast they are growing in number, where they are, how old they are and how the structure of families changes over the years.

The size of the population is a good rough guide to the potential size of the market but, since a lot of products and services are only aimed at a portion of the population, this is not as useful as it may first appear. Population growth, however, is more important. A growing population infers a growing market, but this too is rather crude. Population distribution can effect the potential profitability of a market. The more densely populated a country is, with people geographically close to each other, the cheaper it is to get to them. The more spread out they are, the more expensive it is.

TALKING POINT

It is now an accepted fact that with
the lower birth rate there will be a
greater need to find workers from
'other' areas of the population. The
major source of 'new' workers is
from the female population.

Greater opportunities are now
available to women workers and in
certain fields the retired members of
society are being coaxed back into
employment. What do you think are
the marketing consequences of
these changes?

You will often hear the phrase 'we are living in an ageing society'. This refers, of course, to the fact that people are living longer, at the same time as there is a fall in the birth rate which would have brought new potential customers into the population. Smaller numbers of the young decrease demand for products in the youth market and greater numbers of the older members of society bring about a greater demand for goods and services for the elderly.

Looking at the family itself, the traditional view of the man at work and the women at home with the children is largely a thing of the past. With lower birth rates and the demand for jobs for women, tremendous changes have occurred which have more to do with changing attitudes than population growth.

There are a number of other considerations that are less measurable than population figures and these centre around the buying habits of the customer. Each individual is brought up with a series of values, traits and tastes which are often learnt from either parents or from school. It is likely that if a product or service is offered that does not take these basic values into consideration then it will inevitably fail. Trends are a facet of these values. Certain trends come and go; sometimes certain products are fashionable and then they fade away. Design and style can be equally as important. Even colour has its effect on the level of purchasing.

Technology constantly changes the market. Countless new inventions have revolutionised society. You only need to look at the last few years to find new products that no one just a decade or so before could have imagined would exist or find a market. Going back even further, there are such basics as electricity, television or plastic products which became integral parts of our lives in the twentieth century alone.

New technological breakthroughs open up the market further and further every day. An organisation that cannot respond quickly enough to these changes will find itself left behind and at a severe disadvantage. Manufacturing relies increasingly on automated processes; even stock control is moving into the twenty-first century with the introduction of the Electronic Point Of Sale (EPOS) system. This has required the printing on to every product of bar codes which hold the price and description of the product. When the bar code is read, the system notes the sale and reduces the stock level by one, and from these sales figures a reorder is generated. New materials have also become part of the changing range of products, for example carbon fibres (fibreglass), used in many new products and processes.

A slightly harder concept is that of replacement, or obsolescence. Slide rules are rarely used in class or industry these days – why use the technology of the past when you can use a calculator? Within each specific type of product, like recorders for example, there is a definite demand. The demand for reel-to-reel tape recorders was severely curtailed with the invention of the cassette tape. The cassette tape is about to be supplanted itself by the introduction of the DAK tape, and the compact disc is also taking over many of its markets. No doubt there is already, on the drawing board, the next stage of development that will replace them.

UNDERSTANDING THE MARKET . . . .

A purchase means that someone has bought something. Obvious really, but we have to look at this simple statement in rather more detail. A good start is to examine the different types of product purchases and how they satisfy particular demands.

Types of product

Non-durable   The most common sort of purchase is the non-durable type. This category includes food and all the other goods that can be used up quickly.
Durable   The durable types of goods cover all the other sorts of products that are in use for some time, for example furniture or electrical goods.
Services   The third main category is services. These services include public

transport, education and all sorts of professional advice like consulting a solicitor or doctor, hairdressing, etc.

Goods themselves need more detail. They fall into three main categories:

1 **Convenience goods** are those that are bought on a regular basis. They include most types of food, but also include anything that is a spur-of-the-moment purchase. They are products which are bought with little planning or forethought.

2 **Considered purchases** are those on which people take a little longer to decide before parting with their money. Examples would be clothes, holidays or luxury food items.

3 **Special purchases** are those which people really take some time to buy. They want to have in depth knowledge of the product and to compare competing products. They will tend to buy the best that they can afford rather than search for value for money. These sorts of goods include things like cameras, furniture and housing.

TALKING POINT AND ACTIVITY

Think about the sorts of things you buy. Then try to categorise them into the three main areas outlined above. Where do you think the bulk of your purchases are? What sort of percentage would you place on your purchases in each of the three categories?

Competition

What then of competition? There are precious few areas of business activity that have no competition. Some of the competition that an organisation must face is direct; some is indirect. Almost every product or service that a consumer could possibly need is available from a number of different suppliers.

Competition concerns the various ways in which a particular demand may be satisfied. Consider a person looking for something to cook food with. He or she may purchase a gas oven or an electric oven, a microwave or a solid fuel cooker, or even a barbeque! These are all *direct* competitors. An example of an *indirect* competitor would be a restaurant or take-away, which would satisfy the purchaser's need to some extent only.

TALKING POINT AND ACTIVITY

Identify some other examples of indirect competition. How can you best compete against indirect competition?

There is one other form of competitor which is even harder to fight against. We have already discovered that purchasing power is limited and that businesses must compete for what funds are left available after the necessities of life have been paid for. What happens when someone is looking for a new car and decides to buy a new three-piece suite with the money instead, or perhaps spends it on a holiday abroad? This is known as *competing needs* and we must therefore extend our definition of competition to anything that might induce the prospective buyer to spend money on something other than the product you are trying to sell.

UNDERSTANDING THE BUYER . . . .

If marketing is all about meeting the needs of buyers, then we need to know a lot more about customers, both individuals and organisations. The two markets have different characteristics and we shall have to look at them separately.

The individual purchaser

Let's ask some questions and then try to answer them:

1 **Who buys the product or service?** This question is answered once we have segmented the market and exactly identified our 'ideal' sort of customer. By obtaining this knowledge we can then tell precisely where to find these people and match the product or service as closely as possible to their needs.
2 **What sort of products or services do they buy at present?** This question follows on from the first very closely. Having discovered who buys, we need to know their present buying habits. What other products or services do they consume and is this knowledge useful in persuading them to buy our product or service?
3 **Where do they buy the product or service?** Simply speaking, this is the place where the product is purchased. Is it, for example, bought in a supermarket, a corner shop, at a specialist stockist, a petrol station, through a mail order catalogue or by telephone?
4 **When do they buy the product or service?** Is there a pattern in their purchases? Is the product bought daily, like a newspaper, or is it weekly, like the weekly supermarket visit? Some products and services are only bought very infrequently, like Christmas trees or fireworks.
5 **How often do they buy the product or service?** This is a question of frequency. Does the buyer only buy infrequently, like a car, or quite frequently, as with a monthly magazine? If the business knows this, it can gear its production to fulfilling the demand a lot more closely.
6 **How loyal are they in their purchasing?** This looks at the reliability of people in staying with one product, which is also known as brand loyalty. Certain products rely on loyalty and indeed have strong levels of loyalty. Competitors will attempt to undermine this loyalty by offering incentives to switch brands.

TALKING POINT AND ACTIVITY

Can you identify some examples of 'brand loyalty'? What named brand products do you always buy? Why?

Even though we have looked at these basic characteristics, we still need to answer some other fundamental questions. What makes someone buy something? It is a difficult question, so let's start by stating the obvious: they think that they need it. Fine, but what prompts that feeling that you need something?

The feeling of need can be aroused by a number of different factors. Some are straightforward, like the need to buy food because we get hungry and have to consume food to satisfy that hunger. Other

Washburn put the rock back in the Wall.

WASHBURN

Roger Waters & Friends "The Wall" Concert July 1990

Washburn (UK) Limited Amer Way, Letchworth, Hertfordshire, England, SG6 1UG **WASHBURN**

A magazine advertisement that is a good example of a manufacturer advertising the fact that someone famous uses its product. These are often linked to sponsorship deals and form the cornerstone of many companies' marketing strategies. This is particularly true in the music industry, from which this example is drawn.

feelings of need are slightly more tricky and the key to being a successful business is to stimulate that very essential feeling of need in people. Make them want what you have got! A successful business also knows exactly how to pander to these needs and satisfy the customer, so that next time the customer gets that feeling of need they come back again.

Once you have identified that you need something, what do you do about it? Hunger is easy to satisfy (in most countries) – you just need to find something to eat. But what about more complex needs? The first thing that comes into play is the memory. You try to remember what you did the last time that you felt that need. If you can't remember, you might ask a friend; you might turn to some reference source such as the *Yellow Pages*; you might consult a magazine that has relevant information in it; or go to the local shops to try to find it.

Now that you have discovered the various ways of satisfying your need, you have to weigh up the alternatives. Your cultural values might come into play here, or perhaps your prejudices. Some people will never buy foreign cars; others will not buy the produce of particular countries, or farming systems. In most cases it is an objective decision that determines ultimate choice. Weighing up the pros and cons in making your choice can be a difficult and complex task, and most people make a straightforward, almost automatic decision without such questioning. Businesses need to be aware of the decision-making process and help the customer arrive at the right decision as far as the business is concerned and therefore buy their product.

TALKING POINT

Can you think of incentives that are offered to convince you to make a decision to buy something? Are you won over by these incentives? Do you think that they actually work?

Having decided what to buy, some factors can still stop you. We are all prone to being 'put off' a purchase. Take, for example, that album you really like, but everyone else you know thinks the performer is 'rubbish'. What about that pair of trainers you really fancy, but the trouble is they are the 'wrong' make! What we are talking about is the difference between intention to buy and buying itself. We've probably all really wanted something in life (goods-wise) and then that little problem of cash has got in the way. Luxuries, such as new cars or stereo systems, are most likely to be affected in this way. The successful business must shorten this period of wavering as much as possible and make sure that the prospective purchaser hands over the payment for the purchase as quickly as possible. This often means that incentives are offered to speed up the decision-making and win that sale.

TALKING POINT

Can you think of a company or product that takes its image very seriously and relies heavily on its reputation?

Satisfying buyers will pay huge dividends. If the buyers are pleased with a business's product then they are more likely to buy the same product again. They are also more likely to recommend it to others, and they are more likely to be a fertile source of ideas for improvements and changes in the future. Knowledge of a brand name and, most importantly, knowledge that the product or service is worth while and reliable, gives a loud and clear signal to other potential customers.

The organisation as purchaser

Now that we have looked at the various buying considerations of the individual, let us turn our attention to how organisations buy and look at their buying habits. We will start with the same questions that we posed for individuals:

1 **Who buys the product or service?** This is as complicated as knowing about individuals. The seller of the product or service needs to know as much as possible about the buyer. What size is the organisation? What is its business? Distributor? Retailer? Manufacturer? Service industry? Segmentation in this market is as vital as segmenting consumer markets. Who makes the decisions? Is it an individual or a group of people? Is there one buyer? What about the input of various managers and decision-makers?

We can identify various types of people that are involved in the buying process within an organisation. These range from the person who first brings up the idea that the purchase is necessary through to the decision-maker who approves the purchase. We should not forget all the other people who, to a greater or lesser extent, will also be involved. There are often technical considerations to be thought about, such as whether a machine will be compatible with existing equipment; installation and training costs. There are also other considerations such as delivery time; other suppliers; will they provide a discount; have they supplied the organisation before? The list is endless and the provider of the product or service must be able to answer questions from any of these quarters.

2 **What products or services do they buy?** Broadly speaking, the types of purchases fall into three main categories. Firstly there are basic raw materials and parts; secondly there is what is known as capital equipment. This includes machinery and other accessories which the organisation keeps for some time. Thirdly there are the regular supplies and services, like paper or office supplies, but which may include also services such as those of auditors or solicitors.

TALKING POINT AND ACTIVITY

How important is after-sales service? How do companies stress the support they offer their buyers? Ask this question both for products for the individual consumer and for those for the organisation.

3 **How do they buy these products or services?** This process is rather like that for individual consumers. Starting with the recognition that something is needed, it moves on to determining what exactly is required of the product or service (this may need a specialist to determine what specifications should be considered). The next stage is the inevitable search for suppliers of the product or service, followed by an evaluation of them and what they are offering. The next phase may differ greatly from that of consumer purchasing. The buying organisation now negotiates with the selling organisation as to the exact conditions of sale. This may include obvious things, such as price and payment terms, and more technical guarantees that the product or service will perform in a particular way. Finally, and of vital importance, is the attitude of the seller to the buying organisation and performance in after-sales service, etc. This is likely to trigger further purchases as surely as price.

TEST YOURSELF

1 Name a country that puts up a protective barrier to prevent foreign products penetrating their home market too deeply.

2 How can law affect business?

3 What is the difference between GNP and GDP?

4 What is the per capita income of an average European?

5 List some factors which affect market growth.

6 What is purchasing power?

7 Name at least three countries with small, rich populations and three with large, poor populations.

8 What is demography?

9 What is EPOS?

10 Into what categories do 'goods' fall neatly?

11 What questions do you need to ask about your buyers?

12 What is brand loyalty?

13 List at least ten luxury goods.

14 Name the three basic types of purchases.

15 If determining that someone needs something is the first part of how people buy a product, what are the following stages?

A WORKING CASE STUDY

Dorothy Perkins

The illustration shown comes from a recent point-of-sale display used by Dorothy Perkins to market their latest 'back to school' range.

Dorothy Perkins is a national group of fashion retailers for women, catering for the younger age groups in the mass market range. This is a highly-competitive and image-conscious market. The advertisement is interesting from a marketing point of view – seeking to create an image that would appeal both to the parent and to the child, who will almost certainly be looking for different qualities in the product.

Like posters, this is an area of marketing that relies very heavily on image alone to make a sale.

The imagery in our example should be self-evident, with the rather drab images of the pre-sale contrasting with the happy, high energy imagery after the purchase. The technique is a little basic, to say the least. However, by careful use of illustrations, the method can be wheeled out successfully year after year.

Activities and tasks

1 What we want you to do is produce something similar that will have equal appeal to both the child and her mother. If you succeed, there's probably a glowing career waiting for you; if you don't, then you'll have appreciated yet another problem encountered in marketing: who to pitch at when the person making the purchase isn't the person paying for it!

2 Think of other examples of this problem. What does the organisation do to attract the user and convince the purchaser to buy?

FURTHER READING

Basic Marketing, Principles and Practice, Tom Cannon, Holt, Rinehardt and Winston
Essentials of Marketing, Lancaster and Massingham, McGraw Hill

3 Market segmentation and targeting

CHOOSING A MARKET . . . .

The need to identify and attempt to satisfy the needs of specific target markets is central to the concept of marketing. To do it efficiently is important; to do it more efficiently than your competitors can be vital. Relating the product or service to the needs of the marketplace means that your approach is '*market-orientated*'. In order to do this successfully you must undertake market research and try to forecast your sales. Alternatively, your approach could be '*product-orientated*': in other words, you look at the market as being made up of identical, but potential purchasers of your product.

The single most important factor to have had an effect on marketing, certainly in recent times, is the realisation that markets are made up of very different sub-groups or sub-markets. As identifying these sub-markets has become more refined, the elements of strategy and marketing have been honed specifically to them. Most products are designed for a particular market and not the general public as a whole. Not surprisingly, businesses are interested in the most commercially attractive parts of a market. This is known as *target marketing*. It relies strongly on good research and is, in itself, the logical conclusion of research work.

WHAT IS A MARKET . . . .

This is very difficult to define. Broadly speaking, there are three ways of describing a market. Firstly, it can be the physical (geographical) place where goods or services are sold; for example, Malaya is a market. Secondly, a market is also the actual demand for a specific product or service. Thirdly, it can be the set of conditions which determines the price of a product or service. For example, you could say that the market for personal stereos is £x million per year.

The most commonly accepted definition of a market identifies a group of people with needs, what their purchasing power is and what their buying behaviour is. A further refinement is that this market is not just existing customers but should include those who are potential customers.

TARGET MARKETING . . . .

To target a market, there are three stages which have to be carried out systematically, and we will look at these in some detail:

1 Market segmentation
2 Selection and evaluation of a market segment
3 Product positioning

MARKET SEGMENTATION . . . .

As specialised market segments have developed and been identified, there has been a growth in the number of organisations offering goods and services which are much more closely related to the customer.

It is obvious to say that certain types of goods and services have always been purchased by certain parts of the population and not by others. Initially segmentation was very crude: rich or poor; fashionable or utilitarian; etc. Common sense was the key rather than scientific segmentation. As competition became more fierce in almost every market, businesses paid more attention to their markets.

Having identified a specific market, certain features of that market will be similar to each other, but not identical. As a result it is highly unlikely that one product will be ideal for everyone in that market. Take a look at the products on any supermarket shelf. Just choose one, say the soap. Each soap has its own distinctive qualities, from simple ones such as price to subtle aromas and the creaminess of the lather. More recently, other considerations and approaches have been developed: liquid soap (convenient and non-messy); perfume-free (for sensitive skins); and environmentally friendly (fully bio-degradable). A wealth of different products for different people, but take a look at the labels on the packets and you will certainly see that less than a dozen manufacturers are offering the majority of these soap products. They have identified their market, broken it down and refined their segmentation, and now cater successfully for sub-groups within the market.

DEREHAM
H   O   U   S   E

A unique development of four luxury flats by
ALAN WARD ASSOCIATES in association with
PROPERTY LENDING TRUST PLC.

 FEATURES

1. Entry Phone Communication/ Security System.
2. Windows/Doors fitted with Security Locks.
3. Independent T.V. and Telephone facilities.
4. Fully Automatic Gas Central Heating.
5. Period Architectural features retained.
6. Fire hazard alarms incorporated.
7. Period fire surround with coal gas fire effect.
8. Fitted Kitchens/bathrooms to clients choice if required.
9. Exterior lighting provided.
10. Fully restored exterior period facade and pavement area featured.

 COMMEMORATIVE PLAQUE

A commemorative plaque will be positioned on the exterior building.

Dereham House
Circa 1850
Restored 1989

The first occupants will have his/her name engraved in the brickwork facade.

....
Occupied this Building
1989

 **SALES**

Developers
A development by Alan Ward Associates in conjunction with Property Lending Trust PLC.

Design
H. W. Sankey, Burnham Market, Kings Lynn, Norfolk.

Builders
F. W. Rushbrooke, Norwich, Norfolk.

Sales Agents
Key Property Centre Ltd., 20 High Street, Watton, Thetford, Norfolk. Tel: 0953-881761/884075.

Mortgages
Instant mortgage/insurance services available

A typical sales brochure for an upmarket property development. As well as being informative, the brochure also makes great play on the historic aspect of the development, which the builder correctly perceived to be a major selling point.

The recurring logo theme has also been used well here.

WHERE DO YOU START? . . . .

In order to identify your target market segment, you need to look at a number of variables. The following six variables are known as *demographic factors* and are the basis of market segmentation:

1 Age
2 Sex
3 Family size and life cycle
4 Social class
5 Neighbourhood
6 Education

Then there are four more specialised variables:

7 Benefit segmentation
8 Usage segmentation
9 Loyalty
10 Geographical and cultural segmentation

Each of these variables needs further explanation:

1 Age strongly affects the purchasing behaviour of individuals. In the younger age groups (18–24 for example) fashion, records, take-aways, magazines and newspapers tend to be the big areas of purchasing. This is known as the youth market and is a specific target for certain products. Age is one of the most important considerations, even if it is the easiest to research.

2 Sex is again a straightforward variable to measure, but is, in many cases, crucial. Certain products and services are specifically female (such as women's clothes and cosmetics). Either products do not cater in particular for one sex or another or they are quite clearly slanted in their advertising towards one sex or another. Some drink brands are definitely aimed at males (Holsten and Courage) and others at women (Taboo and Mirage). Even cars may be labelled 'women's cars' and their advertising reflects this.

3 Family size is a straight categorisation of 1–2 members, 3–4 members and 5+ members. The size of the family simply and most decisively determines the size of the pack bought and the frequency of purchase. The family life cycle defines the stage which the typical family has reached and directly reflects their demand for products and their consumption rate. The stages are as follows:

a Young and single
b Young couple with no children
c Young couple, youngest child under 6
d Young couple, youngest child 6 or over
e Older couple with children 18+ at home
f Older couple with no children at home
g Older and single

There are some rather crude assumptions here, as well as the basic assumption that the family unit is still the best social unit to measure. This categorisation may need refinement and eventual replacement.

4 Social class is in fact a mixture of both social class and income. Again, it is a rather crude classification based on the 'head' of the household, and it does not therefore take any account of a second wage earner (in other words married women are ignored for the most part). This socio-economic classification was established by the National Readership Survey:

A Higher managerial, administrative or professional
B Intermediate managerial, administrative or professional
C1 Supervisory, clerical, junior administrative or professional
C2 Skilled manual workers
D Semi-skilled and unskilled manual workers
E State pensioners, widows, casual and lowest grade earners

Although this categorisation has been criticised, it is still extremely useful, despite the fact that some of the boundaries between the categories are a little blurred these days.

5 Neighbourhood classification is a relatively new measure of segmentation. The ACORN system (meaning A Classification of Residential Neighbourhoods) identifies some 38 different types of residential neighbourhood according to their demographic, housing and socio-economic characteristics. The classification is based on the Census of Population in Great Britain:

A1 Agricultural villages
A2 Areas of farms and smallholdings
B3 Cheap modern private housing
B4 Recent private housing, young families
B5 Modern private housing, older families
B6 New detached houses, young families
B7 Military bases
C8 Mixed owner-occupied and council estates
C9 Small town centres and flats above shops
C10 Villages with non-farm employment
C11 Older private housing, skilled workers
D12 Unimproved terraces with old people
D13 Pre-1914 terraces, low income families
D14 Tenement flats lacking amenities
E15 Council estates with well-off older workers
E16 Recent council estates
E17 Council estates, well-off young workers
E18 Small council houses, often in Scotland
F19 Low-rise estates in industrial towns
F20 Inter-war council estates
F21 Council housing for the elderly
G22 New council estates in industrial towns

G23 Overspill estates, high unemployment
G24 Council estates with overcrowding
G25 Council estates with worst poverty
H26 Multi-occupied terraces
H27 Owner-occupied terraces, Asians
H28 Multi-let housing with Afro-Caribbeans
H29 Better off multi-ethnic areas
I30 High status areas, few children
I31 Multi-let big old houses and flats
I32 Furnished flats, mostly single people
I33 Inter-war semis, white collar workers
I34 Spacious inter-war semis, big gardens
I35 Villages with wealthy older commuters
I36 Detached houses, exclusive suburbs
I37 Private houses, well-off elderly
I38 Private flats with single pensioners
I39 Unclassified

The classification breaks the country down into units of 150 dwellings, with the predominant type being the classification that is adopted for that unit. There are certainly some properties and occupants that do not fit into any of the above categories.

The largest users of this system are the direct mail companies; financial institutions; gas and electricity companies; TV rental, credit cards and travel companies; companies holding guarantees for goods; manufacturers with addresses from promotions; charities and political parties.

The ACORN system has further proved to be of use in siting stores and in poster site locations. In general terms it is useful when trying to target without wasting a vast percentage of your mail shot, by having already eliminated areas that are unlikely to be interested in your product or service.

6 Education is a rather less useful form of classification than it has been in the past. In effect, it notes the purchaser's level of formal education, making the assumption that those with a higher level of formal education are more likely to consume wine, recordings of classical music or gourmet food, for example, than those with a 'lower' level of education. On the whole, this is far too crude a measurement. A more useful element is the link with newspaper readership, TV viewing and job types. As a rule (although still a generalisation), better educated people are more likely to read newspapers such as *The Times*, *The Guardian* or *The Daily Telegraph*. They are more likely to watch the more 'arty', 'informative' or 'worthy' commercial TV programmes, such as the *South Bank Show*. Also, with better education usually comes a better job, another target area for the company wishing to reach a specific target.

The Terminal Education Age (TEA) classification system is all but redundant. It works on the basis of noting a person's age on leaving full-time education. With the changes in education over the past few years, and increasing emphasis on part-time study and the opportunities this offers, the question of when you left full-time education is quite irrevelant.

7   Benefit segmentation simply groups together consumers on the basis of why they have bought a particular product. Different people buy the same product for a whole list of different reasons. Some people have had a satellite dish bolted on to their homes because of special offers inducing them to try it; or because they want to watch more sport, or films or twenty-four hour news; or for their children's entertainment; or as a status symbol; or to be the first on the street; or boredom with existing television stations. All are valid reasons for purchasing the product. The key to this segmentation method is for the company to have already identified what the major benefits will be to the potential consumer, then profile those people, measure the product or service against that of the competitors and capitalise on an, as yet, unsatisfied market segment.

8   Segmentation by usage recognises that the consumption rates of products or services are not evenly distributed. If a company can identify the heaviest users of a product or service, it can target its marketing strategy to capture more of this type of person. The fact that beer drinkers tend to watch sport on television has led to the profusion of alcohol advertising during sports coverage.

9   The Loyalty Status divides consumers into four groups according to their loyalty to a product (known as brand loyalty):

   a   **Hard-core loyal**   These consumers have total commitment to a particular product and have been long-term purchasers.
   b   **Soft-core loyal**   These consumers have a divided loyalty, but only between two or three products. They tend not to have a pattern of purchasing; they simply buy one brand or another at a whim.
   c   **Shifting**   These consumers seem to have a pattern and switch their loyalty totally to another product for a period and then switch back after a while for no apparent reason.
   d   **Switching**   These consumers have no loyalty to a brand whatsoever. They may be heavily influenced by special offers and promotional gimmicks.

The key to this segmentation identification is to learn very quickly why consumers are switching from your product to another, or your inability to keep consumers long term, and take steps in your marketing strategy to stop this happening.

10   Geographical and cultural segmentation recognises that certain parts of the UK are substantially different from other areas. The regional differences are marked particularly in food consumption (remember the comments made by Edwina Currie about the unhealthy diets of those in the north compared to those in the south). The differences may be traditional, for example the eating of black pudding! Or they may be economic. In other words, in a poor area people's eating habits are likely to be different from those in more prosperous areas. Purchasing behaviour is strongly linked, of course, to what funds are available to the individual. Areas which have high levels of immigrants or those with different ethnic backgrounds tend to have alternative tastes and therefore need to be treated as a separate market segment.

SELECTION AND EVALUATION OF A MARKET SEGMENT . . . .

To ascertain the viability of a segment, estimates must be made. Essentially, after having worked out the size of the segment, you need to estimate turnover (likely) and profit, and to forecast what the future needs of that segment will be. This will be more fully covered in sales forecasting in Chapter 5.

It is often the case that these specific market segments are not in step with the rest of the market as a whole. The best example of this is the increase in the consumption of low-tar cigarettes in the face of severe cuts in the overall cigarette market.

Organisations which pay particular attention to evaluation of market segments calculate:

- **Cost**   How much it costs to get to the members of the market segment.
- **Revenue**   What the segment is worth in real money terms.

On this basis they then allocate their marketing and advertising budgets.

Once the market segments have been evaluated, the organisation has to make a decision regarding its commitment to that market segment. The response, as far as the organisation is concerned, runs from ignoring the market segment altogether (in other words it has decided that the market segment is either too small or diminishing) to concentrating wholeheartedly on capturing it. There are three main strategies in covering the market segments:

1 **Undifferentiated**   The organisation concentrates on factors common to potential customers. There is no differentiation of marketing mix or marketing strategy. The product itself is designed in such a way as to appeal to the widest possible market. Typical of this type of approach are organisations which mass produce their product. Equally, those involved in mass communication or distribution use this method.

2 **Differentiated**   Having decided to operate in a number of market segments, the organisation offers a slightly different product and marketing mix in each of the segments. Car manufacturers are a good example of this approach. Different styles, performance, extras, etc, are included or omitted depending on which segment is being approached.

3 **Concentrated**   This version has the organisation concentrating on one or very few market segments. By concentrating on a smaller customer base, it relies on being able to cater for this exactly. A very dangerous position to be in if you get it wrong! An example is Rolls Royce.

PRODUCT POSITIONING . . . .

Product positioning is designing the organisation's product and marketing mix so that they are seen by the consumer to fit into a particular place. With market research the company can ascertain the position of the competitor's products and then decide whether to compete by offering a very similar product, or to attempt to fill a gap in the market. *Multi-dimensional scaling* or MDS is an increasingly popular way of positioning a product in the mind's eye. If you can imagine a sliding scale working both horizontally and vertically, with the extremes noted at the end of each line, you can then place a product or service at any point along that scale.

Once a company has established its product positioning, it is ready to finalise the details of its marketing mix.

TALKING POINT AND ACTIVITY

What do you understand by product positioning? Select a product and show how that positioning can be used in the marketing of that product.

Companies find it difficult to cater for the mass market. They have turned increasingly to target marketing, which has enabled them to focus their efforts. By being able to identify specific target areas they can develop an appropriate marketing strategy, advertising, pricing and distribution. The initial research stage is vital. Haphazard or confused results here mean that the entire target marketing exercise is thrown into doubt.

Successful target marketing does have benefit for both parties. For the company it means that it can become more competitive and achieve greater sales and better profitability; while for the consumers it should mean greater satisfaction, since the product or service accords more closely with their specific needs.

TEST YOURSELF

1 What is the difference between being market-orientated and product-orientated, and what must you do to ensure that you are market-orientated?

2 What is target marketing?

3 Define 'a market' in your own words.

4 What is market segmentation? Give an example.

5 List the ten basic demographic factors that are part of segmenting your market.

6 How is the family classified?

7 What are the socio-economic groups to which the following belong?

   a teachers
   b dentists
   c dockers
   d refuse workers

e farmers

f writers

g students

8 What is ACORN?

9 What is TEA?

10 What is loyalty status?

11 What is an undifferentiated market?

12 What is product marketing?

13 What is MDS?

14 How can successful target marketing be benefical to the consumer as well as to the company?

15 How do organisations evaluate a market segment?

A WORKING CASE STUDY

Scott's Sufferance Wharf

Scott's Sufferance Wharf was a building development in London's Docklands (albeit on the south side of the River Thames) constructed by Bovis Homes.

Detail
(From the brief given to the agency.)
The proven success formula for the discerning purchaser drawn to London's Docklands, an exciting locale which is changing and growing with a force that is magnetic. North and south of the Thames, married by Tower Bridge and blending the old with the new.

Scott's Sufferance Wharf is an area that is blooming and undergoing a complete facelift. Local attractions include The Tower of London, Bermondsey Antique Market, HMS Belfast, many historic riverside pubs and a new park just minutes away. There are frequent bus routes nearby with a tube and mainline links at Tower Hill, London Bridge and Fenchurch Street. Across the picturesque Tower Bridge and a walk around the gardens of the Tower, is the new Docklands Light Railway and the West End can be reached by car or taxi. The nearest river bus stop is at Cherry Garden Pier.

Everywhere the tradition and heritage of this busy part of London is represented by restored warehouses, piers, river stairs and massive dock entrances.

The Scott's Sufferance Wharf development has the back-up of several large, well-known companies who are infinitely experienced in their fields, bringing together all their expertise to produce unique state-of-the-art homes in the midst of the exciting community that is the Docklands.

Early roughs of proposed designs (mostly rejected, but note nautical theme).

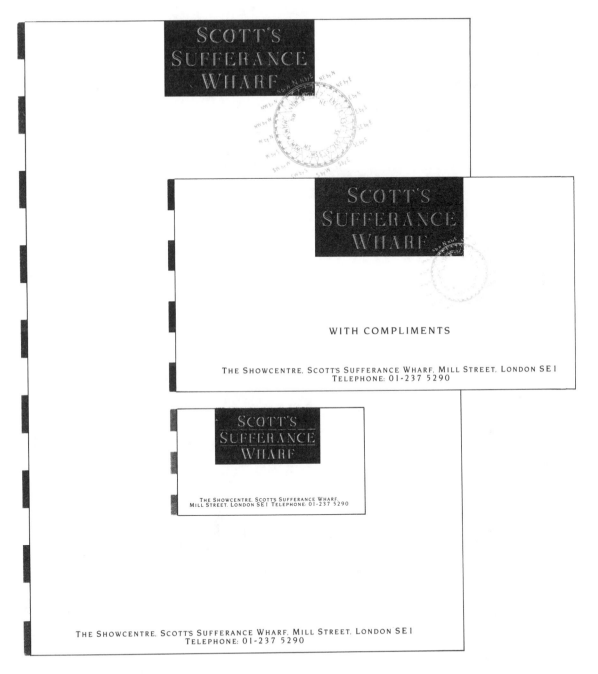

Finished designs for letterheads, compliment slips and business cards.

SCOTT'S SUFFERANCE
WHARF

SCOTT'S SUFFERANCE
WHARF

SCOTT'S SUFFERANCE
WHARF

KOSHE DUCTABLE TODD
CROUCH END WIBBLEY
HARWICH MAYONCI
TEL 267 4587

SCOTT'S SUFFERANCE
WHARF

KOSHE DUCTABLE TODD
CROUCH END WIBBLEY
HARWICH MAYONCI

SCOTT'S SUFFERANCE
WHARF

KOSHE DUCTABLE TODD
CROUCH END WIBBLEY
HARWICH MAYONCI

SCOTT'S SUFFERANCE
WHARF

KOSHE DUCTABLE TODD
CROUCH END WIBBLEY
HARWICH MAYONCI
TEL 267 4587

WITH COMPLIMENTS

SCOTT'S SUFFERANCE
WHARF

MARC DRAKE

Roughs of letterheads, compliment slips and business cards (all rejected in favour of the version on p 35).

Scott's Sufferance Wharf is a joint venture between Gambeta Properties and Bovis Homes South East – part of Bovis Homes Ltd, which operates throughout the UK and overseas.

Specifications

We think that our high specifications set our apartments far above the others you will find in the proximity. All our fittings have been chosen for their high quality, durability and aesthetic value, chic comfort and convenience.

The first thing that you will notice is the front door crafted from American White Oak. This theme is continued throughout the apartment and complemented with brass door handles and fittings. Heating is by effective, economical storage and convector heaters and all windows are double glazed for sound and heat insulation.

The kitchen units are in white oak and appliances include extractor, larder fridge, freezer, oven and ceramic hob. The sink has a waste disposer and a trash compactor. Also fitted is the latest condenser washer/tumble dryer.

The bedrooms are equipped with attractive white wardrobes and vanity units with plenty of storage space.

Brass antique-style taps adorn the luxurious Indian Ivory bathroom suites and wall tiling. Showers are fully enclosed and feature a thermostatic mixer for safety and convenience.

Each apartment has a video phone entry system linked to the outer entrance and a porter will be on hand throughout the day from early morning.

A secure private underground parking space has been allocated to each apartment with entrance to the garage area controlled electronically.

All apartments have been cleverly designed to provide accommodation for your lifestyle and your expectations today.

Above left, design studio's promotional picture of the finished design.
Below left, poster site outside the Scott's Sufferance Wharf project.

Activities and tasks

Now take a look at the material that was produced for the Scott's Sufferance Wharf project and how the image changed and was tightened up.

With the advantage of having seen what was produced and relating that to the extracts from the brief, tackle the following problems:

1 In the role of the property developer's marketing department, what do you see as your profile of a potential customer?

2 With the prices starting at around £100,000, what is the image that Bovis is trying to create? If you were in the position of selling the properties, would you think that this image linked in well with the customer profile?

3 The advertisement was done in colour and in black and white. As a media buyer, where would you place the advertisements?

4 Poster hoardings were used as well as banner hoardings outside the Wharf building itself. Why do you think Bovis decided to do this?

5 Which sort of marketing strategy would you employ: undifferentiated, differentiated or concentrated? As Bovis, how would you test your choice?

FURTHER READING

Marketing – A Behavioural Analysis, P Chisnall, McGraw Hill
Mastering Marketing, D Foster, Macmillan

4 Marketing research

SCIENCE OR SHAM? . . . .

Millions of pounds are spent each year on marketing research in the UK alone. Nearly 10 per cent of the price you pay for goods in the shops is being spent on marketing research in one guise or another. Let's try to define it:

Marketing research is the systematic collection and analysis of data which looks specifically at the customer's attitudes, needs, opinions and motivations within the context of political, economic and social influences.

Got it? Simply put, marketing research is using scientific methods to collect information that is relevant to the product or service in question. Scientific? What information? Is it relevant?

In order to reduce risk, the organisation needs to know about the intended market for the product which it is going to launch. Market research refers to the research into markets specifically but, strictly speaking, marketing research refers to any aspect of the marketing process that requires investigation.

Marketing research covers the obvious markets, but also what we noted in our first definition. There are three main sources of information in which the marketing researcher is interested:

1 Information within the organisation which already exists but may not be in a particularly usable form.
2 Information external to the organisation, which again already exists and is much more expensive to track down.
3 Information which is usually external to the organisation and which does not exist in a usable form at all. Commonly this information is customer opinion, attitude or buying traits.

We can further identify these types of information and categorise them in a more simple way:

1 Information within the company, such as sales figures, is known as **internal information**.

2 Information external to the company, such as government reports or published marketing reports, is known as **secondary information**.

3 The third information source, often characterised by market research opinion polls, is known as **primary information**.

These then are the main sources of information and we will return to them in detail later.

TYPES OF MARKETING RESEARCH . . . .

Marketing research makes a positive contribution to the business by helping in the decision-making process. There are many different types of marketing research; here are the main ones:

1 **Market and sales research**
   - estimating market size of new markets
   - estimating potential growth of an existing market
   - identifying market characteristics and segments
   - identifying market trends
   - sales forecasting
   - collecting data on existing customers
   - collecting data on potential customers
   - collecting data on competitors

2 **Product research**
   - customer's attitude to new products
   - comparing competition with your own products
   - finding alternative uses for existing products
   - market testing proposed products
   - investigating customer complaints
   - packaging research
   - generating new ideas for new products

3 **Research on promotion and advertising**
   - choosing the right advertising medium
   - analysing the effectiveness of advertising
   - establishing sales areas
   - evaluating present sales techniques
   - analysing sales force effectiveness
   - establishing sales quotas

4 Distribution research
- location of distribution centres
- handling products (efficiency)
- transport costs and comparisons
- storage efficiency and needs
- retail outlet location

5 Pricing policy
- demand
- perceived price
- costs
- margins

TALKING POINT AND ACTIVITY

Before you read any further and find out how things are usually done, decide how you would research the following if you were being asked to launch a new product:

a   Is the product needed?
b   How would you set the price?
c   How would you decide on the packaging?

Try to identify the research methods and just how reliable you think they are.

The scope of marketing and market research is very broad. In fact, almost every aspect of the production, promotion, sales and after-sales life of a product is scrutinised at some point for one particular purpose or another.

National Westminster Bank has not 'personalised' its name. It has concentrated, like many other companies, on its logo. Note that the logo is visible from all directions that a customer would approach the premises.

DIY OR GET IN THE PRO? . . . .

Having decided that you desperately need to do some marketing research, you now have a choice. You could get your own people to do it for you, or you might decide that it would be better to get in a professional organisation to do it. Before we look at the advantages and disadvantages of hiring an outside marketing research agency, against the 'do-it-yourself' option, just how do you know whether an agency is *bona fide* (properly run and reliable) or not?

The watchdogs

The Market Research Society was founded in the late 1940s and is the professional body for market researchers in Britain. Its name flies in the face of what we have already said in that market research is just a part of marketing research, but the society was established simply for market researchers and has, over the years, opened its doors to a wider membership.

The Industrial Marketing Research Association, better known as IMRA, in association with the Market Research Society, has published a code of conduct which attempts to lay down the ground rules of market research. It specifically attempts to protect the interviewee from unscrupulous researchers who are trying to use the camouflage of market research as a sales technique. It further warns that researchers should not try to get the response they want by influencing the interviewee; nor should the person interviewed be bombarded by junk mail as a result of being put on someone's mailing list. Market research should not be used to get people to divulge private information about an individual or to let out industrial secrets.

Having laid down these rules the two organisations can only hope that their members do follow them. Indeed the vast majority do, but some companies, although ones that are not all that well-known, give market research a bad name. Have you ever been stopped in the street and asked your opinion, only to discover that they want to sell you insurance? Ever been called to the front door and asked about energy saving and to your horror found that, after twenty minutes of pleasant banter, the person now sitting in your living room is a double-glazing salesman? The big companies, of course, do not resort to these underhand methods of getting your attention, but they can rub off. It gives them a bad name. Let's be honest, wouldn't you close the door in the face of a poor double-glazing or insurance salesperson, or a stone-cladder? Perhaps our reaction to them is a deeper and more complicated fear or dislike?

In their own defence, legitimate researchers have now got identification cards from the MRS, but would you know one if you saw one? The fake researcher can easily claim that the letter they are showing you establishes their credentials and that the information you give them will not be used for any other purpose except market research. It is a difficult and potentially damaging problem and there does not seem to be a readily workable solution.

Considerations in choosing a market researcher

What then of the argument about using insiders or outsiders? There are six main areas of consideration, not all of them necessarily relevant to each case but several of which will be.

1 **Cost**   The first area of consideration is that of cost. An obvious one really as it is more expensive to 'buy in' help from outside; but what about the people you intend to use within your organisation? What should they be doing that they cannot do if they are doing this research?

2 **Expertise** Do your own people have the skills needed? Some research techniques are fairly basic and do not require a great deal of skill or experience, but some are quite sophisticated. Similarly, the analysis of the data that has been collected needs to be looked at by the right person. Perhaps the analysis is beyond your immediately available skills.

3 **Knowledge of the product/service** On the other hand, the question of knowledge of the product or service is much more likely to be the domain of your insiders. You would have to teach the outside organisation about you, your organisation and your products or services. This is both time-consuming and expensive.

4 **Objectivity** Having said that about the 'in house' people and that they have knowledge of the organisation and what it is about, they may be too close. The question of objectivity is an important one. Conclusions drawn from the research may be unconsciously biased and tainted by their own preconceived ideas and prejudices.

5 **Resources** The question of equipment, or more commonly resources, is another key factor. Specialist computer programs or particular testing equipment may be needed, as may the ability to sample a widely separated group of people from all over the country. It may not prove possible or economically viable to train your own people to use specialist equipment or indeed buy what you need just for this one exercise.

6 **Confidentiality** Finally, and by no means less important, is confidentiality. No matter who you use, once information about a new product or process leaves the confines of your own organisation and direct control, there will be a nagging feeling about its safety. In most cases the fear is irrational and unfounded and the information is probably more safe than when it was with you! But people do worry, and not without reason, since a great deal of money can be made through industrial espionage. Many organisations, for a variety of reasons, *never* use outside marketing agencies. These include such household names as Marks & Spencer and Sainsbury's. In their highly competitive market, secrecy is vital and disclosure disastrous.

TALKING POINT

What are the pros and cons of carrying out the research yourself?

THE RESEARCH PROCESS . . . .

It would be fairly obvious to most people that you do marketing research for a reason. That reason should invariably be that you will gain more in the long term from what you have learned than it will cost you in the short term to find out. Easier said than done! Calculating the costs of research is fairly easy. You will know how many people are involved, what equipment you will need, any specialists to pay and what it will cost to process the information in order to get it into a presentable and usable form. The problem is how you work out just what is the value of the information. How can you compare very straightforward costs of collecting and processing data with the benefits derived from your knowledge of this data?

TALKING POINT

What do you think are the benefits of being aware of more of the factors related to your product? Do you think that knowledge through marketing research is vital to making the right decision? How would you weigh up the delay in making a decision whilst the marketing research is going on against making a decision that you *think* is right now?

Two key thoughts are:

- What is the relative profitability of the alternative decisions open to you *before* you undertake the marketing research? After all you might be trying to make one choice or another, and this is measurable.
- How will the information directly affect your decision-making? Will it make a positive contribution or will it just be another factor to worry about?

Perhaps when you see the phases that the research process needs to go through, you will realise that, whatever your concerns about marketing research, the process focusses the mind. In some cases that may be enough for you to get what you want out of the exercise before you have gone through all the stages of the research process.

1   The first task has to be to define the problem. It is here that you, as the client or director of the research, specify exactly what you hope to achieve from the research. What are the major objectives? If these cannot be achieved, then the research is worse than useless.

2   Next you need to decide what methods are to be employed in the collection of the data. As we have already discussed, there are effectively three main sources of information. The primary sources of information are usually the ones that cost you money to collect. This is because they are often specific to your needs and involve the more common forms of data collection, such as surveys, interviews and observations. The secondary sources tend to be cheaper as they are often already collected but are usually less useful and only helpful as background information.

TALKING POINT AND ACTIVITY

How many people do you think would be a representative sample as a minimum? Could you sample, say, ten people and present them as representative? If you interviewed everyone in your class as representative of your age group, would the sample be accurate?

3   The third stage is to decide on the scale of the information gathering. This is know as *sampling*. Basically you need to ask just how many people you are going to include in your research. You could probably interview all Conservative Members of Parliament or the residents of one small area of the country, but you couldn't possibly interview everyone who owns a Ford car or all of Britain's smokers. Sampling decisions are crucial because you will need to make your mind up about how many people would be a representative sample, balanced against the cost of sampling a higher figure.

4   The fourth stage is making your mind up about how the data that has been collected is to be analysed. Which statistical procedures are going to be employed to look at the information? You should consider this in relation to what you wanted in the first place. What are you looking for? The analysis should give you the answers to the questions you have posed.

5 The fifth consideration is time and resources. You may well have considered this already, before you undertook the research, but it could be here that you decide not to pursue the research any further. This is where you will have to put a price on the research so that it is also here that you can finally decide whether the research is worth whatever it is going to cost you. In addition, you may not have considered just how long it is going to take to collect the data to answer the questions that you want answered. Will the process take too long? Can you afford to wait?

6 The sixth stage is the point of no return. You have outlined the parameters of the research. You have decided how much information you are going to collect and how to analyse it to get the answers that you want, and of course put a monetary figure on the whole exercise. It is here that you get the go-ahead or not. Agreement here on the five preceding stages is vital, otherwise the research process comes to an end straight away.

TALKING POINT AND ACTIVITY

How would you decide on the cost-effectiveness of research? Work out a simple research process and try to cost it. The results may surprise you.

The final three stages, 7, 8 and 9, put into practice what you have already agreed in the first five stages. They are: collecting the data; analysing it; and then reporting back on the findings to the person or persons for whom the research was done. We will look at this elsewhere in more detail.

WHAT CAN GO WRONG? . . . .

Whenever people are involved you cannot guarantee 'bug-free' results. By this we don't mean that the researchers can get it wrong (they can though, sometimes!), but if you are asking people's opinions or looking at their behaviour you begin to realise that people can be pretty unpredictable!

Here are some of the more common types of error:

1 **Sampling errors**   These ones are the researcher's fault. The researcher has incorrectly chosen the target sample and it does not represent a true cross-section at all.

2 **Non-response errors**   Again a researcher's error, where this time the researcher has not received responses from all of the intended target sample. This may be partly related to the first error.

3 **Data collection errors**   Most commonly when the respondent in a questionnaire or interview gives the answers which he or she thinks the researcher wants to hear. Alternatively, the respondent may not really understand the question and give an entirely wrong answer. In other cases when the question is read out by the interviewer, intentionally or unintentionally a bias may be introduced into the tone of their voice. Less commonly, some respondents will deliberately give the wrong answer (who can resist it sometimes! 'Yes, I am married and I have thirty

children!'). Equally, an interviewer may be dishonest and put down completely spurious answers for some reason or another.

4 **Analysis errors**   You have wrongly interpreted the findings of your research or you may have incorrectly tabulated the information in some way by overlooking something. In some cases, analysis errors are the direct result of having collected the wrong information or not having asked the one vital question that you should have asked.

5 **Report errors**   Having collected the data and even having analysed it correctly, you can still come to the wrong conclusion! The old saying that there are 'lies, damn lies and statistics!' holds true. You can interpret almost anything from a set of statistics. Ask the Labour Party and the Conservative Party to give you their interpretation of the same unemployment figures and then sit back and watch them swear that they are right and the other party is wrong. Misinterpretation is either a common error or a positive skill, depending on your point of view!

6 **Accidental errors**   These are really no one's fault. What happens if you plan to run your research period over a year and something happens to ruin your research? A competitor may launch a new product, or the weather may suddenly change, or the interest rates might change. Anything can happen, all beyond your control.

TALKING POINT

'Market research is completely unreliable and inevitably prone to misinterpretation anyway, so it isn't really worth doing.' Do you agree with this statement in the light of what you have just read?

TALKING POINT AND ACTIVITY

Visit your local public library or college library and have a look at what is available in the reference section in the way of secondary sources. Try to identify where you might find the following:

a details on the more successful and well-known companies in this country, including their turnover and profitability;
b the name of your local councillor.
c details of unemployment figures?

SECONDARY RESEARCH . . . .

Before an organisation goes to the expense of paying for primary research it is prudent to look at what information is already available. Surprisingly, whatever the subject, there will be something. Secondary data, which is either already in existence under your nose but not in the right format, or is readily available from somewhere else, is massively cheaper than starting from scratch.

Published data is available in most good commercial reference libraries, and in quite a number of main libraries in most towns. It includes some of the more obvious (and weighty) reference books as well as some seemingly boring and starchy items. In the book line there are titles like *Regional Trends* or the *General Household Survey*. Datastream is a computer database facility and Prestel can be accessed via a TV with an adaptor. Other sources are the local Chambers of Commerce, which have good libraries and links to other sources of information.

PRIMARY RESEARCH . . . .

When secondary data cannot provide you with the information that you need, you are left with no choice but to get the information for yourself. This is also known as 'field' research, as the information that you want is actually out there somewhere waiting for you to discover it. There are four main methods of research;

1 The personal interview
2 The telephone interview
3 The postal survey
4 The panel

The choice depends on many variables, which must include the following considerations:

- Your budget.
- The time available – some of the above methods of research will obviously take longer to complete than others.
- The degree of accuracy needed – roughly speaking: the more accurate, the more expensive. 'You pays your money and you takes your choice!', as the saying goes.
- Who do you want to survey? Consider basic problems like literacy or reluctance in putting 'private' thoughts on paper.
- Where are the people you want to survey? They could be scattered across the country (like the readership of a magazine), or concentrated (like the users of a local amenity).

Let's now look at the four main methods of research and try to identify their advantages and disadvantages:

1 **The personal interview** This is a very common method of gathering research information. The interviewer can select the 'victim' and question them face-to-face. The most used method is to ask questions from a formally-structured questionnaire, often with a predetermined range of answers.

Here are the advantages:

- high response rate, due to choosing the respondent each time;
- a fairly low rate of refusal to answer;
- if structured well, the questionnaire is easy to analyse;
- misunderstood questions can be explained;
- deliberate 'wrong' answers can be easily eliminated;
- additional information can be noted without asking the respondent (eg age or sex);
- answers do not have time to be considered – they are immediate and probably more truthful;
- you can ask reasonably personal questions;
- because the respondent does not have to read the questionnaire, it can be longer and more involved.

There are several disadvantages however:

- cost is high, as you will have to pay for the interviewer's time;
- there may be interviewer bias in noting down the answers, if some answers have to be interpreted by the interviewer;
- there may be some inaccuracies if the respondent is in a hurry to leave and will just say anything to get it over with;
- interviewers will need to be selected and trained before they can begin the task;
- speed of collection of information is related directly to the length of the questionnaire and the availability of appropriate respondents.

2 The telephone interview   Very popular in the United States, but very prone to low response rate due to reluctance to be canvassed for information on the telephone. It is after all an invasion of privacy, but you can hang up! Otherwise the technique is almost identical to face-to-face interviewing when the interviewer goes through a set questionnaire and notes down the answers.

These are the advantages:

- it is a very quick way of getting through a lot of interviews;
- the interviewers need only be in one place, and can be supervised easily;
- costs are lower than for personal interviews;
- the sample can be spread across the country without incurring high travel costs;
- you can access those who are hard to track down by other means.

The disadvantages are:

- you cannot get to people who do not have a telephone!
- without asking, you cannot tell age or social class;
- you will inevitably annoy people by phoning at the wrong time of the day;
- it is harder to get the attention of the respondent;
- how can you prove who you are and what you really want?
- ex-directory subscribers are not accessible.

3 The postal survey   Accompanied by a letter, these surveys are sent to a sample of the population in the hope that they may return them answered. Often a second letter is sent after a period of time to remind the chosen sample to fill in the questionnaire. These questionnaires are often found in magazines and are tied to a particular company who will offer discounts or a small free gift as an incentive for filling in the questionnaire. Above all the questionnaire must be straightforward and easy to fill in, otherwise the respondent will not bother to do it.

The advantages of this system are:

- you can reach a wide sample of the population;
- it is much cheaper than the personal interview;
- no field expenses;
- no training of interviewers;
- no bias from the interviewer;

- easier to reach small groups, e.g. readers of specialist magazines;
- the sample is not rushed to fill in the questionnaire and may choose to give more consideration to the answers.

There are, however, quite a number of disadvantages;

- it is unlikely that the sample will be representative. You will only get responses back from those who have bothered to fill them in;
- the refusal rate is high – response will definitely depend on how easy the questionnaire is to fill in;
- there is a strong possibility that questions may be misunderstood;
- questions need to be highly structured, giving less scope for additional information;
- mailing lists are expensive to keep up to date, as they are very labour intensive;
- plenty of time should be put aside for a slow trickle of replies over the weeks;
- personal questions should be avoided as these may stop respondents from filling in the questionnaire;
- the answers may not come from the person for whom the questionnaire was intended. The respondent may be a different person or may have asked the opinion of another person.

4 **The panel** This information-gathering technique relies on asking a range of questions over a period of time to the same people. This is used, for example, to check on changing attitudes. There are three main types of panel.

The first is the *consumer purchasing panel*, where data is collected by a number of methods. This looks at customers' purchases and customers' attitudes to particular products or types of product, such as washing powder or toothpaste.

The second type is the *test panel*, where a group of people is asked to 'field test' new products as these come out, particularly useful in the household product market or for specialist equipment such as hospital products.

Finally, there is the *audience panel*, and this is where audience figures for TV and radio come from. Here viewing patterns are looked at, both for individuals and for members of families.

Geographically, the respondents can be anywhere and you can ask very detailed questions and expect intelligent and useful responses.

These are the advantages:

- good trend indicator;
- you can analyse changes and adjust them according to external factors that have influenced them;
- you can collect very detailed information about the habits and attitudes of individuals, which is very valuable background information.

There are some disadvantages, of course:

- the panel can be easily upset by deaths or by panelists moving areas;
- you are likely to attract the more intelligent panelist and miss out on the less intelligent, and this may affect your sample;

- the panelist may adopt uncharacteristic behaviour, knowing that you are 'watching' them;
- it is expensive to recruit panelists at the outset;
- you will continually have to replace departing panelists;
- you will have to reward the panelists in some way, however small.

QUESTIONNAIRES . . . .

We have talked about questionnaires in general terms but now let's look at them in some more detail. The four types of field, or primary, research at which we have looked all use different forms of questionnaire. The key point to remember is that a well-constructed questionnaire will give far better results than an ill-considered one. If questions are unclear, you run the risk of annoying the respondent and losing their co-operation.

Questionnaires have different types of questions, falling into four main categories:

1 **Closed questions**   The respondent is asked to answer the question from a range of set answers. Usually the answers are simply yes or no, but in other cases may include 'don't know'. The questions could offer a wider range of answers, but the more answers there are, the more likely that the respondent will get confused.

2 **Open questions**   The respondent is given the opportunity to answer the question in whatever way he or she sees fit. There are no multiple choice preferred answers and the questionnaire has to be structured in such a way as to allow plenty of space for the answers.

3 **Direct questions**   Very similar in some respects to a closed question style. These require an exact or specific answer, sometimes a simple yes or no, and at other times a more detailed but specific answer. An example would be:

Would you buy the AX2007 compact disc player?

4 **Indirect questions**   These are very general questions and attempt to discover attitudes that the respondent has about certain issues. A series of questions will be asked that will build up a detailed picture of attitudes or behaviour. As the interviewer has to interpret much of what is being said and will note down what he or she sees as the more important parts of the response, you do need to have well-trained interviewers. Additionally, the time spent with each respondent is longer than that for any other method; hence it is expensive. What this type of questioning does reveal can be very interesting and it is unlikely that the other forms of questions can get so much in-depth material.

Having looked at the different types of question, we can break down the actual types of questionnaire into two basic categories: the structured questionnaire which relies mainly on the closed question, with the occasional open question; and the unstructured questionnaire which mainly makes use of direct and indirect questions.

Structured questionnaires are simple to fill in by just ticking the appropriate box; whereas the unstructured questionnaire must rely on the skills of the interviewer, as the questions themselves are merely a guide to the direction in which the interview should go.

As a guide for the interviewer with unstructured questionnaires, or a way to get an answer that is a little more detailed than a simple 'yes' or 'no', there are two main techniques which questionnaires often employ to measure and record the respondent's attitudes. The techniques are known as the Likert Scale and the Semantic Differential Scale.

Likert Scale

A Likert Scale question measures shades of opinion, and might look like this:

What do you think are the advantages and disadvantages of fresh vegetables against frozen ones? Tick the appropriate box.

	Strongly agree	Tend to agree	Don't agree or disagree	Tend to disagree	Strongly disagree
Fresh vegetables are more healthy	☐	☐	☐	☐	☐
Fresh vegetables are less convenient	☐	☐	☐	☐	☐
Frozen vegetables are better quality	☐	☐	☐	☐	☐
Frozen vegetables are more expensive	☐	☐	☐	☐	☐

The Semantic Differential Scale

The Semantic Differential Scale asks respondents to mark their opinion on a sliding scale of seven (which is the usual). Here is an example:

Please rate your day out at the Theme Park, circling the number you have chosen.

very good value for money	7 6 5 4 3 2 1	poor value for money
very good range of rides	7 6 5 4 3 2 1	poor range of rides
food stalls very good	7 6 5 4 3 2 1	bad food, poor service
staff helpful and courteous	7 6 5 4 3 2 1	staff bad mannered
great family day out	7 6 5 4 3 2 1	not good for families
strongly recommended	7 6 5 4 3 2 1	will not recommend

In both cases the researcher would compile the results and reach an 'aggregate' total for each of the questions. In other words, the researcher would look at the range of answers to the questions as well as discovering which answer was the most common.

SAMPLING AND DATA ANALYSIS . . . .

Sampling

Sampling is absolutely necessary, unless of course you have the time, money and resources to carry out a census of the entire population! Often, though, the reason for the size of the sample may depend on other considerations. For instance, the smaller the sample, the less likely you are to change the attitude of the market which you are investigating. Also, the size of the sample will effect the accuracy of your findings. If the sample is too small or unrepresentative of the market, then your results will be very inaccurate.

So how do you get it right? You have to ask yourself three basic questions. Firstly, what is the target population? Secondly, which of the sampling methods (of which there are five) will you choose? Finally, with reference to such considerations as time and resources, you will need to determine what your sampling size will be.

1 **What is the target population?** Basically this is the part of the total population at which the study is directed. Your prospective respondents should be part of the total population, which you have chosen from directories or maps or perhaps selected after a more general questionnaire to a much larger population.

2 **Which sampling method should be chosen?** Selecting the sampling method is crucial and you will need to pick the one that most closely matches your resources and time:

   a *Random or non-random sampling?* Random samples are simply that – people chosen at random. Each and every member of the total population has an equal chance of being part of the sample. It has two main advantages: firstly, a statistical relationship exists between the sample and the population; and secondly, the composition of the sample is not influenced by interviewer bias. Non-random samples, when respondents are chosen to reflect the characteristic elements of the population at which the researcher is trying to look, can be as effective and useful as a totally random choice of respondents. You need far less in a non-random sample, but true reliability rests on the following: you do need the most up-to-date statistics of the structure of the population; the questions need to be carefully designed; and you have to control the interviewer's choice of respondents.

   b *Single stage or multi-stage sampling?* The larger the sample, the more likely it is that you do not take your entire sample at the same time. A well organised multi-stage sample will look systematically at various areas or classifications of respondents.

c *Single unit or cluster sampling?* Single unit sampling selects each respondent individually, regardless of his/her geographical location. Cluster sampling concentrates on one location and so draws all of its respondents from quite a small geographical area.

d *Unstratified or stratified sampling?* Stratified sampling attempts to segment the population into groups which have the same basic characteristics, and then treats each of these groups as a separate entity when sampling them. It has its advantages, which include making sure that the sample is representative and the chances of choosing the wrong people to sample is reduced. It is most used in industrial marketing research where the samples are stratified to make sure that similarly-sized companies are sampled. The ACORN system provides a useful framework for consumer marketing research if you want to use stratified sampling (*see* p28).

e *Proportionate or disproportionate sampling?* Following on from stratified sampling, proportionate sampling ensures that you use an equal percentage of respondents from each group. Disproportionate sampling is cheaper, as you can sample more or less from one particular group and then simply reduce or increase the sample group results to the correct percentage after you have analysed all the results.

We have already mentioned that the size of sample is usually governed by the amount of money that is available, but it is also affected by the degree of precision that you are demanding from the research. Roughly speaking, the larger the sample, the more accurate the results are likely to be.

The other major factor of precision is to make sure that you have correctly interpreted the responses. Some may have been rather confusing and you will have to make up your mind about how you are going to deal with these. You could ask the respondent to clarify a confused answer, but this is a rather expensive solution. You could, alternatively, decide to sample more than you need and simply discard the useless responses.

Analysis

Now that you have a pile of completed questionnaires, how do you analyse them? The simplest way and the most common is to tabulate the results. This basically means calculating the number and percentage of respondents who choose each of the answers. You will probably have come across averaging methods such as means, medians and modes. These, too, are useful in working out the meaning of your findings.

Most marketing research analysis is limited to working out averages or percentages, but careful coding can reduce the time taken and enable data to be input on a computer. Computers can be put to good use when working out the relationship between different variables.

The marketing research report itself is usually set out like this:

Title page
Table of contents
Summary
Introduction/objectives
Research methods
Findings
Conclusions
Recommendations
Appendices

The technical details of the sampling are usually consigned to the appendices, as the reader is often not particularly interested in these. Sampling design and questionnaire design will often be found here too for that reason.

TALKING POINT AND ACTIVITY

In the role of a marketing researcher you have been asked to design a questionnaire that looks at people's TV viewing habits. You are interested in when they watch as much as what they watch, and how much independent TV they watch compared to BBC TV. Design a questionnaire and test sample it.

TALKING POINT

What are the elements of a useful marketing information system and who would be responsible for its constituent parts and for its overall organisation?

It is important to consider two things before putting pen to paper: don't use jargon or language that your reader may not understand; equally, try to write for your reader and make your report easy to follow. Whenever possible, try to use diagrams or graphs. A good graph will say something that words cannot.

INFORMATION SYSTEMS . . . .

Information systems, if set up correctly, should channel useful information to the marketing department of the company. A marketing information system worth anything should only pass on the useful information and sift out the irrelevant. There are four facets of information that are useful and should make up the elements of a marketing information system:

1 **Internal accounting** Reports orders, sales, stock, incoming cash and outgoing cash.
2 **Marketing intelligence** A firm set of procedures that ensures that new developments that may affect the business are collected and collated.
3 **Marketing research** Systematic collection and analysis of information useful to the decision-makers for the business.
4 **Analytical marketing** A system that analyses relevant marketing data in a scientific manner.

TEST YOURSELF

1 About what percentage of the RRP (recommended retail price) of a product is taken up with marketing costs?

2 What is market research?

3 What is the difference between marketing research and market research?

4 What is internal information?

5 What is secondary information?

6 List five elements of product research.

7 List the elements of pricing policy.

8 When was the MRS founded and for whom?

9 State some basic codes of conduct to which market researchers should adhere.

10 What are the disadvantages of using your own people to do market research for you?

11 What is the first stage of the research process?

12 What is a data response error?

13 Name at least two sources of secondary data.

14 What are the four main methods of research?

15 What are the criteria upon which you choose your method of research?

16 List six examples of the advantages of personal interviews as a research technique.

17 List at least six examples of the disadvantages of postal surveys.

18 In market research, what is a panel?

19 What are the four main categories of questions used in questionnaires?

20 What is the Likert Scale?

21 What is the Semantic Differential Scale?

22 What are the three basic questions to ask yourself when trying to get your results accurate?

23 What is non-random sampling?

24 What is proportionate sampling?

25 What are the four facets that make up a marketing information system?

A WORKING CASE STUDY

BUAV

Take a look at the reproductions of the material which BUAV designed as part of their campaigns to influence two major high street chains, Tesco and Benetton. The approach is different, but calculated to achieve the same end results: firstly, greater awareness of animal testing, and secondly, to encourage the two companies to change/examine their attitudes to animal testing. The situations are different: the intention is to make Tesco consider stocking cruelty-free products, and for Benetton to cease testing its products on animals.

Both campaigns were ultimately successful. They opened a dialogue between the pressure group and the companies. Both companies were deluged with cards and this played no small part in convincing the companies to reconsider their position on this emotive subject. Tesco now stocks cruelty-free products and Benetton ceased testing its products on animals.

Dear Mr Panizzo

I wish to register my protest at the shocking animal tests commissioned by your company for your 'Colors de Benetton' cosmetic and toiletry range.

There can be no excuse for carrying out such experiments. Many companies now produce 'cruelty-free' ranges and as a consumer I prefer to 'Choose Cruelty-Free'. I shall not therefore buy any of your company's products until you undertake to cease such testing.

Yours sincerely

(signature)

Name _____
Address _____
_____ Postcode _____

THE CHOOSE CRUELTY-FREE CAMPAIGN IS ORGANISED BY BUAV 16A CRANE GROVE LONDON N7 8LB TEL. 01700 4888

Mr Paolo Panizzo
Managing Director

Benetton (U.K.)
517 Fulham Road
London
SW6 1HD

Dear Mr MacLaurin

I wish to express my disappointment that your stores are not currently stocking any non-animal-tested cosmetics, toiletries or household products.

As a major retailer I hope that you will consider the growing demand for such products. Like many others, I am appalled that so many ranges, including those currently available on your shelves, are cruelly tested on thousands of living animals.

I would like to have the opportunity to 'choose cruelty-free' at Tesco's. Please offer myself and others that option.

Yours sincerely

(Signature)

Name _____
Address _____
_____ Post code _____

The Choose Cruelty-Free campaign is organised by BUAV, FREEPOST, London N7 8BR.

Mr Ian MacLaurin
Chairman
TESCO
DELAMERE ROAD
CHESHUNT
HERTS

Postcard reverses
with letter to
Benetton (above)
and Tesco (right)

THE TRUE COLOURS OF
benetton

International clothing giant **Benetton** recently commissioned a series of cruel and painful animal tests for their 'Colors de Benetton' cosmetic and toiletry range.

In one shocking experiment their **Mane** fragrance was forced into rabbits' eyes. It proved to be an "ocular irritant", yet it is still being marketted. Rats were also force-fed the product, and guinea pigs and rabbits subjected to skin studies.

Bath and shower gel which proved "corrosive" to the skin of rabbits, was also applied to their eyes.

Benetton deodorant caused redness and swelling of rabbits' skin. Guinea pigs, treated with the same product, died when a heating system malfunctioned (callously referred to as a "pig roast" by lab workers).

Men's cologne caused redness, swelling and discharge from rabbits' eyes.

The true colours of **Benetton** are those of pain and misery.

Many companies now produce 'cruelty-free' product ranges that are both safe and effective. Unlike Benetton, they choose not to cause animal suffering.

You also have the choice. If you would prefer to 'choose cruelty-free' then don't buy Benetton.

The **Choose Cruelty-Free** campaign is organised by BUAV, 16a Crane Grove, London N7 8LB. Tel: 01-700 4888.

ACTION

1 Write to Paolo Panizzo, Managing Director, Benetton (UK) at 517 Fulham Road, London SW6 1HD.

2 Send off for our 'Choose Cruelty-Free' campaign materials – including a list of 'cruelty-free' companies.

3 Send a donation to help us in our campaign to end animal suffering.

4 Join the BUAV and receive our bi-monthly magazine Liberator.

Send to: British Union for the Abolition of Vivisection (BUAV), 16a Crane Grove, London N7 8LB (Tel: 01-700 4888)

I enclose cheque/P.O. for £ _____
£6.00 annual subscription (£3.00 unwaged)
£100 life membership (payable to BUAV)

Name _____

Address _____

_____

Postcode _____

Tick Box

☐ Please send me the 'Choose Cruelty-Free' campaign information pack.

☐ Please accept my donation of £ _____ towards the campaign.

☐ I would like to join the BUAV.
I am against all animal experiments.

Signature _____ Date _____

CODE B1

Activities and tasks

1 The pressure group targeted the two companies as part of a rolling campaign to influence major well-known brand producers and retailers. The companies responded by talking to the pressure group and then changing their policy in this area. No doubt they carried out their own research to see whether the amount of cards they received was representative of the country's feelings on the subject. What do you think was contained in Tesco's questionnaire or marketing research? Design a questionnaire to ask the pertinent questions.

2 From the point of view of the pressure group, what would a questionnaire look like that could be sent to businesses asking them to declare whether they offer or use cruelty-free products?

CUSTOMER QUESTIONNAIRES

Acquiring information about your market is of great importance throughout any marketing campaign.

The customer questionnaire is widely used to obtain this information, and reproduced here are two typical examples. The first comes from the Reflex 'Reds' campaign. In this example the questionnaire has been combined with the guarantee registration card, which (not surprisingly) helps to ensure a high percentage of returned cards!

The second example (*see* p62) comes from *GamesMaster International*, a magazine catering for the fantasy gaming hobby. Although the magazine's readership may be rather specialised, the example is nevertheless typical of such questionnaires.

Activities and tasks

1 The magazine questionnaire is obviously far more detailed than the Reflex one, but why do you think this is?

2 Apart from the ploy of combining the questionnaire with the guarantee card, can you think of any other ways of encouraging customer response?

3 Taking the 'Poppies' example in Chapter 5 of this book, we should like you to devise a questionnaire for franchisees to use with their business clients. You are allowed to ask 7 questions and must devise a way to ensure a good response.

FURTHER READING

Marketing Research, P Chisnall, McGraw Hill
Statistics for Marketing, L Rodger, McGraw Hill.

reflex. PICKUPS

PLEASE FILL THIS IN

Express guarantee cover from our musicians registration system, should you need us for a speedy repair.

To ensure you are registered please post this card to us within a few days – we know how important it is for us to deal with your pickup repairs quickly.

Your Name _____

Street _____

Town and County _____ Postcode _____

Model Purchased _____ Date Purchased _____

Dealer _____ Town _____

In which type of guitar/bass are you installing them? _____

Previous pickups installed _____

Who fitted   Yourself/Dealer

How did you hear about this product?

Shop ☐   Friend ☐   Magazine Article ☐   Advertisement ☐

Your age please _____

Please list your 2 favourite music magazines

1. _____

2. _____   *Reds*

Companies often use their guarantee cards to gain information on their customers. This example is typical and, although the information may seem minor, it is very useful when planning a marketing strategy.

GAMESMASTER INTERNATIONAL READER SURVEY
YOU TELL US WHAT'S WHAT, AND TEN LUCKY READERS WIN A YEAR'S SUBSCRIPTION TO GMI!

GamesMaster International, the independent fantasy gaming magazine, belongs to you. It's your magazine. We take notice of what you think. We welcome the bouquets and the brickbats equally. We may not like or even agree with all the criticisms, but we always read them.
We care about GamesMaster International and we know you care too.
So far we think the magazine is pretty good — not perfect, of course, — but a firm base to build for the future. But what do you think? That's why we want you to fill in this survey. The answers you give will help shape GamesMaster International over the next six months.
The first ten entries out of the bag win a 12-month subscription to GMI!
Thanks for your help.

CUT OUT PAGE

1. Are you? Male ⏘ Female ⏘

2. How old are you? ....

3. Are you:
⏘ WORKING FULL TIME
⏘ WORKING PART TIME
⏘ AT COLLEGE/UNIVERSITY
⏘ AT SCHOOL
⏘ UNEMPLOYED

4. If you work what is your occupation:

5. What is your weekly income:
⏘ UP TO £5   ⏘ £5-10   ⏘ £10-30
⏘ £30-100   ⏘ £100-200   ⏘ £200-PLUS

6. On average how many other people read your copy of GMI

7. How do you get GMI
⏘ SUBSCRIPTION
⏘ RESERVED OR DELIVERED BY NEWSAGENTS
⏘ OFF THE SHELF AT NEWSAGENT
⏘ AT A SPECIALIST SHOP
NAME SHOP

8. Which other magazines do you buy:
⏘ WHITE DWARF
⏘ COMPUTER & VIDEO GAMES
⏘ RAZE
⏘ ZZAP!64
⏘ CU AMIGA
⏘ ZERO
⏘ ACE
⏘ CRASH
⏘ SINCLAIR USER
⏘ FEAR
⏘ SKELETON CREW
⏘ DARK SIDE
⏘ THE ONE
⏘ FLAGSHIP
⏘ SPEAKEASY
⏘ STRATEGY PLUS
⏘ FANTASIA
⏘ OTHER (please specify)

9. Do you read fanzines:
YES ⏘   NO ⏘
If yes, which:

10. What type of games do you play (please tick box)
⏘ BOARDGAMES
⏘ TABLETOP
⏘ PLAY-BY-MAIL
⏘ COMPUTER ROLEPLAYING GAMES
⏘ LIVE ROLEPLAYING
⏘ WARGAMES
⏘ PAINTBALL
⏘ ADVENTURE GAME BOOKS
⏘ TELEPHONE GAMES

11. How much money a month on games/playing do you spend on average:
⏘ £5-10   ⏘ £11-15   ⏘ £16-20   ⏘£21-25
If more than £25, please specify

12. What was the last RPG game you bought:

13. Do you buy miniatures:
⏘ Yes
⏘ No
If yes how much do you spend a month on average

14. Do you own a computer?
⏘ Yes
⏘ No
If so, which one?

15. How often do you go to the cinema:
⏘ ONCE A MONTH
⏘ FOUR TIMES A MONTH
⏘ MORE (please specify)
⏘ NEVER

16. Do you own/have access to a video:
⏘ YES
⏘ NO

17. How often do you rent videos a month:

18. How many videos do you buy a year:

19. What kind of videos/films do you watch:
⏘ HORROR
⏘ SF
⏘ FANTASY
⏘ THRILLER
⏘ DRAMA
⏘ COMEDY

20. Do you buy fantasy books/novels:
⏘ YES
⏘ NO
If yes, how many a year:

For the following questions enter a score of between one and ten — ten being the highest mark.

21. What do you think of GamesMaster International in general?

⏘ MasterWorld News
⏘ MasterPlay (game overview)
⏘ MasterView (reviews)
⏘ MasterMiniatures
⏘ MasterPiece (fiction)
⏘ The Reading Room (books)
⏘ MasterGame (scenario)
⏘ MasterWayne (play-by-mail)
⏘ Live Roleplaying
⏘ Interview
⏘ Conventions/Clubs/Contacts
⏘ MasterMail (letters)
⏘ Critical Mass

22. Is there any other subject you would like to see covered in GamesMaster International?

23. Is there anything you would like to see dropped from the magazine?

24. Which of the following subjects would you like to see covered in GamesMaster International?
⏘ FILMS
⏘ VIDEOS
⏘ RECORDS
⏘ FANTASY ART
⏘ NONE OF THESE

25. What author would you like to see featured in GMI's fiction extract section:

26. Do you attend any games conventions?
⏘ YES
⏘ NO
If so, which ones:

27. Would you attend a GMI Convention/Readers' Meet based in London:
⏘ YES
⏘ NO
If not London where:

Now cut out this page (or photocopy it) and send it to: Newsfield, GamesMaster International Reader Survey, Ludlow, Shropshire SY8 1JW to get to us by November 22.

Make sure we know where to send your prize, should you win — fill in your name and address below:

Name
Address
                              Postcode

Results of GamesMaster International Reader Survey

1 Male   80%
   Female   20%

2 Aged under 17 20%
          17-23   70%
         over 23 10%

3 Full time   40%
   Part time   10%
   At college/
   university   30%
   At school   15%
   Unemployed   5%

4 Professional   20%
   White collar   40%
   (office work)
   Computer-
   related   20%
   Other   20%

5 Up to £5   10%
   £5-£10   15%
   £10-£30   10%
   £30-£100   15%
   £100-£200   40%
   Over £200   10%

6 4 people   40%
   3 people   30%
   2 people   10%
   1 person   10%
   no-one else 10%

7 Subscription 25%
   Reserved   15%
   Off shelf   45%
   Specialist
   shop   25%

8 White Dwarf   30%
   Raze   5%
   Zero   10%
   Ace   5%
   Fear   5%
   Skeleton Crew 5%
   The One   10%
   Flagship   5%
   Strategy Plus 5%
   Other: Dragon 20%
   No meaningful data on
   rest

9 Yes 30%
   No useful data
   No   70%

10 Boardgames   10%
   Tabletop   10%
   Play-by-Mail 10%
   Computer RP   10%
   Live RP   20%
   Wargames   15%
   Paintball   5%
   Adventure GB 15%
   Tele games   5%

11 £5-£10   15%
   £11-£15   20%
   £16-£20   40%
   £21-£25   15%
   Over £25   10%
   Average up to £40

12 No meaningful data

13 Yes   40%
   No   60%
   Average £10 p mth

14 Yes   75%
   No   25%
   No meaningful data

15 Once a month   45%
   Four times   20%
   More often   10%
   Never   25%

16 Yes 90%
   No   10%

17 Up to 4   70%
   5-10   30%

18 Av purchase 10
   0-5   10%
   6-10   70%
   Over 10 20%

19 Horror   15%
   SF   35%
   Fantasy   40%
   Thriller   5%
   Drama/Comedy   5%

20 Yes 95%
   No   5%
   1-10 pa   40%
   11-20 pa   30%
   Over 20 pa 30%

21 MasterWorld   9
   MasterPlay   8
   MasterView   7
   Master-
   Miniatures   7
   MasterPiece   8
   Reading Room   8
   MasterGame   8
   MasterWayne   7
   Live Roleplay 8
   Interview   9
   Conventions   7
   MasterMail   7
   Critical Mass 7

22 No useful data

23 No useful data

24 Films   30%
   Videos   30%
   Records   10%
   Fantasy Art 30%
   None of these
   (no score)

25 No useful data

26 Yes 20%
   No   80%
   No meaningful data

27 Yes 20%
   No   80%
   No useful data on
   other venues

5   Strategy and tactics

MANAGERS AND PLANNING . . . .

Managers, in particular Marketing Managers, are responsible for planning, organising, directing and controlling within their area of influence. All these controlling tasks are fundamental in assisting the manager to make decisions. The formulation of marketing plans, and any strategy allied to them, is strongly linked to managers' ability to control the resources at their disposal. Like most tasks in business, success depends on things getting done by individuals within the organisation. The management of human assets needs careful handling, as motivation, training and selection are the key features of leadership.

We all have ideas of what a manager does; indeed, there are many theories of management. Most managers learn how to manage the hard way through a process of trial and error. This is not a satisfactory method, as organisations need a manager to be effective immediately. Out of this need has arisen some concept of a scientific approach to managerial skills. This professional approach, in theory at least, requires managers to use their experience as a foundation and, from this, to build up an understanding of the basic principles of management. Then they must transfer these fundamental skills to help them, and to help others, in making decisions. Of the basic principles, some are appropriate to all management decisions, and others created to cope with specific problems. The basic principles of management, as we have noted already, are planning, organisation, direction and control. These are all relevant to formulating a marketing plan and, indeed, to marketing management as a whole.

TALKING POINT

'Learning how to manage by experience is the only really effective way of knowing what to do.' Do you think that this is true?

Planning is an essential feature of a manager's responsibilities. Marketing planning requires the manager to set a series of objectives from which to formulate a marketing strategy. Some notion of a timescale has also to be set which considers the implementation and achievements of these objectives. Just how these objectives are decided depends very much on the nature of the business. However, there are a number of basic steps:

1 Analysis of performance, both current and past, of all products.
2 A review of marketing opportunities and possible threats.
3 Relating these plans to the overall corporate objectives.

Once the marketing objectives have been decided, the manager must now determine which route to take to achieve these objectives. Many of the key phrases and tactics are taken straight from military terminology, such as flanking, or encirclement. Broadly speaking, a marketing strategy is the way in which the company or other organisation proposes to achieve its marketing objectives, and should always include consideration of the following:

• The selection of marketing targets
• Market positioning
• An appropriate marketing mix

TALKING POINT AND ACTIVITY

What do you think are the marketing objectives of a newsagent? Compare the approaches of two newsagents in your area. How does their range of goods on offer give you a clue to their objectives?

The choice of the marketing strategy should always take into consideration the company's strengths and weaknesses, together with a good knowledge of the market's needs. These strategies represent the company's overall route to achieving the marketing objectives. Marketing tactics are the fine tuning which adapts the strategy to ensure that the route is as smooth as possible.

The real difference between strategy and tactics is unclear. Tactics can be seen as a part of strategy, but strategies are nothing without a good tactical sense. If a Sales Manager's strategy is to increase the customer base, then an appropriate tactic is needed to achieve this. At the same time, if the company's strategy is to increase business, then the Sales Manager's strategy becomes the company's tactic. In many cases a good strategy has failed because of a company's lack of attention to tactics, or use of an inappropriate tactic. Equally, a poor strategy can be saved by clever tactics. Here are some broad distinctions between strategy and tactics:

1 Tactics tend to be more detailed than strategies.
2 Tactics relate to a shorter time period than strategies.
3 Tactics tend to be more flexible than strategies.
4 The range of tactics is usually wider than the range of strategies.

Timescales for achieving marketing objectives may vary greatly. As we have noted earlier, these marketing objectives are expressed as being short-term, medium-term or long-term, and may range from one month to ten years or more. Setting the marketing objectives and then placing a timescale on them depends on the resources which the company decides to commit to achieving each objective.

TALKING POINT

After having researched the newsagents in the previous talking point and activity, what do you think are their short, medium and long-term marketing objectives?

THE MARKETING PLAN . . . .

Most companies draw up an annual marketing plan, which begins with their analysis of their current situation, a look at their products, and the markets in which they hope to sell them. In developing this annual marketing plan, the following information should be gathered:

- Company sales
- Profits and profit trends
- A detailed analysis of each product
- A detailed analysis of each customer by type
- Market sizes
- Market volume
- Analysis of competitor's share of markets
- Company's sales and profit projections

Sales forecasts are a central feature of setting objectives. Strategy and tactics should then flow from these. Sales forecasts and budgets are very much inter-related with the annual marketing objectives and with any strategy and tactics which are applied to them. Sales forecasting will be discussed later in this chapter.

THE MARKETING MIX . . . .

Marketing mix is the combination of strategies and tactics, company policies, techniques and activities, to which resources are allocated in order to achieve the company's marketing objectives. Marketing mix itself is concerned with the practicalities of achieving the company's marketing objectives; in other words, how can the company's marketing objectives be translated into workable marketing plans and sales activities? The marketing mix should comprise the following:

1 **Strategic considerations** – what products or services should the company produce, and how is it to satisfy the needs of the target market? These choices will be limited in relation to the level of the company's resources; thus the company should limit its activities to what is judged likely to be fruitful for its markets and products.

Re'an

Designers and Manufacturers of
Connectors
Control knobs

Re-an Products Limited,
Springhead Enterprise Park,
Northfleet, Kent,
England.
Telephone: (0474) 328807
Telex: 966143 P.T. Re-an G.
Fax: (0474) 320285

Directors:
J. Jewsbury (Managing)
S. Webb M.I.I.M. Dip.I.M. (Production)
D. Jackson B.A. (Commercial)

Registered in England, No 1973149

With the example in Chapter 1, the Solicitor's letterhead, we simply showed
you the before and after. Here we have the entire creative process! You will see
that there were a large number of ideas floated but in the end the company
decided on something very similar to its previous letterhead above (see
pp68–9). This is often the case when a company already has a well-known
image and wishes to maintain this. Perhaps the best example of this is the 'BP'
logo, the history of which is well worth looking into for yourselves.

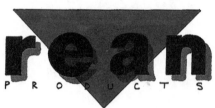

Re an

Designers and Manufacturers of:
Connectors, Control Knobs

PALM
TREE.
COMPANY

Re-an Products Limited

Main Office: 16 Passaic Avenue, Fairfield, New Jersey 07006. Tel: 201-808-0063, Fax: 201-808-6517.
Sales Office: 35 Stillman Place, Suite 102, San Francisco, California 94107. Tel: 415-512-7120, Fax: 415-512-7144.

Directors: J. Weatherley (Managing), J. Jewsbury (Sales), D. Jackson (Commercial), R. Weatherley (Technical)
Registered in England. No 1973149

2 **Tactical considerations** – what sales tactics or promotional tools will the company employ in its attempt to achieve its sales objectives?

3 **Planning considerations** – what is the company's long-term commitment to a product or the development of a new product?

4 **Resource considerations** – how much of the company's resources can be channelled towards advertising and sales promotions, and when can the company expect a return on research and development?

5 **Operational considerations** – to what extent does the company expect the marketing department to generate marketing and advertising copy and material?

The marketing mix aims to ensure that:

• The right product is available
• The price is right
• The product is available in the necessary outlets
• The product is available when the customer needs it

In conjuction with these four basic points, the marketing mix should also be responsible for making sure that the appropriate promotional tool is employed to help persuade the customer to consider the company's product and make the purchase.

TALKING POINT

How does an organisation determine what is the appropriate 'promotional tool'?

THE FOUR PS . . . .

Marketing mix can be more clearly defined as relating to:

- Product
- Price
- Place
- Promotion

The four parts of the marketing mix are extremely inter-dependent and cannot be considered separately. Here are some examples of the inter-dependence:

1 The brand image of a product should be reinforced by the pricing policy. In other words, a customer will be prepared to spend more on what is considered a reputable brand. The price charged is relative to the customer's perception of the product and not necessarily to its quality.

2 The level of advertising and sales promotion can strongly influence the customer's perception of the product.

3 If a company intends to distribute a product intensively, there will be a large sales force promoting the product in every market, and making sure that it is available where and when demand requires it.

TALKING POINT AND ACTIVITY

How would the marketing mix differ when comparing a retail outlet with a wholesale organisation?

If the company makes alterations to one aspect of the marketing mix, this will mean that there will be a knock-on effect to other parts of the marketing mix. If the price is reduced significantly, then this may influence the customer's image of the brand, and the product's standing in the market. This is not to say that a slight adjustment to one of the aspects of the marketing mix will not pay dividends. Slight alterations may be seen in a positive light by the customer, and it is therefore the skill of the Marketing Manager in understanding how the four main elements inter-relate that determines the success or failure of the company's marketing objectives.

FORECASTING – WHERE DOES IT FIT IN? . . .

Businesses must be able to predict their sales. They also need to have some clear idea about their potential profits and their cash flow. Miscalculations can be disastrous. Inefficient use of resources can mean that they will lose out against their competitors. Forecasting sales and budgeting for them is an essential part of the process of being efficient and aware of what may happen in the future. Traditionally, it is the accounts department or the company accountant who is left with the task of sales forecasting. Their approach is conservative in the main and they have a

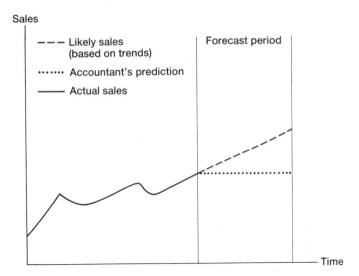

Accountants _v_ trend prediction.

tendency to under-estimate. It is the accountant's responsibility to prevent the organisation from overspending and so the accountant will try to curb spending by under-estimating sales forecasts, and thus turnover from sales and, of course, profit. The other common result is that under-estimating will make the actual sales figures or production levels achieved look all that much better by being 'better than was expected'. There is a danger that, if the organisation gears itself up for the lower figures, then it will be unprepared for the higher demand or the need for increased expenditure on production.

Arguably, then, the marketing department should be responsible for the sales forecasting. Marketing directors did not have, traditionally, to be very numerate and it is perhaps this factor among other historical ones which often prevented the marketing department from having control of this vital area, leaving it to the finance department instead.

Marketing departments are automatically involved if a new product or service is being launched. It is interesting to note that businesses that find themselves with new competitors will often tend to overstate the level of competition in the market and devalue, in market size terms, the potential sales overall.

There are, effectively, three different types of forecast, very imaginatively known as short, medium and long term. Broadly speaking, they fall into two main categories:

1 Forecasting for the whole market or industry and then working out what share of the market your particular organisation might be able to grab. This method is known as the 'top down' approach, as the forecast is obtained from data outside the organisation.
2 Forecasting sales by analysing previous sales data. This method is known as the 'bottom up' approach, as the data is collected from the organisation itself.

Let's now have a look at the three types of forecasting that we mentioned earlier:

1 **Short-term forecasting**   This looks about three months ahead and is done for immediate tactical reasons. It often looks specifically at seasonal trends and tries to smooth out any likely problems with the cash flow and production rate.

2 **Medium-term forecasting**   This looks up to one year ahead and is linked closely to budgeting. Usually this forecast forms the basis of the organisation's planning. It looks at probable sales as well as equipment and manpower needs.

3 **Long-term forecasting**   This can look quite a way into the future, perhaps as long as twenty years, but, more commonly, five or ten years. It is strongly related to the major strategic decisions that the organisation will have to make. The nature of the business will determine how long-term the forecast is. For example, in the car industry it would be no more than ten years, but in the raw materials field, arguably, it could be as long as twenty years.

TALKING POINT AND ACTIVITY

Can you think of a company or a product that was produced wildly in excess of demand? Harder still, can you think of a product or service where demand was well above supply, and which was simply unavailable for some time?

   How can these problems best be avoided?

The forecast determines the organisation's budget, and it is the sales budget that will generate sales. A budget is what is planned to happen and a forecast is just a prediction of what might happen. The budget, therefore, is much more controllable than the forecast, which might be affected by countless unpredicted outside factors. It is vital, however, that forecast, through budget to sales budget, are all linked. Many companies have suffered from an 'over-successful' sales force which has been let down by a serious shortfall in production, so that there are not enough goods to fill orders.

TECHNIQUES OF FORECASTING . . . .

We do not propose to go too deeply into the techniques of forecasting, as we feel this is not strictly necessary for you to know. Sales forecasting techniques are divided into two main categories, qualitative and quantitative techniques. Qualitative techniques rely very heavily on subjective opinion; quantitative techniques rely far more heavily on mathematical computations and have two subdivisions, known as time series analysis and casual analysis. Let's look at these techniques more closely:

Qualitative techniques

1 **Consumer survey method**   This technique asks the consumer or user for their opinion of the product or service. This is a basic market research technique. It is most valuable when there is a relatively small number of consumers and their

opinions are likely to give a better and more accurate forecast than the use of other methods.

2 **The panel or jury method**   In this method a group of experts is asked for its views on the market. Based on the group's opinions, a forecast is worked out. Sitting in committee, the experts will thrash out the various considerations and arrive at a joint decision (which may be an average in the case of disagreements). This is an expensive technique since it tends to be manpower-heavy and is arguably less accurate than some of the more mathematical approaches.

3 **Salesforce composite method**   In this technique each Sales Manager is asked to make a forecast for his/her particular area of responsibility. This is then linked to things such as sales targets and quotas. The salesperson's figures are compared to what the area manager sees as an estimation of the true state of affairs. If the figures differ wildly, as they may, since sales people tend to be pessimistic and to under-estimate, then they will meet and resolve the differences.

4 **Delphi method**   This is rather like the panel or jury method, but the members of the group (usually around twenty or so) do not meet and only correspond or speak to one another on the telephone. The system is designed to get each one of the panel to give his or her true feelings without being exposed to group pressure and the feeling that they should agree with the majority. A truer result should come out of this method than from the panel method. This system is not normally used for product or customer research, as the nature of the technique makes it more useful for research which is far more general. For example, questions could be asked to the panel on what they think will be the impact on the market of a new process or technique of production.

5 **Bayesian decision method**   This is quite complicated to explain, but in a nutshell, a diagram is drawn. This looks like a network of points linked together, and includes all the possibilities which the drawer of the diagram thinks should be considered. The group then looks at all the possible future outcomes, and tries to evaluate these in terms of their expected profitability or advantage to the organisation. The one that is identified as the best outcome for the future is chosen and aimed for. This is both subjective, in the sense that it is your opinion of the most likely future; and objective, since, once you have agreed the range of possibilities, you have to agree the most likely one and the best chances of achieving it.

6 **Testing method**   Usually employed when there are no sales figures to help anticipate demand. Product testing involves a small number of respondents and summarises their opinions and attitudes to the new product or service. This technique is only really any use for new products where the product is launched in a small geographical area. One of the other main problems is that, as with most new products, the cheaper it is, the more likely people are to try it out and not buy it again after the novelty has worn off. It is a brave organisation that bases its future on this technique alone.

Quantitative technique

1 Moving average This is a simple example of time series analysis. Taking a period of sales, say over ten years, you simply add all the sales figures and then divide them by the number of years. In this way you have, crudely, an average. Sales forecasts are then calculated by extending the trend line and following the average into the future.

2 Exponential smoothing This technique helps to overcome the inaccuracies that often plague the previous technique, taking into consideration the different weighting over the period of sales figures (for example, inflation may have distorted the turnover by making it appear, in relative terms, disproportionately high). This technique smooths out the 'blips' and aims to give a much more accurate trend and hence a more accurate forecast.

3 Time series analysis Sales figures inevitably fluctuate. What any forecaster is looking for is the underlying trend. Fluctuations may be simple to identify, such as seasonal changes, but some require deeper investigation. Time series anaylsis looks at any deviation from the average trend, and then adds such deviations back into the forecast once the trend line has been worked out. Not surprisingly, this particular method requires a considerable grasp of mathematics and, as this is a text on marketing, we are gladly willing to say no more.

4 Z chart Z charts provide a year's worth of data. Z charts show the months along their horizontal axis and the number of units sold on their vertical axis. The bottom line of the Z is the monthly sales figure; the diagonal line of the Z is the

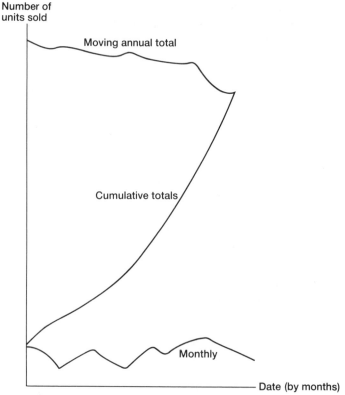

A 'Z' chart.

cumulative sales for all the months up to that month; and the top line is the moving annual average sales figure. In order to make full use of these charts, the forecaster must prepare several, using those from previous years to be able to compare them, and see if there are any common general trends. In this way a prediction may be made. This is, of course, rather subjective and the technique is rarely accepted as a serious forecasting tool.

5 **Leading indicator** This technique uses linear regression to establish a relationship between something measurable (such as sales figures for units sold) and what has to be forecast. On a diagram, one set of criteria is measured on one axis and another on the other axis. The trick is to see if there is a correlation (or relationship) between the two. If the measurements on the two axis lines come close together in a more or less straight line, the correlation is said to be linear, and there is then a close relationship between the two sets of data. The technique is increasingly done by computer and some very useful software packages have taken away the headache of working it out.

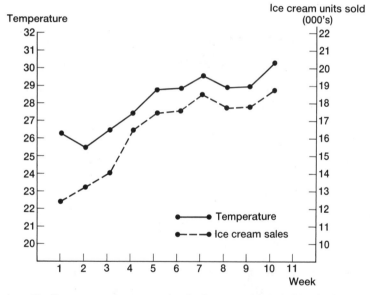

Lead indicator: temperature predictions could thus be used as a predictor or lead indicator for ice cream sales.

6 **Simulation** As with the previous example, this also relies on the use of a computer. The present situation, or a possible future situation, is fed into the computer. Then simulation uses trial and error, systematically going through each and every possibility in trying to work out the forecast. The more complicated the situation, the more complex the simulation, and hence the more variable and more numerous the probabilities.

7 **Diffusion model** This is rather complex. Diffusion theory makes the assumption that new products have four basic criteria:

a the idea which has created the product;

b how this new idea is to be communicated to others;

c the social system in which the product is to be sold;

d any time considerations.

The technique further breaks down the idea or innovation into three further sub-categories which try to identify the product's life cycle. Forecasting is then made from relatively small amounts of data over short periods of time during the launch of the new product. The assumption is made that those who purchase the product after the initial launch period will imitate the early buyers. In other words, buying habits will be similar throughout the life of the product.

Sales forecasts must be incorporated very early in the decision-making process. As competition becomes keener, then planning must become more scientific. Having researched and forecast, the organisation can maximise its efforts in targeting the segment of the market that most closely resembles its potential customers.

TEST YOURSELF

1 What are the basic responsibilities of a Marketing Manager?

2 To what extent do you think that theoretical managerial skills are transferable?

3 What must a manager consider in planning? What are the three basic steps?

4 What is marketing strategy?

5 What is the difference between marketing strategy and marketing tactics?

6 Note five factors that form part of developing the annual marketing plan.

7 What is a marketing mix?

8 List the four main aims of a successful marketing mix.

9 What are the '4 Ps'?

10 What are the dangers of drastically changing the balance of the 4 Ps?

11 How far does medium-term forecasting look into the future?

12 What is a qualitative technique in forecasting?

13 What is the delphi method?

14 What is time series analysis?

15 How does sales forecasting fit into the overall planning that a company undertakes?

A WORKING CASE STUDY

Marketing a franchise: Poppies

Franchising is a form of licensing. The franchisor offers a business package which includes management assistance and marketing services. Franchising need not necessarily be the obvious form which we see in our high streets, such as Wimpy Bars, Benneton and Kentucky Fried Chicken, where the package includes the supply of goods which the franchisee will sell. Perhaps most successful is Pepsi Cola, which franchises canning and bottling plants throughout the world and gives the franchisee the sole right to produce Pepsi Cola's range of products in that country.

Franchising encompasses not only physical consumer or industrial goods but also services, particularly those aimed at businesses. To a greater or lesser extent, the franchisor keeps a close controlling interest in the franchisee. The franchisor must, above all, make sure that the standard of service offered by the franchisee is consistent with the corporate image of the franchising operation.

The exact financial terms and conditions of the franchising agreement will, of course, differ, but the franchisees will inevitably pay an initial 'set-up' fee which buys them the right to operate within a specified area. The franchisees will also pay a percentage of their annual turnover, in addition to contributions to the marketing budget of the franchisor.

By setting up franchising operations, an organisation can dispense with involvement in the physical distribution or servicing of a geographical area.

**Marketing
a
Franchise**

by

Sue M Rorstad
Chairman and Managing Director
Poppies (UK) Limited

Selling a franchise is a complex process. Basically, you are selling someone a new way of life – a means to fulfil a dream, a means to appease their ambition to succeed in business for themself. You are selling to someone who probably has no previous business experience, and no knowledge of your product or service, an opportunity to go into business for themself as part of a franchised network.

You cannot start to recruit franchisees until you know you have a proven successful formula. People will be paying sometimes all of their life savings to buy the franchise – it is completely unethical to sell franchises until:

1 You have a provably successful *pilot operation* which has run for a number of years.

Background Information

Will a Poppies Franchise suit me?

What does a Poppies Franchise mean?

What is Poppies?

What is a Franchise?

Much more than a good idea...

Dear

I am pleased that you are interested in a POPPIES Franchise. This prospectus will give you more information.

It is certainly exciting and challenging to run your own business.

POPPIES offers you the opportunity of providing original and specialist services using a proven and successful business format.

If, after reading our literature, you feel a POPPIES Franchise could be your future, we would like to hear from you.

Undoubtedly you will have many questions and we will be happy to meet you and discuss all aspects of a POPPIES Franchise.

If you also want to meet us for an informal discussion, please contact me to arrange a convenient time. We will be happy to meet you in our Darlington office or in London.

I look forward to hearing from you.

Yours sincerely,

Sue M Rørstad
Managing Director

P2a 6/85

2 You have 'packaged' the steps to success into easy-to-follow *manuals* and *training courses*.

3 You have a *central organisation* with the skills and resources to support your franchisees and help them succeed.

4 You have identified the type of person you want to recruit as a franchisee and have a clear definition of the role of the franchisee.

In the case of my franchise, the concept was founded by me in 1980. I ran a pilot operation in the north east of England for three years before starting to expand through franchising. I had personally done the job of the franchisee and had fully-documented manuals. I had a small but competent central organisation. We had:

- Devised training courses
- Carried out research into potential franchise territories
- A strong and protected corporate identity
- A fair franchise agreement

WE HAD A PRODUCT TO SELL!

All these sound very simple but, in fact, they take years of hard work and substantial investment to perfect.

Just to get to the point of being able to start to franchise took me seven years and cost me at least £50 000 which, in 1983, was quite a lot of money.

To me, successful marketing of a franchise means:

Promoting the franchise to the right people, at the right time and at the right price.

Recruiting the wrong people as franchisees may generate income but will cost a lot more in the long run as people fail or struggle in business.

In the early days, one of our main criteria for franchise recruitment was location. Although we had proved we could run a pilot operation, we had not yet opened and supported franchised outlets. We did not know just how much support a new franchisee would need or how long the learning curve would be. For this reason, we wanted a small number of franchisees close to our home base. Our target number of franchisees for the first year was four, of suitable quality, from the north east of England. Therefore, national advertising was out of the question, as it would generate enquiries from the whole country.

Advertising

Therefore, we had to rely on local newspaper advertising. Unfortunately, as you may have heard, 'the media is the message'. Our experience of local newspapers was that, although they generated enquiries, they were from the wrong people. Our business is a management franchise so we were looking for people with either management experience or with the capability to attain management standing.

A local newspaper was not successful in putting across the correct image of our business. The type, location and colour of advertisements did not do justice to our upmarket and strong corporate identity. The size of an affordable advertisement did not allow a new and unknown business to put across enough information to attract the right people.

Our brochures and promotional literature projected the right image and message but, if we were sending them to the wrong people, we were wasting not only our time but our money.

A further problem in the early days was that all potential franchisees wanted to talk to existing franchisees. They wanted to check out the facts and the claims made by us, the franchisor. The first few franchisees, obviously, were not able to do this and, therefore, our experience quickly showed us that straightforward advertising was unlikely to recruit the type of people who would be right and be prepared to be the first.

People buying the first franchise are likely to take a greater risk but also will pay less than those joining an established and well-known franchise.

In our case the first franchisees paid about £7000 to join Poppies – today the cost is nearer £20 000.

Growth

Faced with these problems – how did we overcome them? Well, after much trial and error, in the end our first franchisees were recruited as a result of personal contact. People who had heard about the pilot operation; people who attended a talk or a lecture; or friends and acquaintances.

For the first year we grew very slowly, creeping down the country. When we were confident that our franchisees would succeed if they followed our method, and when we knew we had the capability to support distant franchisees, we were ready to expand nationally.

This was good for franchise recruitment – as our ideal franchisee is much more likely to read *The Times* than a local newspaper – but the start of a headache for regional staff, who would live out of suitcases for years.

To market the franchise nationally, changes were needed. We:

- Decided to revamp our corporate image
- Changed our name and logo
- Changed our promotional literature
- Increased the price of the franchise to enable us to invest in growth

Our early experiences with franchisees had sharpened our definition of the ideal franchisee. Now, with all the national media available to use, we had to determine which would produce the right response.

> The right people at the right time, in the right numbers. Geography was no longer a major consideration!

This exercise was extremely costly. For the first three years in our expansion programme, we spent thousands of pounds on advertising in national newspapers –

different sections, different days, different advertisements. We were at exhibitions (some specific to franchising, some not), at a cost of approximately £15 000 for each event. We spent on advertising in franchise magazines and, finally, on extensive PR, generating interest and write-ups, and continuing with talks and lectures.

As we grew, we also had to increase investment in research, training and support services and, at the same time, continue to protect our name and identity.

Now:

- We know exactly who we are looking for and how to reach the right people quickly
- We concentrate on seasonally-worded advertisements in strategic places in one or two national newspapers
- We consciously look towards promoting Poppies as the 'Rolls Royce' service to customer's homes
- We concentrate on PR
- We concentrate more on supporting our existing business as a means of future expansion, as this is more likely to come in future from people who already know about our business, either as a service or through knowing one of our existing franchisees

We no longer:

- Attend exhibitions or advertise in franchise magazines
- We rarely use local newspapers unless we are helping to sell an existing franchise

NOW WE ARE A NATIONAL COMPANY!

Because we are a national company, we have to be much more careful to ensure that we select the right people. A bad franchisee will not just cause us a headache, but could risk damage to an already established neighbouring Poppies' business.

ONCE UPON A TIME – TO JOIN POPPIES

YOU HAD TO BE GOOD.

NOW

YOU HAVE TO BE THE BEST!

It has taken us ten years to become a national company and brand lead in our field.

WE INTEND TO STAY

NO 1 IN THE UK

Sue M Rorstad
Chariman and Managing Director
Poppies (UK) Limited
August 1990

Activities and tasks

1 As you may have realised, the Poppies organisation is a franchised commercial and domestic cleaning business. Look through the case study and make a summary of Sue's main points about setting up the operation.

2 In the role of Poppies' Marketing Director, devise an advertisement to attract prospective franchisees.

3 Using the case study as a model, devise a plan which offers the opportunity to set up a Fast Food retail outlet. What qualities would you be looking for in a prospective franchisee? In which ways would they differ from an applicant for Poppies?

FURTHER READING

The Strategic and Operational Planning of Marketing, G Greenley, McGraw Hill
Marketing Analysis and Forecasting, Clifton, Nguyer and Nutt, Heinemann
Marketing Plans – How To Prepare Them, M McDonald, Heinemann
The Marketing Research Process, Margaret Crimp, Prentice-Hall

TALKING POINT

Can you think of a customer need
that has not been met by a product
or service? Perhaps the product or
service lies out of reach (in price) of
the potential market?

6   Products and planning

WHAT IS A PRODUCT? . . . .

As we know, a product is something that satisfies a customer's need.
We should broaden this somewhat and include not only a product but
also a service as being capable of satisfying a need.

The need itself may exist, but there may be no product or service
which exists to satisfy it, or the product or service which does exist
cannot satisfy the level of need at present.

THE PRODUCT MIX . . . .

The product mix is the range of a particular company's products.
Each of these products which make up the product mix is linked to a
particular need within a particular market. This should not be
confused with the product line, which usually refers to the range of
products that is aimed at one particular market.

A collection of product lines make up the product mix and the
extent of this product mix is known as the product mix width.
Everything that has a width has a depth! In this instance the product
mix depth refers to the number of products that make up any one of
the product lines.

The final definition to try to remember is the product mix consistency. This relates to how the individual product lines fit into the product mix. Are they complementary, going with each other to complete the range? Are they different, requiring different approaches in sales and marketing techniques? Perhaps they demand very different sorts of technology or industrial process?

LIFE CYCLES . . . .

Like a living thing, the majority of products have a limited life. A product's life cycle starts with its birth, or introduction on to the market. Then follows its growth into the market; its mature stage when it is a fully-established product; and its declining phase when it is fading out of existence. Let's look at these stages in a little more detail:

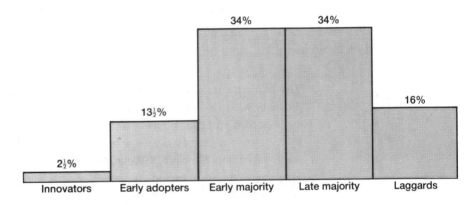

Innovation adoption model (new products) from Everest Rogers.

1 **The introduction of the product** The most important consideration here is to establish the product on the market. Awareness of the product's existence must be built up in the minds of retailers, wholesalers and, of course, the customer. Advertising is the usual method. Once the product is established in the minds of the potential buyers, the product must overcome any resistance to the acceptance of something new on the market. As orders, hopefully, roll in, the focus moves to making sure that sufficient supplies of the product are available. Nothing can kill a product off faster at birth than its non-availability.

2 The growth stage of the product Having successfully launched the product and generated the initial interest and orders, it is often necessary to continue to promote the product in order to maintain its place in the market. This period of a product's life is usually its most profitable, since demand may not yet have reached a peak and most of the initial starting costs have been recouped in the introduction period. It is at this time that the business will look for other potential markets for the product to move into, and also attempt to dislodge competitors from the market.

	High market share	Low market share
High market growth	Stars	Problem children
Low market growth	Cash cows	Dogs

Product classification as a cross-reference of sales growth and share of market.

3 The maturity stage of the product A business will look to this period of a product's life to extend for as long as possible. In this stage the product delivers much-needed profit and turnover for the business. Competition must be beaten off by the strong establishment of a brand image and firmly rooted share of the market. The importance of looking after customers still plays a prominent role. They must be able to obtain the product readily and still be kept loyal to it, to guarantee a steady level of purchase.

Older products which may be on the verge of decline can, by careful thought, be found a new lease of life through being reintroduced into the market or introduced into new markets. We will look at product modification in more detail later.

4 The decline stage of the product Sooner or later something will happen that will forever kill off potential sales. It may be any of the following:

- it becomes technically obsolete
- customer attitude changes towards it
- a better product has appeared on the market
- sales have peaked and are falling off
- it is no longer profitable to produce it

Once any of the above has happened, the business is faced with having to do something about it. Amongst the options are:

TALKING POINT AND ACTIVITY

Identify some examples of products that have declined, stabilised at a low level of demand, and have then experienced an upsurge in demand after a period of time. Can you think of products that have been repackaged successfully and relaunched on to the market, or perhaps been diverted into new markets?

a stop spending anything on the product in excess of paying to produce it;

b raise the price and milk the last possible sales out of it and let it die a natural death;

c divert spending on to other products;

d decide that, once demand reaches a particular level, production will cease and wait until that happens before acting;

e maintain production at a basic level to supply demand arising from brand loyalty;

f maintain the product at present levels and hope that additional marketing activities can rejuvenate the product;

g put the decline down to changes in trends and fashions and wait for the product to become fashionable again.

TALKING POINT AND ACTIVITY

Identify some proactive product developments. An example to help you to get thinking is Barclaycard, which was the first credit card.

Identify some examples of reactive product development – the Access card is the free credit card which copied the Barclaycard.

PRODUCT PLANNING . . . .

A successful business should always try to have a range of products within its product mix at various stages of their life cycles. Businesses which rely on one product and one product alone are in constant danger of getting into a position tnat might mean that they have lost their 'golden egg' and do not have a newly-hatched one to replace it. Businesses need a steady flow of profitable products, the more mature products helping to pay for the new ones, which in turn will pay for the next generation of profit-makers.

In the field of product development there are two major strategies. One strategy is to concentrate on being the first into a new field and is called proactive product development. The other is somewhat safer, as the business responds to changes by copying the leads given by other businesses: this is known as reactive product development.

The dangers of having a proactive policy are that you are forever breaking new ground and taking the risks all the time. There is a high risk of failure, but with that risk comes the possibility of great rewards. The first company to create a product for a waiting market should be well placed to make very good profits.

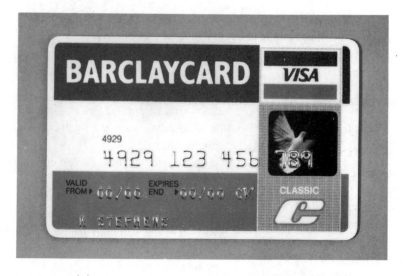

Barclaycard is an example of a successful proactive product.

TALKING POINT

Which do you think is the better development strategy, proactive or reactive? What other advantages and disadvantages of either strategy can you think of?

Reactive policy is a lot safer: you can learn from any mistakes that the proactive business made and avoid these. After all, the proactive business has taken all the risks and if you are ready to react you can profit from the market that it has just opened up. By being a very fast reactor, you can often make as much, if not more, than by being the proactor, and without the inherent risks.

How can you tell whether a product or service is likely to take off? The business must look at the advantages their product might have over the competition and weigh up whether these advantages are promising enough to take the risk. Some of the key considerations are:

1 Does the product accurately meet the requirements of the target market?
2 Does it have advantages in design, style, reliability or quality?
3 How does it perform and stand up to the demands that will be made on it by the customer?
4 Does it make the customer's life easier (in the case of a labour-saving device)?
5 Does it add to the customer's ego or self-image (in the case of a designer product)?
6 Does it offer the chance of respect from others for the customer (in the case of a status symbol)?
7 Is it likely to be seen as a superior product when compared to other competing brands?
8 Is its presentation and image right?
9 Does it cost less to produce than the competition?

10 Can you expect a reasonable profit margin?

11 Can you offer a consistent and reliable product or service?

We will look at launching new products in a separate chapter and you will find further detail there.

BRAND AND PRODUCT MANAGEMENT . . . . . .

A brand is a name that is given to a particular product or range of products. In many cases this brand name is simply the company's name, such as Ford or Heinz. In other cases it may be a completely different name, such as Nescafé, or it may be the overall name for the entire range of goods, such as St Michael for Marks & Spencer.

Branding basically exists to identify a particular product from its competitors. It is all to do with helping the customer identify the product easily. The choice of a brand name is often absolutely vital to the image of the product. Many brand names have become household names; indeed some have become part of the language, such as Hoover (many people now talk of going to hoover the living room, rather than going to vacuum it). Such is the power and penetration of the brand name into our lives.

TALKING POINT AND ACTIVITY

Make a list of the brand names that you can think of, writing down as many as you can in five minutes. See how many of them are company names and how many of them are product names.

Own-label products

With the dominance in the supermarkets of 'own label' products, the brand name has found a new meaning for the customer. If you have the choice of buying Nescafé or Sainsbury's own label coffee, what is there to help you make up your mind? The price is different: the Sainsbury's own label brand is cheaper; you may get more 'bulk' for your money; but what do you really think of the choice? Nine times out of ten you will probably reach for the Nescafé. Why? Probably because you think that the Nescafé is 'better'. Better quality? Perhaps. Now change the situation around and compare Nescafé with Maxwell House. Why do you buy one over the other? Customers go into a shop with a mental list of their preferred brands. What all the marketing, sales promotions and advertising is geared up to do is to put a company's particular brand name into your memory so that your decision-making process when faced with a choice of branded and own-label products is speeded up and you reach for the brand they want you to reach for.

This branding goes further and tries to encourage you to see the company's entire range as having the same reputation (a good one, of course). This multi-product branding really does pay dividends, especially when launching a new product that has the same brand name. The new product will find sales quicker and will be accepted faster. The company must be careful, however, since this is a two-edged sword. A poor product can bring a bad reputation to an otherwise good and reliable brand name.

TALKING POINT AND
ACTIVITY

Visit your local supermarket and
have a look at the 'competing'
brands of washing powder, liquid
and fabric conditioners. You will be
amazed to see just how many of
them are produced by the same
companies. Each brand has its own
identity and advertising campaigns.
Is this just a clever way of selling the
same thing to different people?

Some companies prefer to trade under a range of brand names. They may well be in the same market, but they appear to be almost like competitors, though often with complementary products. A good example of this is United Biscuits, which trades under several 'household name' brand names including Maxwell House and McVities. The same product, in all but brand name, can then be aimed at different market segments with different images, prices and marketing strategies.

As we have noticed, some manufacturers have thier own brand name, while others sell under the brand name of a retailer. The manufacturers which produce particular Marks & Spencer's products will also produce their own brand products. This method of production is very useful to the manufacturers since it enables them to increase their own production runs and simply change the labels. It also means that they can sell a large proportion of their production runs without having to promote and market these themselves. In other cases, producing own-label products for retail chains is the only way for manufacturers to get them to stock their goods.

What this relationship does mean is that retailers like Sainsbury's, Marks & Spencer and Tesco are in a very powerful position. They control the pricing, the distribution and the marketing. The manufacturer is very much in their hands. The retail chain will be able to demand that pricing is in their favour, the specifications of the product meet with their approval, that particular stock levels are maintained, and that they receive priority treatment even above the manufacturer's own-label products.

Product names

The additional use of a name coupled with the brand name also helps to identify a particular product. Ford is the company name and also the brand name, but in addition to this all of their makes or models of car have a name of their own. The Fiesta, Sierra, Escort and Orion are all examples of Ford's product names. This helps the customer to speed up the decision-making process by recognising and selecting the product they want in a potentially confusing situation. Ford could just call all of their cars 'Ford cars' and give them a number, or describe them as the '£13,000 Ford car'. Each product name establishes a specific image by which the customer can identify the product. What you call a product has to be carefully thought out. An inappropriate name is death to the product – after all who would want to ride about in a Ford Trout?

Product name helps to position the product in the market. The name should convey something to which the prospective buyer can relate. A boring or inappropriate name will need much more spent on it in marketing and promotion than a name that inspires the customer to remember it and be inspired by it.

Trademarks

Once you have decided on a name, you need to protect that name. Without trade names being registered as trademarks, there would be nothing to stop anyone giving their product the same name as yours. Successful products can be imitated but they cannot be copied and the same thing goes for names. You cannot even attempt partly to copy a name; for example, you could not name your car the Furd Curtina, or you would find yourself very quickly in court! Registered names and trademarks are very valuable commodities. What the name represents is all the effort and expense you have put into making that product what it is.

PACKAGING . . . .

Packaging has really come into its own over the past few years for a number of reasons. The most important of these are the growth of self-service as a retail tool, and the need to ensure that the product gains as much shelf space as possible. This is done through easy and efficient distribution by virtue of good packaging.

The demand for different and more flexible packaging has led to the widespread use of plastics, foil and treated paper and card. New printing technology has allowed hitherto unusable materials to carry product information, photographs and logos. Packaging has assisted the massive change to self-service supermarket shopping, where nearly 90 per cent of the weekly shopping is now done.

Packaging design itself needs to fulfil a number of functions, which include:

1 **Protection** The product needs to be protected against the environment, rough handling or time spent awaiting purchase.
2 **Convenience** Easy storage – the package should be a regular size, easy to stack and store. Easy to handle and – not to be

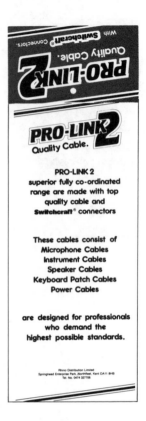

A finished pack design where the product itself forms the main impact of the display. The copy on the packaging itself is kept simple, since much of it will be obscured once the product is in place.

forgotten – easy to open. How many of you have had milk cartons spray you with their contents even if you follow the directions on the packaging?

3 **Information** The package must give all the necessary information on the product, including that required by law such as its country of origin, if it can be harmful, its ingredients, etc.

4 **Easy use** Functional packaging that is easy to use, perhaps incorporating safety features.

5 **Convenient to transport** Costs may be cut by packaging the product in lightweight materials that are still strong enough to survive the journey.

6 **Reuseable packaging** A product's packaging can be designed to be reusable by refills. Other products, such as coffee jars, have a reuse facility as a storage jar. In this case the shape is important so that the container is recognisable even after the label has been removed.

TALKING POINT

Do you think that packaging is important? What makes some packaging work and some not work?

7 **Assisting product image**   The shape, as we have mentioned already, and the wording/design, should be recognisable and help to enhance the product's image.

8 **Corporate identity**   Similar to product image, but a range of products may have packaging similarities to each other, to help foster the image of an overall identity which assists in maintaining brand loyalty.

9 **Display advantages**   An easily arranged stack and display has great advantages in the supermarket. A regular-sized package is likely to be easier to stack in bulk, but at the same time should be eye-catching and attractive to the customer.

10 **Differentiation**   A different shape, or strikingly different artwork, can be used to give the impression that the product is unique, or has changed. The widespread use of seasonal packaging, in particular, is a good example of this.

TALKING POINT AND ACTIVITY

Try to put the 10 packaging considerations into order of priority for the following products:

a   a range of beverages
b   a range of hi-fi and audio equipment
c   a range of self-assembly furniture

How do the priorities differ and why?

Packaging's main responsibility is to protect the product inside. There are several key features to this consideration:

- Damage during handling is perhaps the most common form of hazard to the package. Most damage is done before the product reaches the customer. Damaged goods must be replaced and are both inconvenient to the retailer and to the customer.
- Theft cannot be easily avoided, but certainly a good packaging system will inhibit this. The main problem is the number of handlers there are from manufacturer to customer.
- Contamination of food, clothing and machinery. Sensitive machinery is particularly prone to contamination by dust or other small particles. An airtight package is therefore essential.
- Seepage of liquids, in particular, is a problem and products should be protected from leaks, or evaporation. This holds true for powders too.
- Flavour loss or changes in the flavour may be the result of not having airtight packaging or using packaging that lets in the light.
- Moisture changes can damage the product; frozen foods need a constant moisture level, as do seemingly tough products like paints.

TALKING POINT

Would these considerations regarding packaging and protection differ in hot climates?

- Insects may attack poorly-protected products and do untold damage to them.
- Mould may attack a badly-packaged product and can irretrievably affect its quality.

TEST YOURSELF

1   What is a product?

2   What is a product mix?

3   What are the stages of a product's life cycle?

4   How can a company prevent one of its products from becoming obsolete?

5   What is a proactive policy?

6   State some of the key considerations as to whether a product will be successful or not.

7   List at least ten 'brands'.

8   How have 'own labels' affected the food market?

9   Why are major food chains such a strong force in the food business?

10   What is the importance of a 'good' product name?

11   What has made packaging more flexible in the present day?

12   How does packaging enhance product identity?

13   What is differentiation in packaging terms?

14   At what point in distribution does packaging face the greatest danger?

15   List four 'protective' responsibilities of packaging.

A WORKING CASE STUDY

The Island Spice Company

What we have here is a very good example of a 'pack design' exercise. The client is a well-established food manufacturer and was well versed in the marketing requirements for the product.

The product itself is a range of sauces and spices from the Caribbean; a relative newcomer to the 'ethnic foods' market and as such requiring active marketing if it were to succeed. The brief was therefore to produce something both similar to the client's existing packaging style, yet also conveying the fact that the product was, if not actually produced in the Caribbean, tasting just as if it were!

The proof sheets reproduced here (pages 95–8) give a very good overview of the style designed for the product and how recurring themes were used to create a brand image.

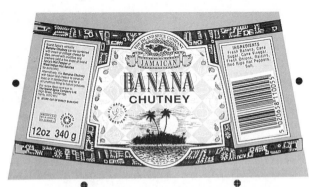

Activities and tasks

1 How important do you think packaging was for this range of products?

2 Investigate the competition that this range faces in the supermarket and how its pricing compares with the competition. For these purposes you will need to compare the range with Indian and Chinese sauces and spices, among others.

3 Do you think that the overall image works? What does the packaging style convey to you?

4 Design a series of packs for a convenience food manufacturer. The product is designed for the ultra-quick 'microwave in the bag in three minutes' type. The major problem is the fact that the client insists that the product portray an image of 'home cooking' yet still appeal to the convenience market! Pricing may be a concern here and you will need to portray a high-quality image in your packaging as the price to be charged will be high compared to the competition.

FURTHER READING

Pricing Strategy, Taylor and Wills, Staples Press
An Introduction to the UK Economy, C Harbury and R Lipsey, Pitman Publishing
First Principles of Economics, R Lipsey and C Harbury, Weidenfeld and Nicolson
Economics – a student's guide, J Beardshaw, Pitman Publishing

7   New products

COMING UP WITH NEW IDEAS . . . . .

Having a good idea is often the basis of a new product. Some ideas
come quickly and others are years in developing. Some products are
innovative, while others are simply copies or adaptations of existing
products. Some products have very little in the way of innovation or
'new product' appeal and are absolute and shameless copies made
just to cash in on the success of the original product.

Good idea or bad, all products start off with an original idea. Any
organisation wishing to develop new products should therefore
address themselves to the problem of creating the right sort of
environment and atmosphere to encourage new ideas and hence new
products. Here are some of the ways in which the development of
new ideas and products may be encouraged:

1 **Brainstorming** can be a very useful and thought-provoking way
of getting people to come up with innovative ideas. Eight to twelve people are put
in comfortable surroundings under the direction of a person who is given the role
of suggesting useful key words or phrases to help stimulate the creative process.
The members of the brainstorming group then shout out the first word that comes
into their heads, no matter how stupid the word might seem. The other members
of the group respond to that word and come up with another word. It works on the
same principle as word association and eventually something useful might come
out of it. The brainstorming sessions are usually taped or perhaps recorded with a
video camera and the results are played back and analysed.

2 **A suggestion box** fixed to the wall of the most used part of the factory or office
may result in something useful being generated internally from one of the
members of the workforce. This has proved especially effective for some
businesses and they now offer financial incentives for good ideas and to help
encourage more members of staff to contribute. Payments to staff are usually
based on how much money the company will save from adopting their sugges-

tion. Indeed the bulk of suggestion box ideas have more to do with cost cutting and efficiency than new product ideas, but a fair percentage of ideas may well be for new products.

3 **Forced relationships**   The concept of forced relationships is an interesting one. With this technique two or more seemingly unrelated items are considered together. Take a kettle, a clock and a radio – put them together and what have you got? A pair of scissors? No, a Teasmade! Brilliant?

4 **Marketing research** should help develop many new ideas. Most, of course, will be utterly impractical or unprofitable. In the consumer field, however, the number of 'free' ideas received from the public is amazing. General market research cannot be expected to generate much in the way of specific ideas. It needs to be taken a step further, asking people specifically about their unsatisfied needs and coaxing the answers out of them.

5 **Research and development** is an area of high cost and employment in certain companies. Some companies need to spend vast sums of money on R & D just to keep up with their competitors. The highest costs are in areas such as electronics, drugs and computers.

6 **The sales force** itself often feels that it is the least consulted and most full of ideas. It is an unwise company which ignores what is, effectively, its 'eyes and ears' in the market place. The members of the sales force are out in the real world day after day; they, above all, know what the market needs and can pass on the thoughts and requirements of the company's customers, as well as their own.

TALKING POINT AND ACTIVITY

Try word association yourself in groups of no more than about six. What do you think are the chances of coming up with something truly original using this technique?

   Which do you think is the most likely source of new ideas?

7 **Competitors**   Looking at what the competition is selling can be very useful, but is also fraught with dangers. Most businesses keep an up-to-date collection of their competitors' brochures and sales literature. Some may even buy and thoroughly investigate their competitors' products. This makes good sense, but, if the product they are looking at has not been properly market-tested in the first place, anyone copying it will just be buying themselves a headache. Who wants another version of something nobody wants? Even if the product is OK, the copier will probably be too late to make much impression on the market by the time the copy is ready for sale.

SORTING THE WHEAT FROM THE CHAFF . . . .

Having thought up all these brilliant new ideas, we must now concentrate on reducing the number of ideas to the most viable ones. Most companies use a screening process to judge ideas as to their suitability for the market. The company should also be aware of how the idea will fit into the company's overall strategy to be an enhancement and not a diversion.

Here are some of the more common screening methods:

1 How compatible is the idea with the existing strategies of the company? There are a great many good ideas that can be eliminated fairly quickly because they do not fit in with the company's strengths and available resources. The company must have staff capable of developing the product, and a sufficient financial buffer to cope with the inevitable costs of development. We must not forget, of course, that the company should also have the necessary marketing skills to launch the product.

If any ideas are allowed to go further than they really should, and it is found that after all the idea cannot be exploited successfully, then this mistake will inevitably weaken the company and add to its financial burdens.

2 How does the idea compare with the company's existing products? If a new product fits well into an existing product line it will create less difficulties and demands on the company's resources. Compatibility means being able to use the same distribution channels, sales teams, sales techniques, etc. A totally different product that is incompatible with the existing product line will cost disproportionately more. A compatible product has several advantages over and above costs: it may fill a gap in the product line, its availability doing much to improve the image of the range; and it may generate additional sales as a knock-on effect to the rest of the range.

3 Will it pay? Even if the product is compatible, there are no guarantees that it will be feasible to produce it. The concept of value engineering looks at all the direct and indirect costs and assesses a product's likelihood to produce a profit.

4 Is the concept sound? There really is no point in making something that no one is likely to buy. The trouble with a new product or idea (the more revolutionary, the greater the problem) is that no one has actually seen it. How can you react to something that does not exist? Customers will not have an understanding of the new product and will, naturally, be biased in favour of a brand or competitor that they already use, as they cannot see yours. However, few companies are prepared to go to the expense of making the product until they have got a customer reaction. A half-way-house solution is to test the concept as it is. The company will make the product as 'real' as possible by using drawings and possibily fake packaging. The new product can then be discussed by the potential customers and a more accurate idea of its potential can be obtained.

5 How many can we sell, then? If all the above hurdles have been jumped, then the final step in the screening process should be to assess the likely demand. The aim of this is to identify any product that will sell, but not in sufficient numbers to warrant actually producing it. Perhaps sales will not even cover the costs of development?

TALKING POINT

How many brilliant ideas do you think
have been lost by businesses not
being prepared to take the chance?
What effect do you think this has had
on new technology and development
over the years?

As a general guide the screening process should be undertaken as
quickly as possible. Time and resources that are pumped into ideas
and products which really have no chance of success are just wasted.
It is very easy to make mistakes and throw out good ideas and take on
useless ones. It is better in the long run to be ruthless, since the costs
of development can be cripplingly high.

MARKETING ANALYSIS . . . .

The cost of developing new ideas gets greater as the development continues from
initial idea through to the launch of the finished product. Since the objective is to
eliminate any potential losers as early as possible, how can a business be fully
satisfied that it is making the right decision to proceed? Comprehensive analysis and
forecasting are the obvious things to do. Once an idea has reached the development
stage, we are talking about big money investment.

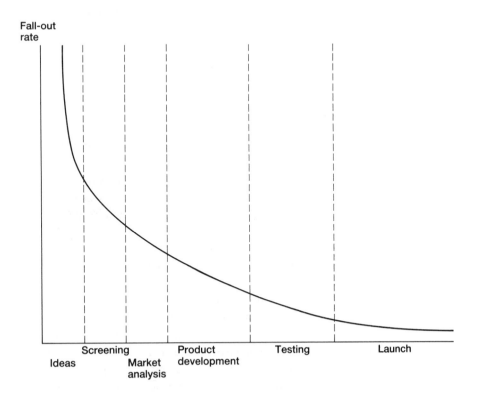

New product fall-out rate.

What are the various stages of development?

1 New ideas.
2 The screening process.
3 Marketing analysis.
4 Product development.
5 Testing the product.
6 Launch of the product.

The 'fall-out' rate from 1 to 6 gets less as the product gets closer to launch. This is the reverse of costs, which get higher and higher as the product reaches launch. In order to make sure that the product goes no further than its usefulness should allow, the business must carry out market research and compile as much information as possible as to the product's potential. Estimates must be made as to costs and the product's price must be set.

The sales potential for the product also needs to be established. This may be obtained by either looking at competing products or consulting the sales force as to potential sales.

By the time the product is reaching the end of its development, the marketing department should have made as many projections as possible. These should include the necessary budgets and the potential profitability.

There are several key ways of working out the sales potential of a new product or service. This form of forecasting is somewhat different from normal forecasting based on 'known' products, which we have already discussed. Here are the main methods:

TALKING POINT

Do you think that the overall revenue that a new product is likely to bring in is more important than the number of units that may be sold?

1 The overall value of the product, in terms of what money it brings in, is one way of predicting the sales potential. Some businesses rely on this value approach and miss the main point. Value just looks at the total revenue generated from the product if every one is sold at full price. It does not take into account many of the more obvious features of sales, such as reductions in price, or inflation.

It is far more useful to look at how many of the product (the number of units) are expected to be sold, i.e. the volume rather than the value. You can then convert the volume figures into value ones at a later date if needed.

2 Forecasting, to some extent, relies on the ability to predict, make guesstimates or assumptions. Price is a prediction, since you do not know what the 'going rate' will be when the product is available. You have to make assumptions on everything, from the economic situation to the impact of a change in government. The reasoning behind these assumptions is as important as the assumptions themselves. This reasoning needs to be looked at and appraised. It is rooted in the forecaster's own view of the future, and the reality of the forecast depends on whether this view turns out to be correct. In order to make sure that the forecast is not wildly out, three forecasts are usually made:

a   The pessimistic forecast, in which all the worst possibilities are assumed to have happened.

b   The optimistic forecast, in which all the best possibilities are assumed to have happened.

c   The 'most likely' forecast, in which the best and worst possibilities are put together and an average situation is predicted. This is the version that is used for most planning exercises.

The forecasting techniques are identical to those which we have already discussed in a previous chapter, but here is a brief description of the most typical ones that relate to new products:

1 **The survey method**   Through market research, a sample of potential customers is questioned about their likely purchases. They are asked to assume that the new product is available for sale and to say whether they think that they would buy it and in what kind of volume. The questions would not necessarily be direct and would include questions which would attempt to look 'behind' the potential customer's buying habits.

2 **The delphi method**   This is a method that attempts to get a general view of possible sales of the product by asking representatives of many different groups of people. This is done by forming a discussion panel, or forum, which may include managers, retailers, wholesalers and sales personnel. In another variant a group of experts is asked to discuss the sales potential, the objective being to arrive at a consensus of opinion. This can be an expensive and time-consuming business but does offer a great opportunity to cover all the aspects and possibilities.

3 **Sales staff predictions method**   This involves the discussion of the product with the sales staff and asking them to assess its sales potential. The method is not often used with a completely new product, since the sales force's knowledge of a totally new product is limited and not very objective.

4 **The trial method**   A particular shop or a small chain of shops in one area is chosen as the ideal average type of shop. The product is offered for sale here, either to anyone who cares to buy or, and more usefully, it is offered to a select panel of buyers who again have the choice to buy or not to buy. This is a cheaper form of test marketing and is slightly more controllable.

5 **The moving average method**   A large number of 'new' products are simply modifications of ones that already exist. If this is the case, then the moving average method is easy to employ. A series of sales figures is looked at, for example over a year or three years, and the underlying trend is worked out, to find the average sales figures. If the sales figures were 10, 12, 6, 8 and 4, the underlying trend would be 8. Uneven daily, monthly or yearly sales can be 'smoothed out' by this method and the true trend can be worked out.

6 **The exponential smoothing method**   This is similar in nature to the moving average method of smoothing of the figures, but it requires a little more consid-

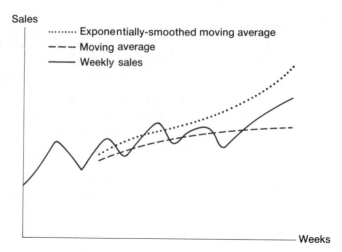

Exponential smoothing.

eration and skill. The later figures are compared to the earlier ones and the researcher then weights the different figures in relation to what he or she sees as their relative importance. If sales were high in a shop during the tourist season and then fell to a lower level after the season had finished, then the researcher would probably decide that the weighting should be placed on the non-seasonal sales figures. The biggest problem with this technique is that it is only as good as the person who is determining the weightings.

7 **The time series analysis method**   The main characteristic of this method is to smooth out the troughs and peaks and come up with an average figure that ignores short-lived increases and decreases. The previous two methods are examples of time series analysis.

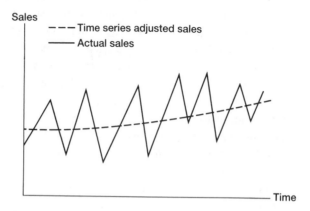

Time series analysis.

8 **The lead indicator method**   When new products come on to the market it is often hard to predict sales. In this technique a similar product is chosen as the

indicator of potential sales. In other words, the researcher finds a complementary product and analyses its sales figures to help predict the sales of the new one.

9 **The diffusion model method**   This is perhaps the most useful for predicting sales of products that have no track record. Products tend to have a life cycle and this method attempts to predict what that life cycle will be like. As the first sales figures come in, any initial prediction of the life cycle may have to be modified or radically rethought.

10 **The general analysis method**   Every business should take a regular look at itself to try to analyse the basic assumptions it makes about its operation, sales and profits. Forecasting is an integral part of this and will be based on the following:

a sales
b direct costs
c gross margins
d development costs
e marketing costs
f overheads
g cash flow

TALKING POINT

If you were a small manufacturer, how long would you be prepared to wait for a new product to start performing well? What factors would you take into account in making up your mind about whether or not to 'pull the plug' on the new product?

New products are slotted into this framework and their contributions, negative or positive, are factored into the calculations. New products are not always expected to pay for themselves immediately, but the lives of some products may be cut very short. This will happen if the projected profitability is not good enough, or perhaps because the waiting time before the product will turn in a profit is too long.

DEVELOPMENT . . . .

Once the product has survived the analysis stage of its life, it changes from an idea to being a reality. The product now has to be developed, made, packaged and given an identity of its own. There are three main stages to consider:

1 Making the product itself will involve a number of different people, such as research and development staff, designers and other technical staff. A prototype is made, which is similar to what the end product is expected to look like and how it should perform. This is tested and, on the basis of the results, the mass production will be approved or rejected. It is important to note that, not only does the product have to work, but it has to do what the marketing department wants it to do.

2 Packaging can be vital. Indeed, in some instances the packaging is as important as the contents! The product may have to fit into the standard image of the company, following its colours or logo. The package must also be functional and protect the product, or keep it fresh.

TALKING POINT

How soon in the development of an idea should it be given a name? Does this matter?

3 Giving a product an identity is very important. The brand name should either help to describe the product or should be a short and memorable one. In some cases it is important to match the brand image with the market segment very carefully, so that the potential customers see this as a positive image that enhances its desirability.

TEST MARKETING . . . .

Test marketing is the last chance to rectify any mistakes or misconceptions about the product or iron out any problems with it. The costs of launching a product nationally can be astronomical and any problems that may occur which could affect the long-term chances of the product need to be eliminated.

The first major way of testing the product is in a test market. Effectively, this is a small area of the country, usually coupled with a low TV advertising cost area like Border TV. The advertising is run in that area alone and the product or service is available within that area only. Some products or services are not advertised on TV but perhaps in the press or on radio only; whatever the advertising media, the principle remains the same. If the test market works out, then a national launch may be attempted. If it does not work out, then the business must figure out whether it is the product that is no good, or whether some other fault in advertising or elsewhere is the culprit. For example, the availability may be patchy or the product may be too pricey. Whatever the cause, it has to be found.

In some cases it may prove difficult to test market the product. Perhaps the product is just a seasonal one, like plastic Christmas trees. Not much point in test marketing them in July, is there! Or maybe the product needs to be kept secret. In the case of technically advanced equipment, it may prove impossible to risk giving the opposition any chance of hearing about the new product.

There is a way to get over this secrecy problem and also to help market test a product that needs to be in use to prove its worth in 'real' work conditions. Potential customers are asked to test the product 'in situ' (where it is) and can test the product under special arrangements with the manufacturer. If the product proves to be capable of coping with the rigours of real use, then it is ready to be fully launched.

TALKING POINT

How would you test market a seasonal product?

UNLEASHING IT . . . .

Launching the product is the most expensive stage so far. So you'd better have got it right! TV costs are enormous; promotional costs ranging from sales promotions through poster campaigns to incentives to stockists often cost more than half of the total revenue that the

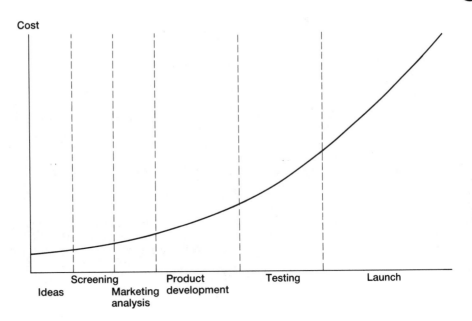

Product costs prior to launch.

product generates in the first year. Manufacturers are looking for a successful product – that's all that counts really. If the product turns in a profit, after taking into consideration all costs, in, say, the third year, then they think that they have succeeded. Lessons are learnt very hard: only about 10 per cent of all products that reach the launch stage can be considered successful. In success terms, this means that they still exist after the first year.

TALKING POINT

If only 10 per cent of products that reach the launch stage and beyond ever make it commercially, then something is going wrong somewhere. What could go wrong that would make a company think that a product is a winner when it turns out not to be? What do you think are the most likely mistakes?

To avoid massive spending and possibly massive losses, the business may wish to mirror its test market launch. Such gradual launches are very popular since the costs can be limited and the returns more accurately assessed. Advertising and PR (public relations) can be mobilised to fill in the gaps in public knowledge of the product.

TEST YOURSELF

1 What is brainstorming?

2 What are the dangers of looking at the competition for new ideas?

3 What are the questions that need to be asked when assessing a new idea?

4 How do you work out the sales potential of a new product?

5 What is general analysis and its usefulness?

6 How important is packaging for a new product?

7 What is test marketing?

8 How can a company avoid launching a 'bad' product?

9 What does a company have to do to ensure good coverage for a new product?

10 Why do so many new products fail?

A WORKING CASE STUDY

Tara: your own product

This assignment is somewhat different from the others in as much as it is entirely fictional. Tara is not perceived as anything in particular. It is entirely up to you. All you have to do is to show that Tara exists and to provide supporting material for its launch as a new product.

Activities and tasks

1 In the role of the research and development manager of the company, create a product (anything is allowable) that will be called Tara.

2 Justify why you have chosen the product and give a physical description of it.

3 Design a questionnaire and test market it with the aim of proving that there is a market for your new product. You will be expected to analyse your results.

4 Create a marketing campaign for Tara and find out the costs of advertising in appropriate forms of media.

5 Present your results in a formal report to the board of the company.

8   Demand and price

WHAT IS PRICING? . . . .

Pricing is placing a value on a product or service. A product or service has to have a price so that the prospective buyer knows what he or she will have to pay for that product or service. In most cases prices will be fixed, the seller having decided on a particular price and the buyer having to pay that price if he or she wants the product or service. The other type of price is the negotiable price. Here the buyer bargains with the seller until they have agreed a price and then the transaction is made.

Pricing occurs at various levels of the distribution chain. The supplier of the product may sell to a wholesaler, who then sells to a retailer, who then sells to the customer (the final buyer in the chain). At each sale a price is set, based on the price that was previously paid for the product or raw material, plus a mark-up to cover costs and to include a profit.

PRICING AND THE BUSINESS . . . . . .

Most business organisations are in the market to make a profit and the financial performance of a business can be measured in the following ways, which all involve pricing.

The first way is to look at the turnover, which means the revenue (money) received from sales. More important is the percentage margin of gross profit that makes up a part of this turnover; in other words, how much profit is being made on each sale. This centres on what the business is charging for the products or services that it is selling.

The other major way is to look at the rate of return on capital assets (like machinery) and how cost effective these are. This centres on what the business paid for the capital assets in the first place.

TALKING POINT

Can you think of some examples of sellers of products who will negotiate a price for their goods with you? How common is bargaining? In certain countries bargaining is the only way to buy goods and there is rarely a set price for anything. Where would you start if you were prepared to bargain for something? Would you say what you want to pay, or start at less than you want to pay?

The generation of sales revenue is determined by what the buyer (the wholesaler, retailer or even the customer) is willing to pay for the products or services that the business is offering. Conversely, the production costs of the business in terms of capital expenditure are based on what the suppliers of those capital assets are charging for their products or services. A value has thus been set at both levels of buying and selling.

A business may be able to distribute well, or to create effective advertising, or be generally efficient, but if it does not get its pricing right it will inevitably fail. If the price is too high, no one will be prepared to pay that price; if it is too low, the business will not make a sufficient profit on its sales. In addition, the pricing may be confusing, in which case sales may suffer or be delayed. It is, above all, imperative to get the pricing right; the very survival of the business depends upon it.

PRICING SITUATIONS

Many different factors determine price. Pricing policies may differ greatly from business to business. Pricing decisions have to be made by suppliers wishing to sell their goods to retail chains, who in turn must set a price at which they will sell the goods on to the customer. In the case of finished goods (like cars, televisions and stereos), the price that the retailer charges the customer has to be agreed to some extent with the supplier of those goods. After all, you would expect to pay about the same price for such an item, no matter where you bought it, although, if you look hard enough, you will always find a bargain. The profit margin that the retailers want will depend upon the needs of the particular retailer and the competition they face. The supplier must allow a standard profit margin for most retailers and a greater one for those who buy the product in greater bulk. We will look at this in more detail in the next section.

TALKING POINT

Is there much deviation in prices? Just how controlled do you think prices are?

WHAT DETERMINES PRICING?

There are several basic considerations when determining price. The main ones are:

1 All prices are dependent on the level of demand. The phrase often used is, 'We'll charge what we think the market will bear'. This means that, if a business can still sell at a higher price than it needs

to make its required profit, then it will. The basic economic rule of supply and demand operates here. Luxury goods that are in short supply will command a higher price than they are perhaps really worth, simply because more people want them than can be supplied. On the other side of the coin, there are many products which are very cheap because they are in sufficient supply and people will not pay exorbitant prices for them.

2 Competition, as we have already noted, plays an important role in the pricing policy of a business. The more suppliers there are, the more likely the price is to be low. The concept of perfect competition, although quite rare, means that the price has stabilised because there is just enough supply to meet the demand and the competing businesses need not price cut, as they cannot supply more even if they wanted to. An imperfect competition in a market means that businesses are vying for more sales by cutting prices in an attempt to control more of that market. The opposite of both of these is when a business has a monopoly in a market. Again, this is rare, but it effectively means that the business can charge exactly what it likes for the product. An example of this is the drugs market where a new drug which cannot be copied by other companies (due to patenting) is the only available cure for a disease or complaint.

Companies are always having to try to double-think their competitors and work out what the opposition is planning price-wise and be ready to react to it. They will also have to be prepared for the customer's reaction to price changes and try to predict any consequent changes in demand as a result of the change. Too low a price, even if the company can afford it, can mean that the customer no longer believes that the product is worth very much or perhaps thinks that the quality is low. The decisions are key ones and may have very dangerous results for the business if not considered properly. It is illegal for rival companies to get together in a 'cartel' to fix prices and drive out other competitors.

TALKING POINT

Can you think of a highly competitive market? Harder than that, can you think of a market that has little competition and the companies in that market do not have to worry about price cutting and can usually charge what they want?

3 The market segment at which the product or service is aimed will often determine its price. Some products aimed at a market that requires cheap and plentiful supply, like most foodstuffs, will demand a low price. On the other hand, some markets rate price very low in their scale of importance and will demand high reliability and good design.

4 Consumer attitudes and behaviour to price are known as 'price sensitivity'. Some look for value for money, in which case price changes can radically change their buying habits. Other customers may consider price to be directly related to the performance and reliability of the product, so that changes in performance and reliability are their measure of value.

TALKING POINT

Can you think of some products
where price is of secondary
importance?

5 As you will already have realised, each time a product changes
hands from raw material through to the 'end user', a price change
occurs. The product's price is different at each stage in the chain of
distribution. Discounts from the 'asking price' of the product are
demanded at each stage. Sometimes these discounts are passed on,
which is why it is often cheaper to buy a radio from Argos than it
is to buy it from the local electrical store. It is not the case that the
local store is marking up the price more than Argos; it is almost certainly the case
that Argos is passing on part of the benefits of its bulk purchase discount.

6 In certain cases products cost a great deal to design and develop. The business
must recoup these costs. The most obvious way is to include a portion of these
costs in its pricing. High prices can be maintained until the company has
sufficient competition to drive the price down to a lower level.

7 An obvious consideration is that of costs. Above all, the costs that a business
incurred in buying, making or growing the product must be integrated into the
price. Simply speaking, the cost plus the desired profit determines the price. We
will look at the cost factor in pricing in more detail shortly.

8 Considerably out of the control of the business are the general economic trends.
These include the following:

   a changes in the price of raw materials that the business needs to make its
      product;
   b changes in the productivity of the labour force;
   c changes in labour costs;
   d changes in the rate of inflation,
   e changes in the interest rate.

You can probably think of a great many more.

TALKING POINT

Can you think of products and
services that have to change their
pricing constantly due to
circumstances beyond their control?

PRICING POLICY . . . .

Pricing is, as we have discovered, closely linked with the value or
perceived value of a product or service. This can often equate to what
people see as the quality of the product or service. The higher the
quality, broadly speaking, the higher the price.

In some cases this quality is linked to the brand name and much
stock is set on the customer's awareness and loyalty to that brand. It
is an accepted fact of life that established brands command a higher price than those
brands which are new and unknown. In order to command a higher price the
business must seek to establish the name of the brand and at the same time stress its
quality and its superiority to other competing brands. If a brand is seen as the
'market leader' or the brand that every other brand is trying to copy, then it can
command a higher price regardless of the pricing policy of the competition.

TALKING POINT

Think of some examples of this where prices are high because the business has the edge in terms of customer awareness and high brand status.

Most businesses sell a range of products that are related to one another. In cases such as this they tend to have a pricing policy that encompasses their whole range. Let's look at this philosophy and how their pricing policy differs from the single product approach:

1 Some of their products may be very competitively priced. In other words, each sale generates only a small profit. The reasoning behind this is that the product has high volume sales and generates useful turnover. As long as the fixed costs are covered and a profit is achieved, then the business organisation is content.

2 The concept of the 'loss leader' is one that is well known in certain markets. The idea is that the product is sold very cheaply, perhaps barely covering the costs, and is available only to stimulate sales of the rest of the product line. Often super-markets will advertise very cheap basic products with the intention that customers are enticed into the store and will buy other more expensive (and profitable) items.

3 The idea of offering products cheaply at the bottom end of their range is again a common tactic, particularly in the car market. A cheap, basic vehicle is offered, hopefully satisfying the customer's initial needs. The customer, if satisfied, will come back to trade in the vehicle for a more expensive model. Good trade-ins are a key to this tactic.

4 The business may decide that one of the products in the product line is the one against which all the other products may be compared. A price is set, usually for the most popular product in the range, and the others have their prices set in relation to that product, more or less expensive.

TALKING POINT AND ACTIVITY

Make a list of the types of products or companies that offer after-sales service. Investigate their prices compared to those that don't offer this. What sort of price difference is there? How much of the price do you think is directly related to that after-sales service?

Another option that is offered quite widely now is the extended warranty. What can this cost as a percentage of the product's price?

Another major consideration is that of after-sales service. In certain markets this is vital and may well be the deciding factor as to whether the customer buys one product or another. The availability and quality of this service and how much it costs must be a factor in the company's pricing policy.

The stage which a product has reached in its 'life cycle' can often determine its price. When a product is first launched, its price is set to achieve as many sales as possible and to grab as much of the market as possible as quickly as possible. Alternatively, the price may be pegged higher than would normally be expected, to recoup the research and development costs, or simply to gain additional profit from the novelty value of the product.

As a product becomes established in the market, the sales policy will change. Perhaps the price has to include paying for a heavy advertising campaign or maybe the product's price rests at an 'acceptable level' and stays there.

When a product reaches the end of its useful life, for example because competitors have produced a 'better' or more modern version (or indeed the company itself may have done), the price has a tendency to fall. This is because the company either attempts to get rid of the last of the stock or finds a another market for cheaper and slightly obsolete products (perhaps abroad).

PRICE AND THE MARKET SEGMENT . . . .

After the business has identified the segment of the market that will be its main target, it may well find that pricing plays an important role. Some market segments are more sensitive to price than others. Pricing should mirror the needs of the segment that is the target. Without considering this factor, the business may discover that the product, although desired by that segment, is not priced correctly. Market research should help to identify the importance and acceptable range of price.

Luxury goods are developed specifically for a target market segment. The pricing policy of the business will tend to depend on factors such as the exclusive nature of the product and its image, rather than the price. In such cases price is not altogether important and neither is competition important to the same degree as in mass markets.

VARIABLE PRICING . . . .

Linked to the patterns of demand for a particular product or service, the price may be different at various times of the year. It is more expensive to go on holiday to Greece in July and August than it is in April or November. This is because the demand in July and August is much greater; hence, going back to good old supply and demand, the holiday companies can charge you more. Conversely, by offering April and November at relatively quite cheap prices, the tour companies are also hoping to attract sales in these off-peak months.

PRICE AND THE CUSTOMER . . . .

One of the golden rules in selling is not to confuse the customer. One of the things that confuses and annoys the customer most is regular price changes. Take the example of the changes in petrol prices during October 1990. Nothing causes greater ill-feeling than weekly price rises and the petrol companies know this. Circumstances, to some extent beyond their control, were to blame, but the damage was done. A stable price structure is vital, as is a consistent price structure that does not charge you three times as much for twice as much in volume!

Added to this is the role of psychological pricing. When we see an advertisement proclaiming 'UNDER £20!' we think, 'Great – what a bargain'. Trouble is, the price is only 1p under £20, £19.99! The point is that we see the £19 . . . and not £20 . . . and the sale is more certain! We all fall for the most simple trick time and time again.

The use of discounts and the quoting of prices excluding VAT are other versions of the same pricing 'trick', as also can be the concept of the 'trade-in'. The true price is hidden and only the wary or alert will spot the real hidden price behind all the 'offers'.

PRICE AND COMPETITION . . . .

Competitors in a market will always try to set their pricing structure in relation to one another. There is nothing to be gained and a lot to be lost by setting a price if it does not closely match the opposition's price. Having compared like products, a business will always try to undercut the competitor's price, although this may mean having to accept lower profit margins.

A way around this problem is to establish a brand identity that does not allow a direct comparison with the competitors. The use of 'own brand' labels in supermarkets is a good example of this.

TALKING POINT

'Offensive pricing strategies are immoral as ultimately they will result in the customer having little choice of products in the market when the inevitable happens and the alternative producers cease trading in that market.' What do you think of this statement?

Often a particular product or product line is dominant in the market. It is this product that 'sets' the price and all other companies wishing to compete must fall in with the dominant company's pricing policy. The key to survival in such cases is to be willing to accept lower margins and have a very controlled set of costs. In some cases the larger or more dominant company has price-cut their product line in order to make it impossible for other companies even to obtain a foothold in the market, or to force out smaller or weaker companies that do not have the ability to survive on lower margins of profit.

TEST YOURSELF

1 What is the most basic method of setting a price for a product?

2 How can companies get their pricing wrong?

3 What are the main factors that determine price?

4 List the main factors that are out of the company's hands when determining price.

5 How can a price be set that is not related to costs?

6 What is the importance of after-sales service?

7 How does price relate to the stage a product has reached in its life cycle?

8 What is variable pricing?

9 What is psychological pricing?

10 How does competition relate to pricing?

Reflex Reds

Reflex Guitar Systems was founded in 1988 with the aim of manufacturing and marketing a range of guitar pickups. The original line, the 'Reds', was to be a 'no-compromise' product designed to a specification rather than a price.

The company itself had limited experience in the type of marketing required for this type of product, but fortunately, being part of a larger group, did have adequate funds for a high-profile campaign.

Since the product was to a high specification, not surprisingly it carried a high price tag and was therefore directed towards the professional end of the market.

The music industry in general has a high degree of brand loyalty, with many potential customers proving to be highly resistant to a changing product.

Some nine months after the launch of the 'Reds' the company followed up with a second range, 'Blues'. This was a lower-priced product designed for the amateur market. It was hoped that the extensive marketing of the 'Reds' would already have created a pool of potential customers for the new pickup. While not having the technical excellence of its more expensive cousin, it still carried the Reflex logo.

The 'Reds' campaign was run in conjunction with extensive user endorsements.

The campaign itself ran for around nine months and was concentrated in the serious amateur/professional music press, such as *Guitarist* magazine.

By comparison the 'Blues' campaign was much lower-key, with the emphasis placed firmly on good retail distribution: attractive displays, prominent positioning and so on.

A mid-stage 'visual' of the proposed advertisement.

Partial artwork for the finished magazine advertisement (see p123).

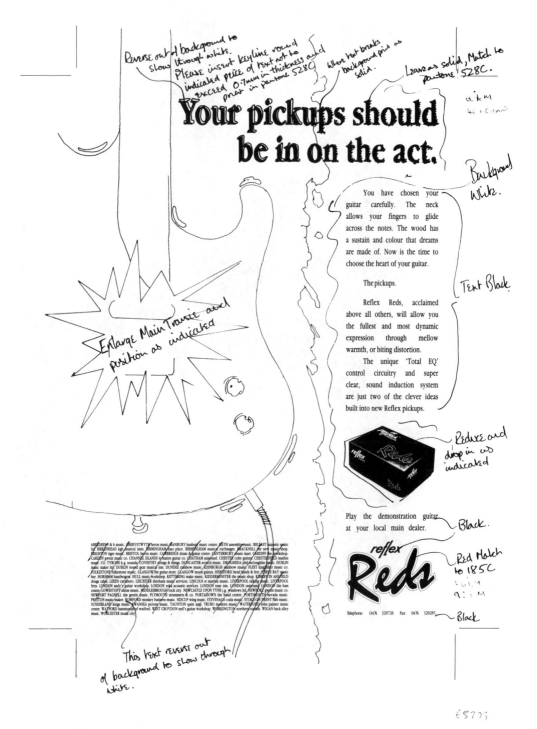

The designer's instructions to the printer. Note how every part of the advertisement must be clearly labelled to avoid confusion.

The finished advertisement as it appeared in the music press.

This guarantee card doubled as a simple market research device.

"HEART AND SOUL" T'PAU

When hit group T'Pau's lead guitarist ordered Reflex pickups for his guitar, we asked ourselves the following question. 'Although we are the new boys in town – how come we got this so right, so early?'

The answer lies in the blending of traditional art with studio technology.

The Reflex 'Total EQ' control circuitry and super clear, sound

Dean Howard of T'Pau has changed to Reflex Pickups.

induction system are just two of the clever ideas built into new Reflex pickups.

When you are playing well, your guitar becomes part of your reflex action.

Because of their sensitivity, your Reflex pickups become your guitar's 'Heart and Soul'.

To get the full story, ask your local dealer about Reflex Reds.

COMPLEMENT YOUR REFLEX ACTION

Reflex Guitar Systems Ltd., Springhead Enterprise Park, Northfleet, Kent DA11 8HB. Telephone 0474 320728. Fax 0474 320285. Telex 966143.

Another magazine advertisement in the campaign. Note the endorsement by the pop band T'Pau.

Another magazine advertisement drawing attention to T'Pau's endorsement.

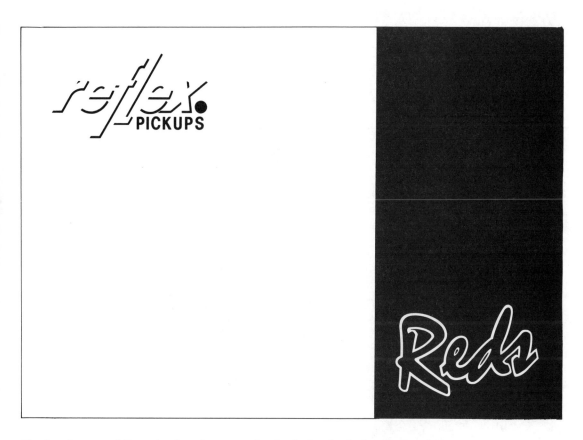

The front cover of the sales brochure – a simple design featuring the two logos.

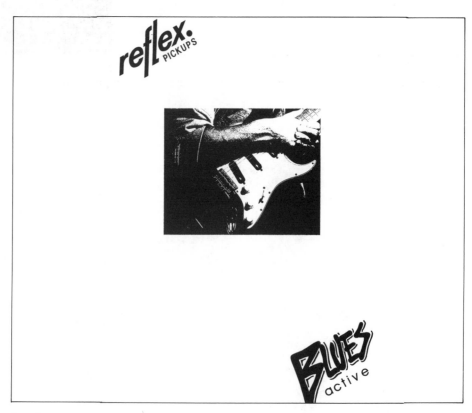

Brochure covers.

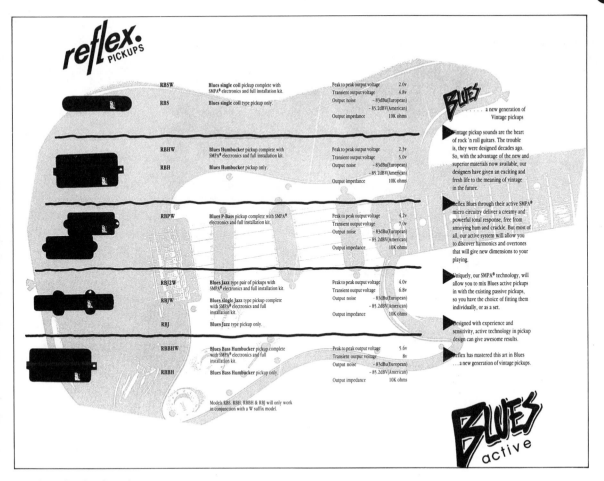

Interior of sales brochure.

Pack design.

Activities and tasks   Looking at the two products, think about the following:

1   How well has the company got across that the 'Reds' range is a high-quality product?

2   How can you package an item to make it look classy *and* affordable at the same time?

3   Does the pack design of each product get the message across?

4   As a further study, pick out a top-of-the-range product – Jaguar cars or Nikon cameras spring to mind – and try out a similar task for yourself. Imagine that your brief is to design a campaign that not only targets the lower end of the market effectively but also utilises the company's existing reputation at the higher end of the market.

FURTHER READING

Marketing Management and Administrative Action, S Britt, McGraw Hill

9 Marketing communications

THE BASICS OF COMMUNICATION . .

The basic purpose of all forms of marketing is to be able to communicate with the potential customer. The idea, of course, is to get the customer to buy the product or service that is on offer. However, to assume that selling is what marketing communications are all about is a gross over-simplification.

What are communications and what are the questions we should ask?

- What are the objective and purpose of the sender of the message? Who is the sender? This is known as the **control analysis**.
- What is the substance of the message? This is known as the **content analysis**.
- Who is the intended audience for the message? At whom is it directed? This is, amazingly, known as **audience analysis**. Segmentation and targeting play their part here.
- Through which media is the message sent? How is the message sent to the target segment? This is known as the **media analysis**.
- Finally, what happens once the message has reached the listener? This is known as **effect analysis** and looks at the response to the message.

Getting the message across

The communicator of the message must succeed in reaching the audience. One of the major problems is that the channels used can often be inadequate for successful communication. For example, an advertisement may be reproduced very badly or in an obscure place in a magazine or newspaper, or perhaps the sales representative may be interrupted by the telephone ringing.

There are some ways around these problems:

1 **The use of attention-getting methods**   This involves the use of a gimmick or something that attracts and keeps the attention of the listener. A good example of this would be the use of a jingle in an advertisement. In visual terms, perhaps the best example is that used by Silk Cut cigarettes, where a slashed piece of silk, with no wording, leaves the viewer to work out the meaning.

TALKING POINT

Can you think of an example of how repetition can work to help you remember the message that is being put across to you?

2 **Repetition of the most important part of the message**   This involves repeated use of a caption, headline or slogan to reinforce the message.

Communication relies on the listener understanding what is being said. Words or phrases should be avoided that are likely to be misunderstood by the listener. Jargon should be avoided or explained. Misinterpretation means that the message will not get through to the listener in the way that the communicator wishes. Advertisers are often accused of being out of touch with the audience, not knowing their attitudes and opinions. In addition, those who have the technical expertise and knowledge of a product may be incapable of communicating with the audience in non-jargon or non-technical terms.

The communicator and the audience need to have some shared idea of the product. Having identified any problems that the audience may encounter in understanding the message, the communicator should be able to adapt the message to suit the audience.

TALKING POINT

Can you think of an example of this? Is it a good idea to shock or challenge people's beliefs and attitudes? Is this good communicating?

Everyone has a slightly different set of beliefs and attitudes: some may be peculiar to them alone; others may be shared with friends, relatives or a particular group. If a message goes completely against an individual's beliefs and attitudes, then it is likely that understanding may be distorted in some way. Some people in marketing believe that a greater effect may be achieved by confronting these beliefs and attitudes. The reasoning being that the audience is more likely to remember the message simply because it was so odd, e.g. the Levi 50ls jeans advertisement that featured the man undressing in the launderette.

The response

Let's look at the different types of communication. It is useful to think of the message as the stimulus (something that provokes action or response) and the reaction of the audience as the response:

1 **Simple response**   This is an automatic response. If you look at a bright light, you will close or squint your eyes. The response is straightforward and simple, uncomplicated.

2 **Operant response**   This is a 'conditioned' response. In other words, the intended response is related to something else that makes you respond. Confused? Not surprised! A researcher by the name of Pavlov experimented in this area with dogs. Every time the dogs were going to be fed, he rang a bell and then fed them. After repeating this over some time, he rang the bell when it was not feeding time and the dogs began to drool in anticipation of being fed. We are really not that different. Sometimes we feel thirsty if we see a film set in the desert. In advertising, we associate certain products with sports events, like Benson & Hedges cigarettes with cricket, or alcohol with some other sports. The association that we make is what is intended; this is an operant response.

3 **Cognitive response**   This is a 'thinking' response. Cognitive responses assume that we are more able to make our own mind up about what we do rather than being conditioned. We will evaluate the choices and then respond.

4 **Complex response**   This is, perhaps, what really happens when we respond. A complex response is a mixture of operant and cognitive responses. Sometimes we respond because of our conditioning; at other times we are free agents with our own ideas and views on the world and respond as we feel.

5 **Planned response**   This is a response that we plan and prepare. If we are aware of the circumstances that will determine a response, then we are more likely to respond to those circumstances each time in the same way. If we have prepared ourselves, the response becomes almost automatic. For instance attending a Tupperware party, where you are likely to buy something.

What then of the way that the customer receives the message? There are a number of different ways: those that are heard or seen – aural and visual messages; and written, verbal or even electronic messages. OK, you might say, that all sounds fairly obvious. Then why is the message often misunderstood if it is so straightforward?

Clear and simple aural messages are easy to understand, but the more complex they become, the more likely that we will misunderstand them. Visual messages can be very much more complex, as they can encompass colour, size and movement. People's movements, known as body language, are the most common visual message. Certain sounds or language become associated with certain messages. The logical extension of this is to write down the message. Writing is a code in itself and the complexity of the written word is enormous.

Note the slanted wording on the side of the train and the none too subtle use of the swift bird logo to suggest speed. Photograph courtesy of InterCity.

Not only are there many different languages, but sub-languages to contend with. As our society becomes more complex, our language also becomes more complex. Our choice of words and word order affect the message we convey. Finally, we come to electronic messages, which are a logical extension of language. Computer language allows machines to talk to one another, and this can be converted into a form which humans understand.

COMMUNICATION AND THE ORGANISATION . .

There are many potential problems in getting the marketing message across. Knowing the problems is part of the fight. Even the most sophisticated and effective means of communication will not reach all of those at whom it is aimed. The organisation must attempt to come up with a strategy to overcome as many of the problems as possible. The organisation needs to ask itself a number of questions:

1 At whom are we aiming our message?
2 What information will they need to make up their minds?
3 What are our objectives in trying to communicate effectively with them?
4 How much is it going to cost us?
5 How big should the budget be?

6 How should we apportion the costs?

7 How much of the responsibility to communicate should lie with us and how much with our wholesalers/retailers, etc?

8 How can we evaluate our communications campaign?

By planning the communications campaign in a systematic way, the organisation is taking a professional approach to the problem. Many organisations do not do this, for a number of reasons. Firstly, their structure may not be geared up to monitoring the communications campaign. Secondly, they may not be able to realise the benefits of approaching the exercise in a more professional way. It is amazing that, while an organisation may spend much time and resources in considering such matters as pricing, it is incapable of sorting out its marketing communications. Often the problem lies in the management structure. It may be that the organisation is too hierarchical and that decisions are left to those who do not have the time or the knowledge to do anything about the problem.

In having a product strategy, you should assume that the organisation has a view of the direction in which it wishes to move. Equally you should assume that the efforts made by the various parts of the organisation are coordinated in some way. Marketing communications strategy should be a part of the organisation's coordinated strategy, as planned and considered as the production, finance and other parts of the organisation. Alas, it is often not so.

TALKING POINT

What do you think is the inevitable outcome for an organisation that does not communicate with itself?

Product strategy is usually long term, looking at the possible changes in demand, attitude, price, etc. The marketing communications strategy is more short term, It is there to deal with all the problems that may crop up. Often, however, marketing communications objectives are too general or do not exist at all. Unless all the people involved in the organisation know its objectives, they will tend to work to their own targets. They may very well have good ideas and may realise their goals, but they are not coordinated with those of the rest of the organisation.

Objectives for a consumer market

We have talked about having marketing communications objectives, but what are they? Here are some of the more common ones in the consumer field:

1 To tell customers about a new product.

2 To put the record straight about a product (in other words to correct any misconceptions).

3 To get the customers to use a product more often.

4 To remind customers that the product exists!

5 To tell customers about special offers and promotions.

6 To educate customers about a product, e.g. how to use it.
7 To build a company image.
8 To build a product image.
9 To try to obtain a degree of customer loyalty to the product.

Objectives for a trade market

The objectives may differ slightly if the marketing communication is aimed at other organisations:

1 To provide information about your organisation.
2 To provide information about your product(s).
3 To pre-warn about forthcoming promotions.
4 To give trade incentives or offers.
5 To educate the trade on the uses of your product(s).

Targeting communications

There are, of course, limitations on how effective your communications will be. Not all of your communications will get through to the right person, consumer or trade.

Once the objectives are set, the organisation has to decide which are the best ways to reach the intended audience. Before we can look at the different ways in which to communicate, we will need to consider a number of points. Firstly, the basic ground rules:

1 Once we have identified our audience, by what methods can we ensure their interest in the information we have on offer?
2 How can we maximise our expenditure? We have to try to make this as cost-effective as possible.
3 How much of the information can be communicated to the audience in ways that will not cost us anything? We may be able to secure editorial coverage in newspapers and magazines. We may be able to offer promotions that other agencies will willingly handle for us, or we may be able to offer support to charities, sporting events, etc, for little capital outlay.

Budgeting

Setting a budget for marketing communications is important. In deciding how much money to give to a promotion, the organisation will need to consider the following methods:

TALKING POINT

Why do you think that cars have a lower percentage of expected sales revenue allocated to promotional activities? After all, they are advertised on television too?

1 **Allocation of funds in relation to the sales revenue**   Organisations tend to set a marketing budget at a fixed percentage of the expected sales revenue. This is usually around 10 per cent for basic TV-advertised products, falling to only 1 or 2 per cent for expensive items such as cars. Industrial products often have an allocation of less than 1 per cent.

TALKING POINT

Why do you think it is important to increase promotional spending when your competitors do so? Can you think of some examples of markets that need this?

2 **Reacting to the competition**   Often organisations will increase their spending on promoting products in relation to what their competitors are doing. It is important in some markets to make sure that your spending increases in line with that of your competitors.

3 **Setting specific objectives and tasks**   Deciding what you want to achieve, and how much it will cost, is the safe way. Setting an objective, and then spending as much as is needed to achieve it, is dangerous. Organisations should tread the line carefully and be willing to shift their objectives if the cost becomes too great.

4 **Affordability**   What can the organisation afford to spend? Rather than setting objectives, as in the previous method, a budget is set. When this money is gone, that's it – the marketing exercise is over. This is a method often employed by smaller businesses with limited resources.

THE WAY TO COMMUNICATE . . . .

Now that we have allocated a budget, we have to decide how we are going to spend it. Let's look in detail at the methods competing for our cash:

1 **Personal selling**   Cost-effective if the number of customers is small (you don't need so many sales people). If a product is expensive, the likelihood is that it will take longer to sell the product to someone and require personal selling skills. Cars, houses or computers are therefore best sold this way. It is a useful method of making sure the sale is completed and that questions regarding price, delivery dates or credit are covered. Technical questions may be answered and a good relationship can be struck up with customers.

2 **Telesales**   A more economical version of personal selling where selling is done over the telephone rather than in person. It is useful for efficient order taking, reminding customers to reorder and closing sales that are a result of an initial personal call.

3 **Exhibitions**   A great chance to communicate with lots of people in a very short time. Exhibitions are a good place to demonstrate complex goods, and help to enhance the organisation's image by showing its 'face'.

4 **Direct mail**   Useful for sending out 'personalised' messages to a large number of people. Target markets can be identified, complex messages can be sent, and special offers can be used as a 'bait'.

5 **Public relations**   Useful to convey more complex messages. PR increases the audience's understanding of the organisation or its products and helps generate awareness and image. PR will liaise with the press and other media, using press releases and organising special forms of promotion.

6 **Literature or brochures**   Again these are useful for passing on complex messages. Explanations may be detailed and illustrated, interest can be stimulated and image can be built.

7 **Sales promotions**   Cost-effective in putting over simple messages. These get the attention of the customer and help to encourage repeat buys.

8 **Advertising**   Similar in many respects to sales promotion, but may often be even cheaper. Advertising reaches a larger audience, helps generate awareness, interest and image enhancement.

TALKING POINT AND ACTIVITY

Match up products or services to each of the eight different types of marketing communication methods. Which methods do you think are the most effective, overall?

Now we need to figure out whether all this carefully-prepared decision making and communicating works!

IS IT WORKING? . . . .

The organisation needs to know whether the message has reached the target. If it has got this wrong, then two things may have happened: either no one has noticed the campaign or, even more annoying, people have noticed it but have got the wrong message! There two main ways of evaluating this:

1 **Pre-testing and post-testing**   A sample of the intended target audience is asked a series of questions before and after the campaign. If the campaign has been successful, then the target's knowledge of the product afterwards will be greater than before.

2 **Direct response**   Have there been increased orders for the product? The organisation looks for measurable ways of assessing the effectiveness of the campaign. Looking again at our eight different types of marketing communication, how is their success measured?

   a *Personal selling*: the number and level of sales achieved.
   b *Telesales*: as (*a*), or the number of sales leads for the sales force.
   c *Exhibitions*: direct sales and sales to stockists.

d *Direct mail*: the number of positive responses.
e *Public relations*: increased awareness and visible 'knock-on effect' in more sales.
f *Literature or brochures*: similar to PR in many respects.
g *Sales promotions*: purchase of the product on offer.
h *Advertising*: interest, increasing sales and attracting customers to stockists.

Communicating with the target audience can be very difficult. A good campaign should have very broad objectives which can then be adapted to specific objectives. The marketing manager must attempt to choose the best technique most closely matching the specific objectives that have been set. After the campaign is over, the evaluation period is vital in assessing whether the target was reached, the message was understood and the campaign was effective.

TEST YOURSELF

1 What are the main considerations in marketing communications?

2 How do you get around the possible interruptions when personally selling a product to someone?

3 What is operant response?

4 Apart from language, what are the other methods of communications which can be used?

5 List some of the questions which an organisation should ask about its communications strategy.

6 List at least six main objectives of communications.

7 How do the above differ from communications between industry and industry? List a further three of these.

8 What are the criteria in setting a marketing communications budget?

9 What is personal selling?

10 How do you evaluate personal selling?

A WORKING CASE STUDY

Boosey & Hawkes' poster campaign

Boosey & Hawkes is a very well-established company. It has several clearly defined branches in its operation, including music publishing, instrument manufacture and retailing. This particular poster was used by the retailing branch.

It was important to the company to appear modern and up to date, without losing the kudos of its long company history. In addition, the actual address of the shop in Regent Street was perceived as a selling point by the company and was to be emphasised where possible.

Posters are a very specialised section of marketing, where image is by far the most important factor. There are, after all, few people who will actually stop to read a poster unless the graphic content is sufficiently striking to catch their eye.

The poster.

(Opposite is some background on the company, given on a bookmark.)

Activities and tasks

1 What did Boosey & Hawkes try to achieve with the mixture of the elements in the design, including the picture of Beethoven?

2 Where would this poster be best sited?

3 Design a poster for a new model of compact camera. Unfortunately for you, the manufacturer is very 'anti-design' and wants to concentrate on the engineering quality of the product. Slick images are out! It can be done, but you'll have to think about it!

FURTHER READING

The Complete Guide to Advertising, T Douglas, Pan
Advertising, R White, McGraw Hill
The Fundamentals of Advertising, J Wilmshurst, Macmillan
Advertising, F Jefkins, M + E, Pitman Publishing

10   The world of advertising I

HISTORY AND EVOLUTION OF ADVERTISING AGENCIES . . . .

Advertising agencies can trace their roots back to agents or 'space-brokers' who sold space for newspapers to potential advertisers. These brokers did not really need to know very much about advertising. This is amply borne out by looking at some of the early advertisements. There was nothing technically clever or interesting about these advertisements. A favourite approach was simply to repeat the same word, like 'Sale', in a large typeface, and then put the address of the business at the bottom of the advertisement. Press advertisements started to appear in the 1660s, when *The London Gazette* carried advertisements for coffee, chocolate and other delicacies. These advertisements had no more merit than a simple classified advertisement of today. By the beginning of the eighteenth century rather more elegant advertisements were appearing in magazines such as *The Tatler*.

The first advertising agency

The Government, desperate to raise funds to fight off the threat of invasion by Napoleon, ran advertisements for lotteries at the beginning of the nineteenth century. The first advertising agencies began to appear at about this time. James White and Charles Lamb set up the very first agency in London in 1800. White's job as a clerk at a school was supplemented by being paid as a freelance copywriter for these government lottery advertisements. Newspapers themselves were still very provincial. There were no national newspapers until halfway through the nineteenth century.

Two crucial changes in legislation helped to spawn the advertising agencies of the nineteenth century. In 1853 advertisement tax was abolished and in 1861 stamp duty was removed from newspapers. With these two hurdles gone, the incentive to sell advertising space was renewed, London became the main centre for advertising agencies, but even as late as the inter-war years, the average size of the advertising agencies was still very small.

Space-brokers had by now given way to 'contact men', and the creative side was the domain of the 'wordsmith'. The main characteristics of this period up to the 1950s were the absence of any statistics or testing of advertising copy. The key word was 'clever'. The copy had to stand on its own merits and in the final analysis depended on the client's reaction to it.

The 20th century

During the 1930s the trend was to entertain the reader of the advertisement. With the backdrop of high unemployment and general depression, 'make them laugh' was a good approach. By the late 1930s and early 1940s (notwithstanding the Second World War), technological leaps brought cars, electrical goods and a host of other products on to the market. Advertising broadened out, encompassing public relations, marketing plans and research. The British advertising scene died down considerably during the war, while the lesser effects felt in the United States meant that American agencies forged ahead. The leading British ad-men headed the ministry concerned with British propaganda, using and refining their public relations skills to pull the country together in a time of great crisis.

After the war, with rationing still in place, the newspapers were restricted as to the number of pages they could print. Sunday newspapers were dominated by the big advertisers, and those advertisers who could not afford the rates charged stuck to the provincial daily newspapers.

Magazines were in heavy demand, by both advertisers and readers. Financially, they were a cheap product, using thin paper and colour gravure printing. They had combined sales of over a million.

Posters were often the only outlet for advertising budgets that could not compete with the big companies. Radio advertising, principally based on the Continent of Europe, had all but disappeared, with the notable exception of Radio Luxembourg. Commercial British radio had not yet started.

Cinema, very popular in the 'forties, backed by a strong British film industry, pulled huge audiences and considerable advertising. Television, however, was still largely out of the price range of most Britons, and in any case commercial television did not yet exist.

Losing control

The Labour Party lost the next election and the controls which, in the opinion of most advertisers, had restricted the media were abolished. The Festival of Britain in 1951 seemed to herald a new era of plastic, carpets, cars, and all the other paraphernalia of an affluent society, and with it, advertising on a grand scale.

The old-fashioned British agency rapidly disappeared as advertising agencies strove to emulate their American counterparts. Trying desperately to encompass market research and public relations, crucial mistakes were made in these early days of the 'service' advertising agency. They simply had no idea as to what was involved in providing a complete service.

At about the same period, and for the first time, potential advertisers could now delve deeply into the readership of magazines and newspapers. Readership surveys, pioneered by Sir Edward Hulton (who owned several titles including *Picture Post*), gave vital information on the life-styles and aspirations of the reader. Furthermore, estimates could be made as to the 'pass-on' rate – in other words, how many people actually read the publication beyond the original buyer.

As industry produced ever more new products, a boom in the technical and trade press meant fresh outlets for advertising. The pressure and need for advertising often outstripped available space, leading to magazines even reducing their editorial pages to accommodate advertisements. The additional revenue meant that magazines could grow, and public relations specialists stepped in. By providing editors with technical articles, the gap was filled and the 'advertorial' was borne.

Television brings change

Television entered the scene in a forceful way in the early 1950s and, when independent television arrived in 1955, the advertising agencies had great new challenges to cope with. Quick lessons were learnt from America, where there was not only the Hollywood tradition, but soap opera radio shows which were sponsored by advertisers. As television took its hold on the public, money flowed into television advertising from other media. Magazines began to lose their circulation, and many were forced to cease publication. Cinema was perhaps hit the hardest. Not only was there the loss of money from advertising, but also the loss of public interest. This was the fate of many 'old' forms of leisure pastime.

As several newspapers folded, this left the remainder as the only routes to the public in that media. As many magazines ceased publication, a new 'breed' of magazine came into existence, the new-look women's magazine such as *Woman's Realm*.

Advertising agencies made a vital change to their operations yet again. They became media planners and buyers, as well as creators of dramatic advertising material. Armed with scientific statistics, the agency could now pinpoint the target, choose the medium and construct a suitable package to fit the client's needs and pocket, with maximum efficiency.

TYPES OF ADVERTISING AGENCY . . . .

There are several different types of advertising agency, from full service agencies to the specialists. Some of the types of specialist have only subtle, but important, differences. Some specialist agencies are independent companies; some are subsidiaries of larger agencies which have snapped up the opportunity to cash in on new client needs. A few of the categories listed below are purely theoretical and serve only as an indication of what the agency covers.

The full service agency

This is the traditional type of agency. Generally it concentrates on 'above the line' advertising, but does offer a full service which encompasses marketing and market research, and it is capable of handling television advertising.

The media independents

These types of agency concentrate on media planning and buying, i.e. organising and ordering advertising in the press, TV, radio and other media. They tend to work on a commission basis, or as a reflection of the workload undertaken for the client. This flexibility enables clients to buy the best media for the lowest cost.

The à la carte agencies

These agencies concentrate on creativity and planning, for which they charge fees. They do not tend to buy media, leaving this to the media independents. They usually take on *ad hoc* jobs ('one-off' jobs), especially new product launches. Because they pick the jobs they do, they are known as à la carte agencies (like choosing from à la carte menus).

New product development agencies

These agencies offer a full service from the birth of a new product or service to its eventual launch on the market. Work includes product design, packaging and pricing as well as market research, advertising and sales promotion. New product development specialists are particularly useful because they have vital knowledge of how to launch a product successfully, which full service agencies may not have.

Sponsorship agencies

These are somewhere in the grey area between public relations agencies and normal advertising agencies. They seek sponsors for specific clients, and clients for sponsors. For example, they link up sports events with a company wishing to gain promotion through the sport.

Poster agencies

These agencies offer a poster site booking service, coupled with the planning of a poster campaign to gain maximum coverage at an economic rate.

Direct response agencies

These agencies specialise in direct response advertising, including direct mail, catalogues, mail drops, and radio and television instant response telephone advertising. Credit card sales are a new speciality.

Industrial agencies

These agencies concentrate on specialist areas of industry, usually technical accounts, and have writers and artists skilled in these particular areas.

Studio agencies

These cater for clients in need of specialist technical advertising, and specialise in design, production and promotional material as opposed to consumer advertising.

Sales promotion agencies

These agencies concentrate on designing competitions, premium offers, redemptions, demonstrations and charity promotions. They create original schemes to help boost sales.

Overseas press agencies

These agencies specialise in the production of international advertising. They can offer translation services and are expert in handling the press of foreign countries. They also offer assistance in organising export campaigns.

Recruitment agencies

These agencies operate by placing advertisements for clients who are seeking staff, either as classified or display advertisements. They also handle the initial interviewing of applicants.

Financial agencies

These agencies concentrate on placing advertisements for new share issues and other financial advertisements such as company results.

Radio and television agencies

These agencies specialise in buying advertising space on these two media. They also write scripts for commercials and offer production skills for television and radio commercials.

Telephone sales agencies

These agencies are a relatively new phenomenum. They provide facilities for telephone selling and telemarketing.

TALKING POINT

Most agencies now offer nearly all of these different services. Under what sort of circumstances would you go to a specialist agency and why?

WHAT DO AGENCIES DO? . . . .

As we have already mentioned, advertising agencies originally sold advertising space, on a commission basis, for newspapers and magazines. It was a natural progression therefore to assist in creating that advertisement for the client.

Agencies now exist to produce advertising material for their clients and place this in the appropriate media. Beyond this basic function they also offer a range of other services to support their client's marketing and sales needs.

STANTONS
of
KING'S LYNN

PREPARED STOCKS
&
MOULDINGS

J.T. Stanton & Co. Ltd.
Cross Bank Road,
King's Lynn, Norfolk
Tel: (0553) 763261   Fax: (0553) 761310
Telex. 81179

PRICE LIST — JANUARY 1989

The original and now rather dated design. The company recognised the need to update their image.

Opposite (p149) are various 'roughs' for the new design to change the company's image.

Russian Softwood To Arrive

J.T.Stanton & Co. Ltd, Cross Bank Road, King's Lynn, Norfolk, PE30 2HD. Tel. 0553-763261. Fax. 0553-761310.

0553 - 763261

Softwood

Sheet Materials

0553-763261

0553-763261

The finished sales folder.

STANTONS

Sawmillers and Importers of
Timber and Sheet Materials.

J.T. Stanton and Company Limited
P.O. Box 11
Cross Bank Road, King's Lynn,
Norfolk. PE30 2HD

Telephone King's Lynn 763261
Telex 81179
Fax 0553 761310

All prices quoted are exclusive of Value Added Tax, and any Value Added Tax payable in
respect of goods and services supplied will be borne by the buyer.

Registered Office Malden House, Radlett Road, Park Street, St. Albans, Herts AL2 2JE   Registered No. 58598 England.

**The old letterhead. Note the similarities with the lettering of Stantons opposite
(p150). What does this tell you?**

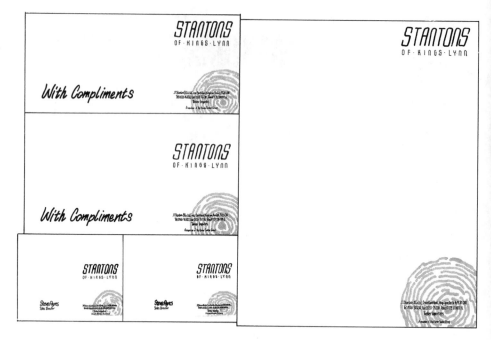

Roughs for the redesigned letterhead and other stationery

The advertising agency offers, among others, the following services:

1 Marketing consultancy service
2 Business planning
3 Advertising material
4 Sales promotion
5 Point-of-sale material
6 Public relations
7 Exhibitions

In order to offer these services, the agency employs specialists with the knowledge to perform these tasks. Smaller agencies will tend to use freelancers to cover tasks with which their own staff cannot cope. A large agency (of around fifty people) will have staff to cover most of the specialised functions. Smaller agencies need strong and experienced managerial ability to juggle the sub-contractors that are vital to them in order to offer a full range of services.

Advertising agencies are specialists in communications of all kinds. They are creative groups of people who produce ideas that sell for their clients. Success depends on being able to provide the clients with what they need. The agency must produce new ways of presenting their client's products and sell them effectively to the public.

TALKING POINT

What are the advantages and disadvantages of using freelance personnel?

AGENCY ORGANISATION AND PERSONNEL . . . .

An advertising agency is just like any other service business. Despite the image of a group of creative types slouched in comfortable chairs reeling off brilliant advertising copy (there must be some!), the reality is that an advertising agency most needs to be organised.

Organisation falls roughly into two categories. One is the formal, departmental structure. The other is the 'account group' approach, which is a fluid system drawing together staff who are working on a particular client's account. The second version is the most popular and seems to work well for the vast majority of advertising agencies.

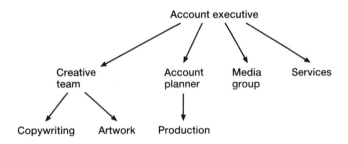

Typical advertising agency structure.

THE FORMAL OR STANDARD ADVERTISING AGENCY STRUCTURE . . . .

Management

Advertising agencies tend to be headed by large boards of directors. Most of these 'directors' are in reality account executives. It is a great selling point if the client thinks that a director is working personally on their account. In small agencies, directors will be in charge of the sort of things that you would expect, such as creativity, media liaison and financial control. In larger agencies there will be a small 'management core' who will support the efforts of a greater number of account executive directors. The word 'director' is very prominent in job titles, as are other high-sounding names for fairly mundane jobs.

Account Manager

Every account has a manager. The Account Manager's job is to make sure that the agency makes a profit, while catering to the client's needs.

An Account Manager (or Account Director) tends to supervise; it is the account executives that do the bulk of the work, with the help of lower level staff and trainees.

The Creative Department

Commonly, a group of specialists, including writers, artists, photographers, etc, will work together on a job. These teams are centred around the copywriter and under the guidance of the Art Director. They work in all forms of media, but will call on the services of agency producers for TV work or for cinema and radio which might be outside the normal experience of a creative team. They exist as teams rather than as a true department.

Design work tends to be subservient to the creative team and receives tasks from them. They would deal with pack design, devising promotion and point-of-sale material, etc.

The Media Department

Responsible for both planning and buying, the media department works closely with the creative department. This liaison is important as the media department decides what is most appropriate for the client and may help direct the creative teams. Negotiation with the media for the best price as well as the position of the advertisements is a separate skill and sometimes therefore the buying is separated from the planning.

Production Control and Progress Chasing

This is the department that makes everything happen, or makes sure that it continues to happen! It works closely with all of the other departments, especially the account executives.

The jobs includes progress chasing (ensuring work schedules are adhered to), production, record-keeping, etc. Without a tight rein being kept on the work, the agency would be incapable of functioning. This is perhaps the most unsung job in the agency. Not only does the client never meet you (perhaps not even realising you exist), but everyone will blame you when things go wrong and ignore you when they go according to plan.

Planning, Marketing and Research

The planner's role is to develop the advertising strategy for the client and to evaluate the success of advertising through market research.

Advice on market research and its interpretation usually comes from the account executive, as few agencies have their own market research department any more. Separate, although subsidiary, research companies have taken over.

Accounts

This is the straightforward and more usual use of the word 'accounts'. As with any organisation, an efficient accounts department means that money flows easily into the company from its clients with the minimum of fuss.

Other departments

Depending on the size of the agency, here are some of the other departments.

- Information and library: useful for research, etc.
- Data processing
- Legal
- Personnel
- Art buying
- Contracts with clients and freelance workers
- Exhibitions
- Overseas specialists
- Direct mail
- Merchandising and sales promotion
- PR
- Administration: secretaries, receptionists, telephonists, messengers, dispatchers, etc

TALKING POINT AND ACTIVITY

Try to draw up a flow chart of how the different personnel in an agency inter-relate. What different departments and specialists would handle a client's job?

THE AGENCY ACCOUNT GROUPS . . .

The account group usually consists of five or six people, fronted by the account executive, and will undertake all the tasks involved in creating and placing the client's advertising.

Broadly speaking, the group operates as a self-contained unit, liaising with 'outside' groups, such as those responsible for media, and with the rest of the creative team. Central to it all is the planner and often this responsibility lies with the account executive.

The account executive

As we have already said, the account executives are the 'front' men. It is they who not only plan the campaign, but make sure that the agency does what it said it would do. A well organised, perceptive and efficient account executive should be able to pull all the strands together and see problems ahead and avoid them. The account executive is the link between client and agency and, as such, will attract all the problems, misunderstandings and disagreements, and have to sort them out. As a result he or she must be the master of diplomacy, getting the best out of people and generating interest in the client's product, thus stimulating the creative team to come up with something new and original.

When the agency has produced any proposals for the client to look at, the account executive will present these, sometimes calling upon members of the account group to introduce their specialities.

Customer liaison is vital. The occasional meal, drink or call pays dividends in keeping the client committed to using the agency. Directors, when they are not the account executive responsible, will keep a close eye on the progress and working of the account. They will offer advice and share their experience if needed.

The creative team

Members of the creative team are not often seen – usually only at the beginning of the relationship with the client. After this initial contact the liaison and presentation fall to the account executive. Consisting of at least a writer and an artist, the creative team will do the lion's share of the work for the client. It is rare that the team will follow the job through to the very end. The team will produce 'roughs' or basic pictorial designs, accompanied with slogans and headlines to give the impression of how the advertisement, etc, will look.

Genuinely creative people are few and far between. Agencies, particularly the smaller ones, will use freelance writers and artists, controlled and directed by the account executive and/or the account planner.

The account planner

Strategy and development of a campaign is the responsibility of the account planner. In large agencies, the planner makes all these decisions and is a specialist in his or her own right. In smaller agencies, the account executive's and planner's jobs are rolled into one, or at least the account executive and perhaps an assistant will take overall responsibility.

Basically, the planner has to put together all the information about the client, the product(s) and the market in which the client operates. The sources of information are, first, the client's brief, giving details of what is required. Then there are the generally available information sources and, occasionally, market research undertaken by the agency or the client. After having analysed the material, the planner is in a position to help direct the account executive and creative team in devising the ideas and designs. It is the planner's job to work closely with the creative teams, interpreting the client's brief, looking at the customer's view of the client's product, identifying gaps in the market research, and obtaining information to fill these.

The media group

A media group, or more often a media specialist, will be included in the account group to decide which type of media should be used. This decision is vital since it will direct the creative group to concentrate on the right type of advertisement.

Once the advertisements have been developed, it is the media group's or specialist's job to identify the places to advertise, the cost, etc. In short, they must undertake the media planning. After agreement has been reached between the agency and the client over the scope of the campaign, the media group must now purchase the advertising space on behalf of the client. Their expertise in dealing with the media should get the client the best possible deal. Positioning of the advertisement, possible discounts and any other incentives to advertise in a specific media can be crucial.

Job allocation

One final point is that many agencies have an average staff level of no more than thirty. In such agencies a large number of the jobs which we have talked about will be part of an individual's responsibility. Larger agencies, particularly in the United States, with 400–500 employees, are more likely to split up these tasks and allocate them to individual specialists.

CHOOSING AN AGENCY . . . .

The client's pitfalls

Picking an agency is perhaps one of the most important decisions that you have to make (after having decided that you actually need one!). This choice will not only affect what you will get for your money, but also how important you are to the agency.

Realistically speaking, if you are spending a few hundred or a few thousand pounds, then you will rank pretty low on their 'importance scale'. If you have a limited budget, it may be better to pick a smaller agency as the converse will be true.

It will be you that is the big spender and your 'paltry' few thousand compares very well with their other clients' few hundred.

Accessibility is vital. The agency does not necessarily have to be close geographically, but remember that all travel expenses are ultimately going to have to be paid for, by you. London is inevitably seen as the centre of the UK's advertising universe. Advertising agencies outside the capital have a massive burden of credibility heaped upon them. This is patently unfair. They are no less competent than their London counterparts and, in fact, an increasing number of them are satellites of London agencies. The trend has been towards these 'out-of-town' agencies in recent years. After all, why pay London prices if you don't have to?

Perhaps your choice is restricted from the beginning because of what you want to advertise. It would perhaps be a little self-defeating to engage a city-based agency to look after your tractor spares' advertising campaign (unless, of course, they had particular knowledge of the market and the product). Specialist agencies cover virtually all specialisms. These include financial (for your share floatation, company reports, etc); 'business-to-business' advertising; direct response; technical; medical; and, for those with the tractor spares, agricultural specialisms. Having said you might need a specialist agency, that might be exactly what you do not want. Standard agencies have their advantages even in the specialist market; they do offer a broader perspective and may have greater general experience.

Choosing the right agency

Apart from deciding whether you do need an agency or not, it is worth while dwelling on the question of what you need one for. Do you need creative help? Assistance in choosing and liaising with the right media for your product? Someone to take the brunt of arranging everything for you? Market research? Analysis of the market? Targeting your potential customers? The problem, especially if you have answered 'yes' to all of these questions, is that there are few agencies that are good at all of these tasks. It is perhaps better to try to consider what you need the most, and then take on an agency.

One of the major sources of friction between the advertiser and the agency is misunderstandings or fundamental mismatches of skills and requirements as a result of choosing the wrong agency for the job. The Incorporated Society of British Advertisers (ISBA) offers some useful guidelines to advertisers in their booklet *Choosing the Advertising Agency*.

Having decided that you think you need an agency, the ISBA believes that the next stage is the most vital one. Just how good is the agency? What is its marketing capability? Knowledge of the media? Experience of the market? What specialist skills does it have? How creative is it? Is it a communications expert? Does it offer the full range of services if you need them? What about its research competence? If a mistake is made at this point, then a small miscalculation 'could be magnified into a large one at the end'.

The next task is to draw up a short-list of suitable agencies. There are numerous sources of information, but they should include the ISBA and the IPA. Cutting down your short-list is easy in the first instance. If you are selling lager, you do not want to use the agency that handles Fosters! Or any other competitor. Not only do you not want them, but ethically they will not want you.

Getting the agency to perform is a good idea. If you persuade it to show you what it can offer in a proper presentation, you might even pick up some free ideas while you are at it!

The last stage, that of the final decision, is a matter of personal preference. If there is nothing in price or creativity to choose between them, then it is down to whether you like the people at one agency more than another. Can you work with them? How does your organisation get on with theirs? If you fit together well, then look no further.

PAYING THE PRICE . . . .

After having settled on your 'ideal' agency, the next step is to tell them exactly what you need. For their part, they will want to know how you are going to pay them! There are potential sources of friction here for the unwary.

Copyright.

First, there is the question of who will own the copyright (the legal right) in any material that may be created. Generally speaking, and this is both an ISBA and IPA guideline, copyright belongs to the originating artist, designer or photographer, unless it has been assigned to someone else (usually the company for whom the specialist works). The client is given reproduction rights only and that is what the client pays for. The two guiding bodies further state that if the work is used for another purpose (presumably not part of that campaign), then additional charges are payable.

The most awkward and significant question is what happens when the client and the agency part company? As a client, you should have made sure that you have a binding agreement concerning the ownership of the copyright before you terminate the relationship.

Methods of payment

Since advertising agencies do not produce anything as such, they sell their time and expertise and that of their employees. Broadly speaking, the agency charges the client for the time which staff have spent on the client's work.

There are two ways of paying for the staff time. Traditionally, the commission system worked well. Commission was collected from the media (newspapers, for example) when an advertisement was placed. In return, the agency would design and write the advertisement and liaise with the media for the client. The commission system really worked only for agencies which had clients that were spending large sums of money. For clients who needed an agency's skills, but only advertised in specialist media which did not charge large sums for space, a second way of paying emerged. The fee system, based on the cost of time spent, seemed much fairer. Fees, it is argued, are fairer and more rational.

The ISBA set up a working party in the 1970s to look specifically at the advantages and disadvantages of the two opposing systems and came to the following conclusions:

1 The advertising agency, in collecting its 15 per cent, cannot guarantee that the effort it has put in will have any relationship to what it will earn.
2 The larger accounts inevitably subsidise the smaller accounts.
3 Less profitable accounts may be maintained only for turnover they produce, to keep money coming in, and the more profitable accounts subsidise these.
4 Operating on a 15 per cent commission may mean that money has to be saved by using staff of a lower calibre.
5 When the agency is not really doing much for its commission, there is the temptation to 'pad out' the list of work it has undertaken.
6 Unscrupulous advertising agencies may try to convince clients to increase their advertising budget just to generate more income for the advertising agency.
7 The advertising agency may be tempted to advise the use of 'above the line' activity rather than 'below the line', again to keep income up (see Glossary at the end of the book for these definitions).
8 Advertising agencies have a buffer (a hidden extra charge), at the expense of the advertiser, against inflation and rising media costs.
9 The fee system can breed inefficiencies, since the charges made are cost plus profit. With the commission system, the advertising agency must be disciplined and keep costs down.
10 The fee system can cause price wars between agencies.
11 Fees are quite difficult to work out and administer.
12 Settling fees can cause friction between client and agency.
13 The client may try to get the advertising agency to rush through the work, to save money.
14 With the commission system, as far as the advertising agency is concerned, increasing profits are linked directly to the success of the client. If the client is successful, there will be more work for the agency and thus more money and more profit.

15 The commission system, if everyone makes the same 15 per cent charge, will mean that cost is not a part of choosing your advertising agency. The decision relies entirely on the quality of work and service.

CURRENT TRENDS IN AGENCY WORK

The massive changes in the advertising world in the last few years perhaps begun with the Restrictive Practices Act 1976, which extended the law against restrictive practices to include services. Before then, the media used to undertake to pay the agencies a commission of 15 per cent on advertising space sales. In 1979, this was ruled illegal on the basis of being monopolistic and restrictive. The requirement to adhere to the British Code of Advertising Practice, recognising that agencies were credit-worthy, and allowing the agency to negotiate on commission, led the way to great changes.

Specialists emerged with the relaxation in the law. The growth was phenomenal. In 1981 the Association of Media Independents (AMI) was founded; three years later a dozen members had a billing of £300m or more each.

Creative agencies have sprung up which have no interest in media planning and buying services. They concentrate on the creative side of an agency's work, operating on a fee structure for work done.

Some agencies have been floated on the Stock Exchange, attracting strong interest. Others are now on the Unlisted Securities Market with mixed fortunes: some good, some bad.

Saatchi & Saatchi was the 'big news' agency of the 1980s, peaking in the mid-eighties when they boasted pre-tax profits of £10m+. After a period of acquiring American businesses and dominating the market and the public image of advertising, their position is now far less certain.

As the 1980s limped on, television advertising ceased to be cost-effective for many products and organisations. Public relations were taking over, whereas for many years they had only prepared the market for the advertisers.

Sponsorship became important too, replacing advertising almost completely in some areas. Cricket was the first to attract sponsorship on a major scale with Cornhill's injection of cash into the sport in 1978. By 1983 the Football League had succumbed to Canon's £3m.

TEST YOURSELF

1 What are the historical roots of advertising agencies?

2 Who founded the 'first' advertising agency in 1800?

3 How many of the different types of agency which are listed in this chapter actually exist as separate entities?

4 List at least five functions which an advertising agency performs.

5 What is done by account executives?

6 List at least ten services an agency can perform.

7 What is an agency account group?

8 How far does the amount of money that you spend with an agency determine your relative importance to that agency?

9 What is the ISBA?

10 What is the AMI?

A WORKING CASE STUDY

Scotts Sufferance Wharf

Take a look at the brief from Chapter 3 about the Scott's Sufferance Wharf development, and then tackle the following problems.

Activities and tasks

1 In the role of an account executive, what specialists would you have used to design, create and place the Bovis advertisement shown here?

2 In the role of the advertising manager at Bovis, put together a brief to the agency which would direct it to place the advertisement.

3 Where would you place the advertisement?

FURTHER READING

The Complete Guide to Advertising, T Douglas, Pan
Advertising, R White, McGraw Hill
The Fundamentals of Advertising, J Wilmshurst, Macmillan
Advertising, F Jefkins, M+E, Pitman Publishing

11   The world of advertising II

THE CREATIVE SPARK . . . .

The message that a company wishes to communicate to its target audience is central to an advertising campaign. The advertising will, hopefully, be that mixture of words, colour, images, sound, etc, which best gets the message across. If a company expects to get its message across to everyone that it has targeted, it will surely fail. Certain types of advertising will simply not be appropriate for certain parts of the target segment. More importantly, there are two major problems to overcome. The first is getting the message noticed by anyone and the second is getting the right message noticed. If you go too far in trying to get the advertisement noticed, you can often leave a confused message. Only a basic message needs to be remembered, and an overly-clever gimmick may leave the audience only remembering that.

TALKING POINT

Can you think of examples of advertisements which have been confusing or too clever?

A good advertisement tries to put over the message clearly and accurately, without actually diverting the attention of the audience to the advertisement itself. It is the message that is centre stage and not the advertisement.

No one has really been able to get this mix right every time. There are, however, many examples of advertisements which have done so; they are the exception rather than the rule. Here are a few pointers to help you get the balance right:

1   The first and most obvious point to consider is the amount of exposure to be given to the advertisement. The concept of 'threshold' maintains that, unless an advertisement is shown often enough, people will simply forget it. On the other hand, advertisements can be shown too often, which can lead to the product being

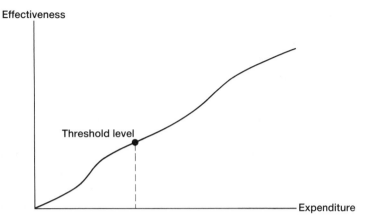

Threshold concept.

considered irritating and boring. Budgets are an important consideration here, as few companies can afford to show their advertisements frequently enough to get the impact that they want. In these circumstances they will have to rely on other methods of getting their message across.

2 If a company cannot afford to saturate the media with its advertisements, it must look to the long-term impact instead. Prolonged and gradual exposure can be equally as effective. As time goes by and the advertisement is shown over and over again, people will remember it. The boredom and irritation factor is minimised. This technique relies on the consistency of the advertising and the memory of the audience.

3 People remember and respond to things that interest them. Advertisers try to find out what interests their target audience and adapt their advertising accordingly. This rapport with the audience can pay dividends. Typical methods are using well-known people to whom the audience will relate, or music that they know and enjoy.

4 Creativity itself plays no small part in all of this. The problem is in putting together the brilliant idea with the best method of getting across the message simply and clearly.

TALKING POINT

What advertisements can you remember as being particularly brilliant or clever? What makes them stick in your mind? Can you remember the whole advertisement, or just the product, or just the gimmick?

Out of the above techniques the most effective is the frequent exposure method. As most organisations cannot afford this technique, they have to rely on spending heavily to begin with and then resorting to the repetition of the advertisement over a period of time. Even with a limited budget, an organisation can have effective advertising by paying attention to the interests of their target audience and establishing that very important rapport with them. These days, the role of creativity can be vital. It may mean that an advertising campaign can be successful with lower overall costs, while being very effective for the short time it is shown.

THE MESSAGE . . . .

There are three main stages in the development of the advertising message: generating the idea; selecting the idea from the various options; and making the idea a reality. Let's look at them in a little more detail:

1 When the message is first discussed, the creativity of the advertising agency is given full rein. The objective is to come up with an idea for communicating the message in the most interesting way. It should be different from anything that has gone before, if possible, and have the strength of impact to be noticed. Above all it should be remembered. Attributes that the product or service has over its competitors should be stressed as heavily as possible.

2 Having partially developed several ways of communicating the message, the competing ideas have to be tested. Sampling is done by showing 'rough' versions of the ideas to members of the target audience. They are asked to compare the idea with existing advertisements for competing products. The idea that they remember best should be the agency's best idea.

3 Advertisements need to be produced well. A high standard of work is demanded, with the best technical skills available. Good ideas can be let down by poor photography or sound. In magazine and newspaper advertisements, the balance of words and picture is important and these should never look cluttered or messy.

There's an awful lot more to the creation of a logo than meets the eye! These pages show approximately 5 per cent of the designer's roughs for a single project, and there's still more work to come!

TALKING POINT

Do you think that the organisation which is paying the advertising agency should always have the last say about the finished advertisement? If the agency is the expert in the relationship, then surely it knows best? What happens if the organisation violently disagrees with the agency on this?

MEDIA AND MEDIA PLANNING . . . . .

Having decided on the creative side of the advertisement, the next decision is to choose the media. There is a very wide choice of media, including over a dozen daily national newspapers; hundreds of regional papers; some sixteen independent TV stations; satellite TV; over fifty independent radio stations; around one thousand cinemas; hundreds of magazines and periodicals; outdoor advertising opportunities; and much more. Quite a choice. Where do you start?

When planning your media campaign, the first two things to think about are how many of the target audience you would like as a minimum to get your message to, and the number of times that you intend to run the advertisement. In other words, the two key considerations are coverage and frequency. There are a considerable number of factors to look at which will affect this decision:

1 The budget available can be a very limiting factor. On a low budget, the more expensive forms of media must be ruled out. The choice for the planner on a low budget is between the cheaper forms of media, such as newspapers. Television, for example, must be ruled out completely.

2 It is important to have an accurate idea of the profile of the target audience. The amount of information to be amassed about the target audience will depend on the particular product.

3 By comparing the media's profiles of their audiences, the planner can then attempt to match the product and message with the right media. It is unlikely that any one medium will get the message to all of the proposed target audience, so several different media will have to be used. Here are approximate figures based on the number of adults that might see advertisements in particular media:

   a Outdoor advertisements (posters, buses, etc): nearly all of the adult population
   b Television advertisements: over 90 per cent
   c Sunday newspapers: around three-quarters
   d Daily newspapers: nearly 70 per cent
   e Radio: nearly 40 per cent
   f Weekly magazines: around 40 per cent
   g Monthly magazines: between 30 per cent and 40 per cent
   h Cinema: less than 3 per cent

This is known as 'opportunity to see' or OTS and is the basic measure of the potential coverage of each major medium.

TALKING POINT

Why bother to advertise in any other media than either TV or outdoor? After all, aren't you likely to reach the bulk of the target audience?

4 Unfortunately it is not quite as simple as this. If the planner could choose the medium only by considering its effectiveness, then life would be easy. The question of cost-effectiveness must also be considered. Amazingly, it costs more to advertise in certain media than in others. Not surprising, you might say. Your £1 goes further in some media than in others and these costs are compared below. The cost is per thousand (CPT) of the adult population:

   a Outdoor advertisements: around 30p
   b Television: about £3.25 (varies according to region)
   c Newspapers: nearly £3
   d Magazines and colour supplements: roughly £1.40, but differs greatly according to the magazine's popularity
   e Cinema: a massive £18+!
   f Radio: around 80p

This price comparison is not entirely fair as we have not considered the size and length of the advertisement or the colours used. Here are examples of the typical sizes and methods of use, on which the prices above are based.

- Newspapers: a full page, black and white advertisement.
- Colour supplements: a full page, colour advertisement.
- TV: a 30-second slot.
- Outdoor is a very rough average since the costs of the advertising position differ enormously.

TALKING POINT

What is unfair about the percentage that is shown for cinema audiences seeing advertisements? What is there about cinema audiences that makes it so expensive to get to adults?

5   As we have already mentioned, you can advertise on television, or elsewhere for that matter, and still not make an impact. You can look at the cost-effectiveness of different media, choose the best for your budget and still not have an impact. The key is the frequency with which you advertise. Marketing writers, as we have already discussed, have called this the 'threshold'. What they mean is that you have to advertise beyond a certain limit in order to have any effect at all. This is worked out on the OTS (opportunity to see) basis, so if you wanted the target to have ten OTS, you would have to show the advertisement far more often than ten times.

TALKING POINT

How could you work out the OTS and make sure that your target audience does see the advertisement the required number of times?

6   Having worked out the CPT, this still isn't enough. As we have already seen, we are not comparing the different media fairly. We can only make assumptions and make very rough comparisons between the different media. Certain media have advantages over others for certain products. When working out a media plan and schedule, the planner must consider the following factors:

a   The budget
b   The right media to reach the right target audience
c   Covering the whole audience (in other words making sure all of them are reached in some way)
d   Making sure that the target audience has the opportunity to see the message
e   Achieving this in a cost-effective way
f   Making sure that the particular medium helps in increasing the impact of the message

Taking account of all these considerations means that the media planner has to compromise. The key considerations are the continuity of the campaign, the overall coverage (in different media, etc), the impact and the frequency. It is a rare media planner indeed that is capable of satisfying all these considerations.

In order to take account of the relative merits of each of the media, you need to look at all their advantages and disadvantages.

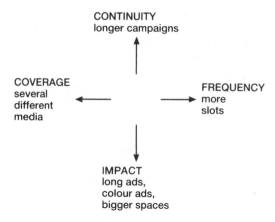

CONTINUITY
longer campaigns

COVERAGE
several
different
media

FREQUENCY
more
slots

IMPACT
long ads,
colour ads,
bigger spaces

The media planner's dilemma.

Television

Up until quite recently, viewing was almost equally divided between the BBC and the IBA. The IBA, of course, includes the fourteen regional independent stations, plus Channel 4 and TV AM. Naturally, ITV's regional viewing figures are reflected fairly closely in the demographic spread of the population, i.e. the number of people living in each regional area. The station's share of the audience ranges from some 22 per cent in London and the Thames area to less than 1 per cent in the Channel Islands.

Advantages

a Television is extremely useful in getting simple and uncomplicated messages to the vast majority of the population. Most homes have a TV set and therefore, on a purely statistical basis, everyone has the opportunity to see your advertisement.

b Generally speaking, the impact should be good. The standard of creativity is high and is assisted by the use of colour and sound.

c It is widely agreed that people are more receptive to advertisements in a relaxed atmosphere (homes are usually relaxed, but not necessarily so).

d The sophisticated collection and analysis of viewing data helps the media planner target the audience more accurately.

e In a highly competitive market such as this, attractive discounts are offered to new or, for that matter, regular advertisers.

f The regional nature of independent television further helps the planner to segment the country into manageable advertising areas.

Disadvantages

a Production costs, unless for the most basic of advertisements, are high.

b Air time can be extremely expensive at peak times. For example, in the Thames region a 30-second peak time slot would cost in excess of £40 000, dropping to as little as £2000 in the Border region which only caters for 1 per cent of the population.

c High-income and well-educated groups tend not to view as often as the rest of the population. Therefore, television may not be the right medium for them.

d Tests have proved that viewers' attention wanders during advertising breaks.

e The wide use of the video recorder may mean that advertisements are not viewed at all when a programme is played back.

TALKING POINT AND ACTIVITY

Do you think that the BBC should offer advertising opportunities? Research the costs of TV advertising and try to find out the 'peak viewing' periods.

The available advertising time is at present strictly limited. Only 7 minutes per hour is allowed for advertising purposes. Charge rates are calculated according to particular times of the day, assumed audience size, and demand from other advertisers. To buy a 30-second slot on all regional television stations in peak time would cost well in excess of £100 000.

Newspapers

There is a considerable choice in national newspapers available to the potential advertiser. Sales figures (or circulation figures) differ widely. Far and away the most successful newspapers are *The Sun* and *The Daily Mirror*, both boasting sales between 3 and 4 million per day. Several other major papers have sales in excess of a million, with the 'heavy' newspapers barely mustering half a million each. A distinction should be made between the daily papers and the Sunday papers as some 3 million additional sales are made on Sundays. Nearly 15 million newspapers are sold daily, whereas over $17\frac{1}{2}$ million are sold on Sunday.

Advantages

a Over 85 per cent of the population can be reached by the combined sales of national and local newspapers. However, a great many individual advertisements would have to be placed in different papers.

b Each newspaper has a distinctly different readership which allows for accurate segmentation.

c The flexibility of giving short or long notice in booking advertisements is a key feature of daily newspapers.

d Many people tend to believe the printed word more than any other form of advertising.

e Many national newspapers offer the facility of split-runs – in other words, you may advertise in *The Daily Mirror* just in the North of England should you wish.

f The message which you are trying to get across may be long and complex, such as in financial advertising, making it most suitable for this medium.

g Many newspapers have now begun to offer special features and advertising on certain days, e.g. Monday may be 'jobs', Tuesday may be 'property'.

h An increasing number of newspapers offer colour supplements. Despite the fact that many papers have gone 'colour', there are grave misgivings about the quality of colour reproduction on to newsprint. The availability of advertising in colour supplements helps to alleviate this.

Disadvantages

a Most people view newspaper advertisements as boring. They lack impact, although the introduction of colour has helped this.

b Most newspapers are only read on the day they come out; therefore, the advertisement has a very short life.

c The growth of the free newspaper market has diluted available income. Further, it has meant that many newspapers simply consist of advertisements with very little editorial content. Advertisements simply 'get lost' in the mass.

Reader loyalty can compensate for a number of the criticisms. Equally, certain prestige newspapers attract a disproportionate amount of advertising compared to their readership. Editorial support for new products is very much a feature of certain newspapers and greatly enhances the impact of the advertisement itself.

TALKING POINT

Is there any point in advertising in local weekly 'Advertisers' or free-sheets? Are they just a paper full of advertisements pretending to be a newspaper? How would you assess their value?

Magazines

With well over a thousand magazines available in the UK alone, the advertiser has the choice of specialist or general interest magazines, published from weekly to quarterly. The range of magazines is really quite bewildering and constantly changing. Many have done a lot of the work for the advertiser by specifically catering for a particular audience and giving the right sort of editorial material.

Advantages

a Segmentation and targeting can be precise, as the magazine may well have done this for the advertiser already by providing a full reader breakdown.

b Special interest magazines have a considerably longer life than most other magazines. The editorial is well read and the advertisements are given much more attention than in general interest magazines.

c Magazines tend to have a longer life than newspapers and have a much higher 'pass-on' rate (more than one person reads the magazine).

d In the case of well-known and respected magazines, advertisements may well gain increased impact and credibility by being in them.

e Compared with newspapers, the better-quality paper and more sophisticated printing techniques in magazines allow the advertising of up-market products with full colour advertisements.

Disadvantages

a There is quite keen competition to be noticed by the reader, with other high quality advertisements and interesting editorial.

b The readership breakdown is far less complete than for newspapers. Indeed, for smaller circulation magazines, independent audits of their true circulation figures may not be available.

c You should not expect an instant response from an advertisement, as the 'shelf-life' of the magazine is comparatively long and so is the 'digesting' period after the buyer has purchased the magazine.

d Magazines often have long lead and cancellation times, advertising copy being required sometimes weeks or months in advance, which makes 'spur-of-the-moment' advertising very difficult.

e High-quality advertisements inevitably mean high production costs to create the original artwork for the advertisement.

TALKING POINT AND ACTIVITY

Compare the relative costs of magazines and TV advertising. What are their advantages and disadvantages over each other?

In many respects the world of magazine advertising is much like that of the newspaper. Magazines tend to vie for advertising far more agressively than newspapers. They will often offer special deals for new advertisers and regulars far more readily than newspapers. As pointed out, one of the disadvantages is that magazines have relatively early copy dates and may require advertising copy as much as two to three months prior to the publication date. Costs vary enormously. Women's weekly magazines can be as much as £20 000 per full colour page. The range and scope of advertising in magazines is huge and there should be something that will suit everyone's pocket.

Radio

The late 1980s signalled (no pun intended!) an explosion in radio and there are more changes to come.

Independent radio, as run by the IBA, tends to be very middle-of-the-road in its appeal. Networking (rather like the TV version), where the same programme is simultaneously broadcast across the entire Independent Local Radio network, is becoming more common and offers very exciting possibilities for the advertiser.

Advantages

a This medium is ideal for urgent and immediate advertising announcements.

b With the widespread use of stereo, sound-effects and gimmicks are far more effective than on television.

c You can advertise precisely to a set area (independent local radio has clearly defined broadcasting areas).

d Production costs for radio advertisements are comparatively cheap.

e Good discounts are available for both new and regular advertisers.

f Short notice may be given to the stations for bookings and cancellations, so flexibility is high.

Disadvantages

a National campaigns are difficult to plan and co-ordinate, due to the local nature of the ILR network.

b Radio has the reputation of being a 'low impact' medium, used as background 'sound' and not concentrated on as much as the TV.

c As with TV, national advertising can be expensive if you add up the air time across the whole network.

TALKING POINT AND ACTIVITY

Radio advertising is a relatively young medium. Do you think that you can accurately target the segment to which you wish to get the message? How well do radio stations detail their audience?

There are two main routes through which radio air time sales are made. Firstly, there are 'brokers' who handle the sales for each of the stations through their contacts with the London advertising agencies. Secondly, the stations sell air time locally through their own offices and sales force. Capital Radio in London heads the price league with a cost approaching £1500 for a 30-second peak slot; this drops to under £10 for an off-peak slot on one of the smaller and more remote stations. Discounts can be very attractive as it is rare to buy a single spot. The most common advertising package offered is known as the Total Audience Package (TAP), which aims to reach a cross-section of the listeners at various times of the day over a period of time.

Outdoor advertising

Outdoor advertising is not just static poster sites. It also includes advertising carried on buses, taxis and trains, and at railway stations. Other 'sites' include sports stadiums (such as football pitches), hot-air balloons (the really big ones!), milk bottles, and even parking meters!

The most obvious form of outdoor advertising is the poster and you will find these literally everywhere. They may lack the impact of TV, magazine or newspaper advertising, but do serve to remind people about the advertising message.

Advantages

a Very high OTS.

b Very low CPT.

c Wide range of colours available.

d Wide choice of sites.

e Good opportunities to be the only advertisement in view at any one time, with little direct competition.

f Sites tend to be sold on a quarterly basis. The gradual effect of the poster may make people sub-consciously notice the advertisement and take note of it over a period of time.

g Great opportunities, particularly on large hoardings, to have very innovative advertising, such as the '3D' advertisement with models, cars or similar items 'stuck' on to the poster.

Disadvantages

a Printing costs are high on the short runs needed for the posters.
b There is a long booking and cancellation period.
c Very debatable research into site 'audiences'.
d Can be missed easily and not even looked at by the 'audience'.
e Only short, snappy messages tend to work.
f Graffiti writers can be a problem.
g Prime sites are often monopolised by 'big' advertisers.
h Sites are usually not available individually and a package of sites is sold to the advertiser, who has no control over where their advertisement is shown.

TALKING POINT

Do you notice poster or bus advertisements? How effective do you think they are? How would you assess their effectiveness?

Most of the outdoor space is sold by a handful of contractors. They sell a package of mixed sites which are meant to get the advertiser's message across to the intended target audience. Popular sites are often tied up for literally years with the TC (till countermanded) system. This can be frustrating.

Costs vary immensely, of course. For example, some 400 sites sell for around £70 000 per month; bus rears cost around £50 each per month and are usually available in multiples of 50.

Cinema advertising

There are now under 1000 cinemas in the UK, but the medium is gradually fighting its way back as a form of entertainment after a period of decline. Attendance figures show that it is a medium that tends to attract the younger age groups.

Advantages

a Local advertising is possible, and cheap.
b Ideal for targeting the younger age group.
c Great impact – the audience's attention is held by the 'big screen'.
d Sound and picture reproduction is very good.

Disadvantages

a Low audience figures.
b Production costs are high – as expensive as TV advertisements. In addition to this, prints of the advertisement are needed for each cinema and these cost several hundred pounds each.
c Buying 'space' can be difficult as the medium is not as developed as others in this area.

TALKING POINT

Do production and duplication costs outweigh the advantages in cinema advertising for the average-sized advertising budget? Can you get away with just showing your TV advertisement?

There are two main sellers of cinema advertising space, but data on audiences is still sparse. Packaging of advertising 'slots' is popular and you can either buy slots in similar towns or areas (such as seaside towns) or all the cinemas in a particular city. If you wanted to buy a 30-second slot on all of the available screens in the UK, it would cost you in excess of £40 000.

SCHEDULING . . . .

Now that the message has been created and the correct medium chosen, the media planner must work out how to time the campaign. Sorting out the timing of the whole campaign is known as macro-scheduling and the detailed timetabling of everything within the campaign is known as micro-scheduling.

Many advertisers decide that the best form of impact is to assault the audience with a sudden burst of activity. This is useful, particularly for seasonal advertising. However, the slower and softer approach can be just as effective and usually a great deal cheaper.

TALKING POINT AND ACTIVITY

Devise a schedule form which would detail the media schedule for an advertiser.

The media schedule details every element of the campaign, such as the magazine space booked and the TV advertising slots ordered. Schedules show the timing and the pace of the campaign and detail the costs and nature of each element piece by piece.

TEST YOURSELF

1 What are the essentials of a 'good' advertisement?

2 How important is creativity in designing an advertising campaign?

3 What are the stages in developing an advertising message?

4 What are coverage and frequency?

5 What is OTS?

6 What is the CPT for advertising and what is the basic slot time?

7 List five advantages of television advertising.

8 Identify the best medium for targeting specialist interest groups.

9 List three disadvantages of magazine advertising.

10 Compare newspapers and magazines as useful mediums.

A WORKING CASE STUDY

BUAV cosmetics cinema advertisement

The stunning BUAV cinema commercial starring Angie Hill, a top model, was designed to take the cruelty-free message to a new audience throughout the UK. The commercial was conceived and produced free for the BUAV by a supporter, Anita Davis. It was launched nationwide in December 1989, and attracted considerable media interest and screenings on television on such programmes as *The Clothes Show*. The commercial was screened again in March 1990 in a packaging slot with the film *The War of the Roses*.

The cosmetics' animal-testing commercial was a key feature in the BUAV's campaign and proved to be a turning point in the campaign.

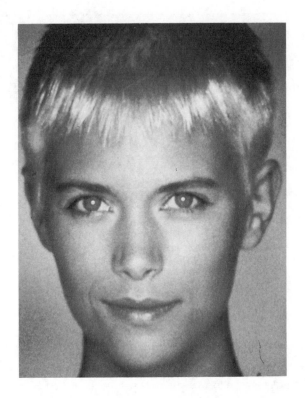

Progressive close-up stills of Angie Hill, from the BUAV cinema advertisement.

Steve Mclvor previews the BUAV's stunning new cinema commercial UGLY PAIN.

Audiences first believe they are watching yet another cosmetic industry promo. In the opening shot we see a beautiful woman smiling gently. The camera then closes in and focuses on her applying an eyeshadow. As she does so the eyelid suddenly transforms as the flesh becomes bruised and discoloured. Haunting, atmospheric music adds to a sense of unease as she brushes blusher onto her cheek only for the skin to bleed with each stroke. She next applies lipstick and when she removes the tissue paper from her lips, they emerge cracked and sore. Finally, she rubs perfume onto her neck which turns red raw. The camera then pulls out slowly revealing her bruised, ravaged face. She is clearly in pain. Until this point however it is unclear what the message of the advert is. The voice over then cuts in to state "Every year thousands of other animals suffer this ugly pain in the name of beauty. Please use cosmetics that are 'cruelty-free'." This is followed by a pained scream as the woman throws back her head. Finally the BUAV name appears on screen. The audience is left with a clear impression of just how animals suffer for human vanity. The role reversal is a powerful medium and is superbly worked in the commercial.

This one-minute advert is the BUAV's latest powerful weapon in the campaign to end cosmetic, toiletry and household product tests on animals. Its launch on the 29th November at the Bijou theatre in the heart of London's film land created great interest. National press, women's magazines, radio and television were on hand to cover the event. What they witnessed was the product of almost a year's work, great dedication and generosity. The advert was conceived and arranged by Anita Davis – art director for one of the country's largest advertising agencies. Her decision to put her talent to work, was sparked by the extensive media coverage at the end of 1988 surrounding the BUAV's *True Colours of Benetton* campaign. She decided it was time to use her own ability to help progress the campaign. With support from her boyfriend Stephen Worley, the film's producer, and his colleague, director John Swannell, the project became a reality. They were able to recruit one of the world's top models, 23-year-old Angie Hill, to star in the commercial. As with all the other participants she waived her fee and took on a gruelling 18-hour filming session in order to produce the advert.

Her previous work had included appearances in television adverts, cover features in many European and US women's magazines and recently a part in the hit TV series *Boon*.

Others who gave their talents to the project included Britain's leading make-up artist and owner of the Colourings range, sold in the Body Shop International – Barbara Daly. Voice-over for the commercial was provided by internationally renowned Shakespearian actress Anna Massey, and the Cocteau Twins granted permission to use their song *The Thinner The Air* for the soundtrack. Special effects for the ad were provided by Maralyn and Aaron Sherman who are better known for their work on films like *Brazil* and *American Werewolf in London*.

It is hardly surprising with such an abundance of talent that the commercial is so polished and professional. It was a great surprise however, when Anita Davis first contacted us about the project. She telephoned on the recommendation of Barbara Daly who has been an active supporter of the *Choose Cruelty-Free* campaign since its launch in 1987.

Our initial reaction was a mixture of surprise, hope and concern. To be offered a cinema commercial on the cosmetic testing issue was the stuff of dreams. We had been committed to producing our own advert for over two years, but meeting the cost of such a venture was a major obstacle. Nevertheless, we were concerned that the commercial might be completely unsuitable, wasting considerable time and expense on everyone's behalf. It was therefore with some trepidation that we arranged to meet Anita and view the recently finished advert. As we sat waiting for it to begin, it was difficult to tell whether it was Anita or ourselves who were most nervous. A few minutes later and the tension was gone – the ad was a winner. We immediately agreed to promote and distribute the film, and the next stage in the process was underway.

A few short months later, all the trials and tribulations of securing music and a distribution deal for cinemas were behind us. However, only a few days before its launch the ad was given a 15 certificate by the Board of Censors. Sadly, this meant that our hopes of running the commercial with hit films like "Ghostbusters II" and "Back to the Future II" were scuppered. Furthermore, the commercial had earlier been banned by the Independent Broadcasting Authority (IBA) for screening as a television advertisement, because of the 'political' nature of the film and the BUAV! Nevertheless, the ban did not apply to broadcast of the commercial as editorial content in a television programme. Clearly, this is a ridiculous situation and makes a mockery of the IBA decision. We can only continue to press, along with other pressure groups, for reform of the rules that constrain groups such as our own from putting across our message in paid television advertising space, in a way that our opponents already do.

Nevertheless coverage of the ad has been excellent. On the launch day articles appeared in *Today* newspaper and the *Daily Mirror*. *Sky News* and Radio One's *Newsbeat* also plugged the ad, with Sky showing it in its entirety on their evening news slot. Magazines, including *Look-In, Cosmopolitan, More* and *Essentials*, were also in attendance, as were cosmetic trade and healthy living journals. Further coverage followed with the screening of the film and a studio debate on the issue of animal testing on ITV's *The Time, The Place* programme – watched by around 1.6 million people.

Once again cosmetic companies that continue to cruelly test their products on animals have suffered a major blow to their image in the run-up to their key Christmas sales period. The growth in support and activity on the issue continues and, thanks to people like Anita Davis, Angie Hill, Stephen Worley, John Swannell and Barbara Daly, we move closer to our goal of banishing such tests once and for all.

Reprinted by courtesy of BUAV from *Liberator*, Winter 1990.

Activities and tasks

1 In the role of an account executive of an advertising agency which has received an enquiry from BUAV, do you think that you have a conflict of interest because you have regular bookings from cosmetic companies? How would you handle this and any potential complaints from the cosmetic companies? Does this matter?

2 Try making a simple 30-second advertisement to be screened in the cinema or on television, sticking strictly to the time limit and limited funds.

3 How would the BUAV measure the effectiveness of the commercial? In the role of a media buyer, how could you prove the effectiveness to the organisation?

FURTHER READING

Sales Promotion, P Spillard, Business Publications, Texas
A Guide to Consumer Promotions, A Morgan, Ogilvy and Mather
The Practice of Public Relations, W Howard, Heinemann

12   Sales promotions and public relations

SALES PROMOTION . . . .

Sales promotion, known as 'below the line expenditure' in sales and marketing, is hard to explain in theoretical terms. It is easier to describe by giving examples. If you buy something that says '10p off!' or 'Save wrappers from this snack bar for that nifty Wurzles tape' or 'Buy two, get one free', these are all examples of sales promotions.

Sales promotions account for up to half of all marketing expenditure. This half includes sales promotions that most people never hear about. Trade sales promotions are very common, such as bulk order discounts, or rebates based on the amount spent over a year with a supplier. In the latter example, a target amount for the year is set by the supplier and, if the buyer reaches that level of purchasing over the year, the buyer will obtain a higher (retrospective) discount level from the supplier. In strict terms, these types of sales promotion should not really be counted.

Sales promotion has one main aim – to increase sales. Fairly obvious, but the tactics are more complex than those for advertising. Sales promotions try to encourage larger and more frequent purchasing by the buyer.

Most sales promotions are short-term campaigns. Some types of goods regularly dominate sales promotions. For example, cereal producers offer sales promotion, but not specifically to increase sales, since they keep one promotion or another going for virtually the entire year. So why? By offering plastic Turtle figures, one brand of cereal temporarily has an edge over the cereal that doesn't. Sales promotion for cereal producers, and indeed for petrol companies, replaces the need to cut their prices to attract more sales. Price wars do nothing for any of the companies involved except reduce their profits, and no one wants that. Having said this, price reduction is itself a sales promotion tactic which is very successful. Let's have a look in some detail at the various forms of sales promotion and their relative merits.

TALKING POINT

Why bother with sales promotions? Surely these show that your overall marketing strategy and advertising campaigns aren't working?

THE DIFFERENT FORMS OF SALES PROMOTION . . . .

The major types of sales promotion fall into two main categories. There are those which seek to put pressure on the consumer (or distributor) to buy more. There are also the types of sales promotion that aim to increase goodwill.

1 **Money off**   This can be a very simple form of sales promotion. The pack can be reprinted to include a 'special price' on it. If the budget does not run to that, stickers can be printed to be slapped on to the pack, which avoids the cost of changing the pack's original artwork and reprinting it. The key to this technique is to let the distributors know in good time about the sales promotion and to back up the 'special pack' or sticker price with point-of-sales material and any displays.

TALKING POINT

Do you think that money-off promotions actually work? Are you convinced to buy something just because the price has been 'reduced'?

Money-off promotions are a very effective way of inducing customers to try a new product, or perhaps persuading them to change brands. Indirectly this form of promotion can help to persuade existing stockists to take larger orders as a result of expected increased demand.

2 **Self-liquidating premiums**   This form of promotion offers the product at a greatly reduced price, providing that the customer has several proofs of purchase (usually part of the packet) of the product. The manufacturer is able to offset the cost of this form of promotion by buying in bulk. The offer must be attractive in order to ensure that the target market segment responds well. This form of promotion can be used in two main ways:

a   It can act to counter a price cut by a competitor.
b   It can aggressively increase the level of purchase among existing customers.

TALKING POINT AND ACTIVITY

Do you think that many people bother to follow through the self-liquidating premium offers? Devise a self-liquidating premium for a consumer product of your choice.

Eye-catching displays and point-of-sale material greatly increase the customer's awareness of the brand which is being promoted in this way, and will also work as an inducement for the retailer to devote more shelf space to the product. Self-liquidating premiums are less common now. In the past they were the major form of promotional activity, second only to money-off promotions.

TALKING POINT AND ACTIVITY

Visit a local store and see how many free premium offers you can find. How do the free samples relate to the product to which they are attached? Are they similar products?

3 Free premium offers This promotion's objective is to encourage a customer to sample a new or existing product. The most common form that it takes is attaching a sample of the product to another product. In this way the customer cannot avoid the free sample, and may be encouraged to purchase the other product and get something free. This type of offer is often used when the product is being launched for the first time.

TALKING POINT

How would you assess the effectiveness of free samples?

4 Free samples Teams of door-to-door distributors are employed to push the free sample through the customer's letter box, or a special charge is made for delivery through the Post Office. An important point to note is that the sample pack is smaller than those available in retail outlets. This ensures that the retailer is not deprived of potential business. Retailers may take great exception to the distribution of free samples in their area if they feel that this will diminish their own sales, and it is vital that their permission is gained before delivery is made. This particular form of sales promotion is most common when geographical availability of the product is patchy and it seeks to stimulate demand in new areas.

TALKING POINT AND ACTIVITY

Devise a realistic competition. How does the competition relate to the product you have chosen?

5 User competitions This form of promotion has a twofold objective. Firstly, it seeks to maintain brand loyalty. Secondly, it hopes to increase the frequency of use and purchase from existing customers. It is unlikely that new customers are attracted by this sort of promotion. The idea for the competition must be attractive and this is directly related to the desirability of the prize or prizes. Each and every entrant must have (or at least feel that they have) a fair chance of winning. Competitions are subject to tight legal controls and must conform to such legislation, which says that an element of skill should be involved. For instance, putting the features of a product in the best order. Competitions are useful in encouraging retailers to give shelf space to displays related to the competition.

TALKING POINT

Make a list of fictitious characters related to products. Did you remember the product first and then the character, or the other way around?

6 Personality promotions Several companies create a fictitious character which is associated with their product. Point-of-sales displays and other advertising material feature the character and, by association, seek to enhance the customer's awareness of the product range. Celebrity endorsements or associations have a similar effect.

7 Quantity discounts This form of sales promotion is aimed at the retailer or distributor specifically. Higher discounts are offered on orders made in bulk. This is meant to encourage higher stock levels, thus increasing sales and freeing the manufacturer's warehousing for other products.

TALKING POINT

How would a company offering a trade premium work out how much they can 'give away'? What considerations should be taken into account?

8 Trade premium offers These can be seen as a form of quantity discount, but actually give away additional stock if the buyer purchases a specified amount. This can be an attractive offer, as the retailer will not have paid for the free bonus products and can achieve a better profit margin on the whole order overall. An additional benefit is that stock levels in retail outlets are increased.

9 Trade competitions These are a form of competition which is aimed at the retailer as opposed to the consumer. The retailer may be required to devote additional space, perhaps a window display, to promote the product. The prizes must be attractive to ensure retailer interest, or may perhaps offer the chance of additional discounts. The objectives are threefold – firstly, to increase the retailers' efforts in selling the product; secondly, to gain larger display areas in the outlets; and, thirdly, to educate the retailers about the product.

TALKING POINT

How can the effectiveness of consumer fairs be assessed?

10 Fairs and exhibitions There are two main types of fair. A trade fair seeks to increase retailers' goodwill and attract new stockists and distributors. A consumer fair, such as The Ideal Home Exhibition, endeavours to persuade customers to sample the product and perhaps to see it in operation, as in the case of a household appliance.

Each of the above forms of sales promotion has specific objectives. Most relate to sales and distribution of the product, but some have the much wider aim to increase goodwill, perhaps through sponsorship. This form of sales promotion is particularly popular in the sporting field and many physical activities have benefitted from the injection of resources and the subsequent interest created by sponsorship from organisations.

Sales promotions can be easy to mount, or they can be very complex and intricate operations. Whatever the level of complexity and time allocated to organising them, it is still very difficult to measure the effect they have on sales. So many other variables affect customer demand that it is almost impossible to quantify effectiveness. One way of overcoming this is to define objectives clearly and judge changes in product demand in relation to all other trends. There may be clearly laid out objectives, such as increasing brand loyalty, or simply increasing sales. Whatever the objective, a careful monitoring and evaluation process must be put in place to determine the level of success.

Sales promotions have become increasingly popular in past years. There are three main reasons for this:

Fast food outlets often wish to associate themselves with 'fun' images. This Wimpy promotional photograph shows how a theme can be followed through. Why has a wide-angled lense been used (common practice in advertising photography)? Photograph courtesy of Wimpy International.

- Costs in reaching consumers through other more conventional forms of advertising have rocketed over the last few years.
- Sales promotions can appeal directly to the consumer, or to the trade, very easily.
- Sales promotions can be used as an adjunct to other forms of marketing and advertising, and they are often used in conjunction with advertising campaigns.

PUBLIC RELATIONS . . . .

Public relations, better known as PR, attempts to create a strong and positive image for the company. This image, sometimes known as a 'corporate image', is the public face of the company and it is vital that the general public has a favourable impression. The general public's image is a reflection of the company's ability to satisfy customers and to make the public aware of the company through successful marketing.

PR AND THE WORLD . . . .

The world outside the company can seriously affect its operations. Factors which may affect the company include the following, and you will probably think of many more:

- Economic
- Political
- Social
- Technological
- Ethical

The exact nature of these influences or external forces will, of course, depend on the nature of the company's business. The company must evaluate these forces, once they have been identified of course, and figure out the best way to react to them. PR aims to smooth out the effects of these forces and influences. This creates and maintains a climate in which the company can get on with its business without interference. Better still, PR may change the external forces to the benefit of the company. This is a two-edged sword, as the company has to be seen favourably not only by its customers but by the 'world' in general if its working environment is to be improved. At the same time, improving its working environment will bring the company to the attention of larger numbers of people and other external forces, and these in turn will scrutinise the company and demand ever higher levels of service and satisfaction. In brief, PR tries to achieve acknowledgement for what the company does and appreciation of this.

Here are some targets for the PR machine, and the techniques which are used:

1 The general public, often targeted by community relations exercises such as sponsoring public events.
2 The company's employees, increasingly important as the workforce is perceived as an asset rather than a necessary evil and/or a source of confrontation.

3   The banks and the Stock Exchange, to whom the company must look financially sound and with a reasonable future.

4   The customers or clients of the company, for whom work must run alongside the advertising and general marketing policy. Educating customers as to the superiority of the product or service is vital, as well as maintaining general interest and awareness in the target group of the general public.

5   The media, an integral part of a well-organised PR campaign. PR aims to strike up an understanding relationship with the press, be they newspapers, radio or television.

TALKING POINT

Companies which have a large and active PR department have a disproportionate share of coverage in the media as compared with smaller and less active companies. Is this fair, and how could this be offset by the smaller companies?

PR AT WORK . . . .

There are some typical forms of PR activity which show the range of tasks which are part of PR:

1   Identifying specific interest groups which will be able to influence the attitude of the public towards the company. The company will have to identify the objectives of these interest groups and assess the resources available to them. Examples of these interest groups are pressure groups and investors. Once the interest group has been identified, the group's attitude towards the company must be ascertained. How does the interest group operate? What are its strengths? The PR side of the company must now devise a plan to influence these interest groups and, hopefully, encourage them to project a favourable image of the company to the public at large. The company must be able successfully to deflect any of the criticisms that may be levelled at it by the interest groups, and at the same time try to build a strong company image in the eyes of the individuals that make up the interest groups.

2   PR should also offer counselling or advice to the management of the company and keep it updated on attitudes and opinions in society that may well have an influence on the company's decision-making. The creation of forecasts of what may happen in the future should be a vital part of this and the use of these predictions should enable the company to offset any possible problems.

3   Publicising the company's products or services is an integral part of the overall marketing policy. PR plays an important role in the launch of a new product and can also be a key factor in the development of new ideas. PR aims to keep interested segments of society informed of trends, developments and launches on a rolling basis.

4   In the field of media relations, the PR element of a company tries to get editorial coverage in newspapers and magazines or, less commonly, on either TV or radio. Media relations are used to inform or educate the public about a particular product, service or activity in which the company is involved.

5   Creating awareness and fostering a positive attitude towards the company on a corporate level is extremely useful. This activity seeks to increase overall interest

and awareness that is not specifically related to any of the company's products or services.

6 PR also aims to lobby the decision-makers in both government and professional organisations, to persuade them to promote legislation, regulations or attitudes that are favourable for the company.

TALKING POINT AND ACTIVITY

Certain companies in particular fields find it easier to get coverage than those in more obscure fields. In the role of an oil company PR Manager, who would you attempt to contact to gain coverage for your company's new 'Super Green' lead-free petrol?

PR AND PERCEPTIONS . . . .

PR is also responsible for developing a favourable corporate image to the general public. This image tries to adapt, change or amend the public perceptions of the company by redefining the public's image of the company and offering a positive view to them.

The company should always appear to be acting in a socially responsible manner. The public now demands this as a result of a more educated awareness of the issues, the demand for more information to be made public on the operations of organisations and, most importantly, the changing attitudes to what is acceptable and what is not.

The public's perception of the company leaves the company with a problem. It must be able, and willing, to respond to the public. It leads to some very important questions:

- Should the company simply respond to changes in attitude, such as environmental awareness?
- Alternatively, should the company try to be in the forefront of such changes?

Many organisations have discovered to their cost that they should not sit back and wait for things to change before doing something about them. They have to take the lead; public demand is gradually growing that they should do this. It can mean obtaining great advantages over the competition by being seen to be in tune with the public and not simply reacting to demands.

By building up the corporate image of the company, the PR department may be able to fulfill the following broad objectives:

1 Instilling in the public's mind that the company is socially responsible and has the flexibility and foresight to adapt to changing needs and demands made by the public.

2 Building public goodwill which may induce people to look more favourably on the company's activities in general.

3 Greater image awareness, leading to many additional benefits in areas such as general marketing activities, by having a head-start over competitors because of the public's knowledge of the company and the company's broad policies.

TALKING POINT AND ACTIVITY

Some companies have a strong and positive corporate image. List as many of these as you can. Now try to list those that have a negative corporate image.

PR IN THE MARKETING CONTEXT . . .

Marketing plays an important role in enhancing the corporate image. An effective and well-managed company should be market sensitive and should aim to create greater customer satisfaction. PR cannot possibly succeed in its goals if the company is unable to show itself as performing well and demonstrating reasonable efficiency. Good trading performance coupled with strong customer loyalty goes a long way in maintaining a sound and positive corporate image. Marketing can help PR in the following ways:

1 **Product publicity**   Getting your products (particularly new ones) on to the TV or featured in newspapers and magazines.
2 **Informing**   Continually feeding information to the public and to interested groups.
3 **Media relations**   Co-ordinating advertising, sales promotions, press releases, etc, with the PR effort. It is in the company's interest to release as much information as it can, in order to counteract the possibility that lack of information causes public misunderstanding or a negative image of the company.
4 **Creating awareness**   By fostering a strong and positive attitude to the company, to add to the reputation of the company's products and services. In circumstances where the company's reputation is not very good, PR and marketing can make sure that the company's name is kept away from the brand name of a product and that the product does not suffer as a result of the company's poor reputation.

TALKING POINT AND ACTIVITY

How do companies begin to build their corporate image? Where would you start? In the role of a company new to the market and involved in importing cheap Eastern European cars, devise a brief corporate image-building campaign.

5 **Developing a corporate image**   Marketing can be involved throughout the whole process, starting with market research to try to find out the expectations for the company. Following from this will be the analysing of customer behaviour, targeting policy, advertising and selling, and trying to readjust the perceptions of the company. The next step is to make the most of the marketing opportunities and then broadcast the company's successes, at the same time being honest about mistakes. Finally, by using promotional skills, pass on information about successes and failures and develop the company's powers of information dissemination.

TEST YOURSELF

1 What is sales promotion and what else could it be called?

2 What is a self-liquidating premium?

3 What is a trade premium offer?

4 What are the objectives of trade competitions?

5 Why have sales promotions become more popular in recent years?

6 What is PR?

7 List at least three targets of PR and say why they should be targeted.

8 Why are some specific targets lobbied by PR departments?

9 How does marketing help PR?

10 What part can PR play in establishing a company's image?

A WORKING CASE STUDY

Boosey & Hawkes woodwind folder

Boosey & Hawkes is a very well-established company operating within the music industry. As well as being involved in the manufacture and retailing of instruments themselves, the company is also active in the field of music publishing, and it is from this branch that our example is drawn. (*See* pp192–3).

The product itself is a general-purpose folder, used as a means of projecting a unified image when sending information to other people, mainly customers. It is, to use a rather glib expression, a way of 'prettying up' communications and fostering a strong image to the buyer.

Because of the wide number of uses intended for the folder, the brief received by the agency responsible for its design was wide, yet also tantalisingly difficult; how to get across the image required without becoming too specific.

The examples shown here illustrate very well the creative process involved in such a work, from the original roughs, through to the finished product itself.

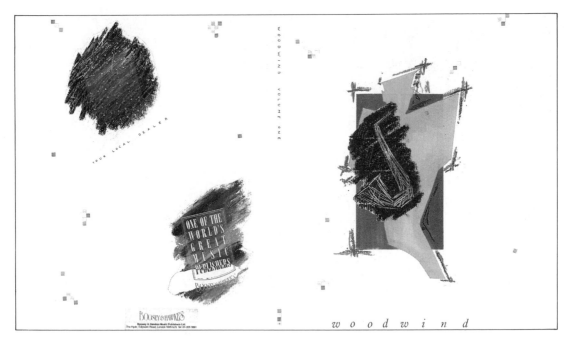

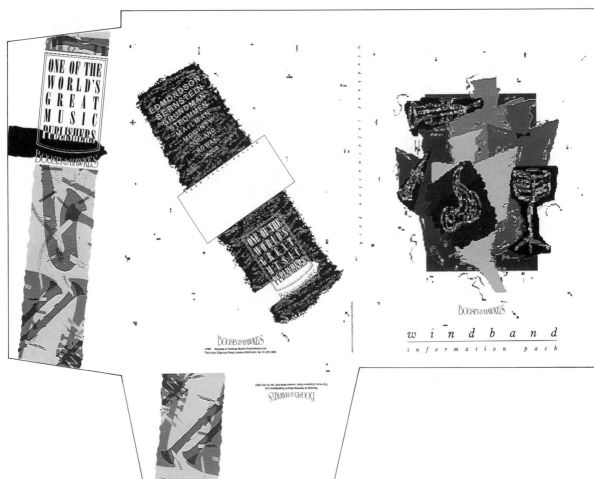

The finished folder design.

On opposite page: rough visual of the folder design (above), and intermediate stage design, later amended (below).

A PRESS RELEASE

The Haunted Dungeon

An effective press release should be just long enough to maintain interest and precisely written to be easily paraphrased by an editor who wishes to feature the contents of the press release in amended form.

Press releases are one of the methods of gaining regular publicity in the media, and are often used simply as a sales letter to potential customers.

PRESS INFORMATION
Border Television plc

CARLISLE: The Television Centre Carlisle CA1 3NT Tel. (0228) 25101
LONDON Sales and Marketing 18 Clerkenwell Close, London EC1R OAA   Tel. 01-253 3737

THE HAUNTED DUNGEON

Networked on ITV from Sunday 2nd April 1989 to Sunday 27th August 1989, at approximately 9.45 am, The Haunted Dungeon will be a regular feature on The Ghost Train.

The twenty-two roleplaying games (running time around six minutes per week) are filmed by Border Television and produced by Tony Nicholson. The main Ghost Train programme is a mixture of features, cartoons and interviews.

The Haunted Dungeon sets a series of tasks for two children, a boy and a girl aged 10-13, to complete within a time limit. The game requires the children to work out how to escape from the room, aided and taunted by Stinker. The puppet is operated by Spitting Image and Labyrinth puppeteer Simon Buckley.

The game has an educational slant to the problem solving, with the children figuring out how various weird and wonderful machines, processes and logic puzzles work. As time runs out, the children must try to complete the series of puzzles or face a forfeit before Stinker will let them out of the room.

Presenter Shauna Lowry is at hand to congratulate or commiserate with the children at the end of the game.

The game is specifically designed for television and has, to date, received a very good response from the general public and the networks alike. It is hoped, by both the writers and Border Television, that an opportunity will arise to expand the concept to a full twenty-five minute version as a programme in its own right.

The writers, Jon Sutherland and Nigel Gross, are prolific children's book authors, having had nearly twenty books and dozens of articles published since they began working with each other only three years ago.

If you require any further information please contact Border Television on (0228) 25101.

Don't miss **Haunted Dungeon**,
the weekly TV roleplaying game
in ITV's new Sunday morning
children's show. It's written by
Jon Sutherland and Nigel Gross,
who regularly write scenarios for
GM. Here they tell the story of
the making of the programme.
Catch it every Sunday at 9.25 am.

THE MAKING OF HAUNTED DUNGEON
by Jon Sutherland and Nigel Gross

It all started back in November 1988 when a rather cryptic message had been left on
the ansaphone. It turned out to be a researcher for Border Television in Carlisle;
they wanted a roleplaying game to feature as part of the twenty-two weekly
programmes they were putting together.

After an initial meeting in London with the producer, **Tony Nicholson**, we set
about creating a series of 'roleplaying' segments which, within the very tight
specifications of five minutes duration and very little in the way of rules, provided a
daunting but exciting challenge. A further provision was that it had to have a

Stinker with Shauna Lowry.

From left to right, Nigel Gross, Stinker, Shauna Lowry, Jon Sutherland, Tony Nicholson, Charlotte Dymond and competitors.

vaguely horror-based feature to it. That in turn not only ruled out mainstream fantasy, but brought up extra problems, as the programme was due to be transmitted on Sunday mornings with an audience of eight-year-olds and up!

We originally offered three proposals, from a quiz show style format to 75mm scale haunted house in which the contestants would move 'characters' around and solve tricks and traps. The format that Border opted for was, on reflection, the most feasible, controllable and above all filmable. **The Haunted Dungeon** revolves around two contestants (note one female and one male!) aged around 10–12 being dropped onto a set containing a wide variety of props and traps, roughly 16' x 16' and having a limited amount of time to 'escape' via the grill-gate to the rear of the room.

When we arrived at Border TV in Carlisle for the first time in January, we met the team that was to make our game a reality. We test ran one of the sample adventures on two pairs of contestants (who were to be the first two pairs filmed for the series proper). With bated breath, we watched as the guinea-pig tried the game for the first time. It worked! The kids enjoyed it, Border were delighted (and we're sure – very relieved!).

The next day and a half were solid meetings, with Tony Nicholson, and our main contact and lynch-pin with Border TV, **Charlotte Dymond**. The other member of the team were gradually introduced, associate-producer **Cathy**, researchers **Jo** and

Jeanette, contracts people, props, cameras, lighting, etc. By the end of the two days we were exhausted, but raring to go.

The set designer and props man **Ian Reid** proved to be a great asset to the whole project, his enthusiasm tinged with the solid practical approach of what was possible and what was not, pulled out all the stops as we began to create twenty-two puzzles for the series. Wood, fibreglass and plastic in his people's hands took on the guise of wickedly cunning machines, suits of armour and dank dungeon walls swimming with damp and slime, all built and ready by the time we came up again in March to film it for real.

It had been agreed that there should be no adults on the set; it would inhibit the contestants and distort the game too much. We settled on a compromise, which in the end worked out very well, a puppeteer. **Simon Buckley**, whose credits include **Spitting Image** and **The Labyrinth**, would work the specially designed taunter and presenter – Stinker. The origins of the said beast are best left to the imagination.

The first two games would be filmed on the same afternoon. We checked through the props for 'Diamond' and 'Map' nervously and then stood back for the experts to get on with it. The studio was packed, three camera crews, several props men, lighting, make-up ladies, sound and several others. Hidden at the back were two, now very nervous writers. The two games went brilliantly, Stinker taunting and then chivvying the contestants along at just the right level. We breathed an immense sigh of relief.

The main presenter, **Shauna Lowry**, although not having a direct involvement in the game, interviewed us on roleplaying, the books we have written, the hobby in general and the game itself. The interview, after having filmed the first two games, was nerve-wracking, but went smoothly enough.

So, there you have it, from conception to execution. We did, of course, fail to mention the late nights and early mornings writing the games, but that was all part of the job. Whatever our input into the game, Tony, Ian and Charlotte actually made it happen.

Hope that you enjoy the game. We would be pleased to hear your comments and suggestions.

Reproduced by kind permission of *GamesMaster International* magazine.

Look at the two different styles of press release illustrated here. The goal in producing the second one was to publicise the TV programme via the games magazines, whose readers would know the reputation of the authors of the TV programme. The magazines produced the contents of the press release without alteration.

Activities and tasks

1 An assignment relating to Boosey & Hawkes. Seeing how the agency managed to fulfill the brief tends to make the task easier than it actually was, so we thought it might be a good idea if you tried doing one yourself! Assume that the company which has briefed you is involved in the production and manufacture of high-quality furniture. The firm has been established for over 100 years and has a strong reputation as a 'traditional' manufacturer. Of late, however, it has started to manufacture more 'modern' pieces, but still with the same emphasis on quality. The company wants to get this across without alienating its loyal customer base, whose members are more familiar with the company's traditional activities.

2 An assignment based on the first press release. In the role of an editor, rewrite the contents of the press release as a news feature of no more than 250 words. How easy is this task? Do you think it a good idea to copy the contents exactly? Do you need to rewrite totally?

3 A joint assignment. In the role of the PR Manager of the furniture company, write a press release explaining the changes in company policy, and the availability of the new range of furniture. Make sure that you stress that quality will be maintained despite the change in style. You are free to devise the company's background. Use your imagination to make the company seem real.

FURTHER READING

The Rise and Fall of the British Manager, A Mant
An Introduction to Sales Management, D Smallbone

13   Selling it straight

DIRECT MARKETING . . . .

Direct marketing is a type of direct supply. It involves promotions, sales and supply made direct to the customer or other end-user of the product. In essence, all the 'middlemen' are cut out and the supplier directly contacts the customer. There are three main types of direct marketing and we will look at these separately:

TALKING POINT

Are there any advantages to the customer in buying from a mail order company? What can the company offer to induce customers to make the purchase through them?

1 **Mail order**   This is one of the most common and well-developed forms of direct marketing. It often relies on a catalogue which describes the product and details its price, availability and how to order it. The catalogue in conjunction with an agent marketing system is very popular, particularly in the case of general mail order companies, such as Littlewoods or Freemans, or the cosmetic company, Avon. The relationship relies on the agent obtaining orders and then passing them on to the mail order company, who then supplies the agent with the product, and the agent then passes it on to the buyer. The agent, naturally, receives a payment from the mail order company as a reward for obtaining the order. A variant of this is party selling, where products are demonstrated at home by the agent and sales are generated from a group of invited guests.

TALKING POINT

Think of some examples of direct response advertising. Take a look at a Sunday newspaper and find as many examples as you can, not just in the paper itself but also in the colour supplement. You will notice that the value of the products on sale through this medium range from a few pounds to literally thousands of pounds.

2 Direct response advertising   The object of this form of advertising is to generate sales of products or services by receiving orders directly from the customer. Typical versions of this form of selling are the newspaper or magazine advertisement, although there are several examples of this technique being used on television and radio. Records are a common product sold this way. The ordering process is made very simple to enable the customer to make a telephone call and order by credit card or simply to put a cheque in the post, almost as an impulse buy.

3 Direct mail   This covers a wide range of different marketing activities, but all are based on the use of the postal system. Here are some varieties of direct mail:

- Sales letters
- Brochures
- Personalised mail

Much of this direct mail is unsolicited, but is carefully targeted at what the company considers may be potential customers. A well-presented mailshot can be a very effective method of promoting and selling the company's products or services.

Many household names, such as the Automobile Association and the *Reader's Digest*, use direct mail on a regular basis. Direct mail has had a very bad press recently, and the Office of Fair Trading has issued a damning report on certain direct mail users, such as time-share. Time-share companies tried to lure customers to sales presentations with promises of valuable gifts. Further concern has been expressed over the influx of foreign 'junk mail' from countries like Holland and the United States. In 1990, the Data Protection Registrar received a 250 per cent increase in complaints about direct, unsolicited mail. The industry itself has tried to put its own house in order by drawing up new codes of conduct which lay down some guidelines, such as:

a Direct mail is not to be sent to deceased persons.

b Direct mail is not to be sent to those who have opted to be registered in the 'ex-directory', known as the Mailing Preference Service, which attempts to stop all direct mail being sent to people who do not wish to receive it.

c in co-operation with the Advertising Standards Authority, the industry has laid down what may be sent as direct mail, and has agreed with The Post Office that companies which break the code should be penalised by not being given their bulk postal discounts.

The category of 'junk mail' can be described as follows:

advertisers who send out mail indiscriminately;
those who send out very poor-quality mailshots.

Most mailshots are boring, unimaginative and not very useful to the person who receives them. It is a generally-held belief that, if the mailshots were of better quality, the public would be more tolerant of them. The problem is that, while TV and printed advertisements can concentrate on interesting and well-thought-out campaigns that are entertaining, the poor old mailshot has to concentrate on selling something and just that.

Some of the richer and more extravagant direct mail users can afford expensive holograms, tapes and other gimmicks to make their mailshot stand out. Most advertisers, however, are reluctant to invest in the same level of spending as for other advertising media. It is a rather odd attitude when a company may spend hundreds of thousands of pounds making a TV advertisement and then send out a boring letter in an envelope. What tends to compound this is that the letter is often badly written.

Mailing list sources

Direct marketing has increased in volume enormously over the past few years and this increase can be put down to two major changes:

1 Direct marketing makes the dependence on wholesalers and distributors less critical, because you are actually dealing with the customer 'face-to-face'.
2 Technology has made far easier the job of producing the mailing lists and producing and personalising the material that will be sent out. Databases and other related computer software and hardware is now available to speed up the process, from compiling the list to printing the letter itself.

We have just mentioned databases as a main reason for the easy availability of mailing lists of potential customers, but where do these names and addresses come from? Here are some of the major sources:

1 Order forms
2 Enquiry coupons
3 Product guarantees
4 Product warranties
5 Pack offers which require the customer to fill in his or her name and address
6 Magazine subscriptions
7 Membership of organisations, such as the Automobile Association
8 Buying a list from another company or a list broker

Having compiled your list, you cannot use it straight away. You must first check on your computer's database management system to make sure of the following:

TALKING POINT AND
ACTIVITY

How would you go about defining
your target for a mailshot? Where
would you go to get the names and
addresses for this mailshot?

- The list is relevant to the proposed target
- The list is as accurate as possible
- The list is up-to-date
- The list does not duplicate names and addresses as far as can be
  seen

Presentation

So what does a mailshot look like? After all, the presentation of the package is of
critical importance. The customer should be able to understand the message and be
able to act easily upon it. If the message is confused then it will only annoy the
person who has received it. The result of annoyance is a quick journey to the bin!

To avoid the possibility of being recycled, the mailshot is often very glossily
printed and quite creative. Very visible items such as the telephone number of the
company are important to try to convince the customer to ring and order the product
or service *now*! Personalised letters which accompany the package further help in
terms of making the package seem special and worth reading and acting upon.

Developing the business

The business generated by direct marketing operations accounts for over 3 per cent
of the total business done by companies in the UK (most of this is mail order).
Having noted this, we can see that the mail order business is an integral part of the
selling scene of this country and is here to stay. Recently it has been further boosted
by retail chains getting in on the act by offering some of their range of stock via mail
order. Examples of this include Next and Marks & Spencer. There are three main
reasons for this development:

1 Mergers have taken place between mail order companies and retail chains.
2 Modern technology and computerisation of the mailing business has streamlined
   and speeded up trading.
3 The high level of competition for prime retail sites has driven some companies
   into the mail order business, because of economic considerations. Mail order is
   seen as an alternative way of reaching customers without going to the expense of
   setting up and paying running costs on expensive retail sites.

Who is a typical direct mail customer? Target segments vary across the whole of the
socio-economic range. Traditionally C and D groups were mail order catalogue
customers; now upmarket mail order catalogues cater for A and B groups. Mail
order grew well until the end of the 1970s, when the recession caused the mail order

business to suffer badly, showing a poor increase in turnover. This was directly related to the higher levels of unemployment in the North of England in the late 1970s and 1980s, where the main users in the C and D groups lived. In addition to this, the mail order companies had lost out in almost every way to the very competitive high street retailers.

Several strategies to turn the tide have been considered, and the merger between mail order companies and retail chains is just one. Here are some of the others:

- Greater efficiency and quicker delivery
- Increasing the range of goods offered, to attract new customers and create new markets
- Giving more attention to the image of the mail order company

TALKING POINT

What other techniques could a mail order company employ to increase its market share?

TELEPHONE SALES . . . .

Because of the high costs of keeping a sales force 'on the road', coupled with the relatively short time that the salesperson is actually selling, companies have looked for other ways to increase the efficiency of their sales effort. Sales made over the telephone, known as telesales, have grown rapidly and are now a key feature of many companies' sales approach. The advent of telesales has not meant the total replacement of the more traditional forms of selling. Telesales' techniques are usually employed to sell relatively low-cost items on a repetitive basis.

Telesales tend not to be a totally separate operation, but part of the sales force's overall responsibilities. The aim is simple – to increase the individual salesperson's selling time as a whole. The experienced salesperson, who follows up the initial contact made by the telesales people, is able to concentrate on 'live' leads and not waste time in first trying to get an appointment to see the prospective customer. The usual procedure is something along the following lines:

1 Initial 'cold' call from the telesales representative of the company with the aim of drumming up interest in the company's products or services. Alternatively, a mailshot which describes the company's products or services is sent out speculatively and then followed up by the telephone call.

2 Once a prospective customer has been identified and convinced to make an appointment with the salesperson, the responsibility of closing the sale goes to the salesperson, and the telesales people begin work on new batches of potential customers.

PERSONAL COMMUNICATIONS . . . . .

The question of personal communications is an important one when assessing the effectiveness of your sales force. Key features of personal communications, some of which we have already mentioned, are:

1 The ability to identify prospective customers. This can be divided into:

   a Cold calling, where the salesperson systematically knocks on all 'likely' doors in the area. To knock on every door would be a pointless and enormously time-consuming activity. Marketing research should help to identify the target and avoid wastage of time and resources.

   b Word-of-mouth contacts, particularly in the industrial market, where there are good opportunities to make sales this way. The more successful and experienced, the more likely it is that the salesperson will have useful contacts who will be interested in what he or she has to sell and will tell others about the company and what it offers.

   c By using direct mail or advertising compaigns to stimulate interest in the company's products or services, a number of useful enquiries may be received which the salespeople can follow up. Usually these enquiries are 'screened' to discover just how interested the enquirer is in the product or service. From this brief (usually telephone) communication, the salesperson can grade the emergency of the enquiry, and whether the interest is serious and likely to lead to a sale.

2 The second major consideration is that of preparation. It was once a widely-held belief that selling was simply a matter of having the 'right' personality. Most companies now do not trust to luck and have extensive training programmes. Here are the key elements to make sure that your salespeople are ready for the challenges ahead of them:

   a Systematic and well-thought-out training programmes which cover the principal features of selling and how to cope in certain circumstances.

   b Greater product or service knowledge. All the aspects of the company's range of products must be learnt, in order for the salespeople to be ready to answer any potential questions thrown at them.

   c Customer knowledge is as important as knowing about the product itself. The sales force should be continually made aware of the needs and attitudes of the buyers and, as importantly, know their names and a little about them personally.

   d Knowledge of the competition can prove to be very useful too. The members of the sales force should know the relative advantages and disadvantages of what they are offering against those of the competing business.

Elan's vehicles are its business and all carry the prominent logo and company name along with a standardised livery. Photographs courtesy of Elan International.

Being a 'good' salesperson goes further and must take account of the way in which the salesperson approaches and communicates with the customer face-to-face in pursuit of closing a sale. These are known as the active selling skills of the salesperson and include such elements as making appointments; opening the conversation with the customer; identifying what the customer wants and matching that to what you can offer; fielding and responding to questions and criticisms; and negotiating the price and terms of the deal. Finally, as vitally important is the closing of the sale.

Once the sale has been made, the company itself swings into operation in close liaison with the salesperson. The problem of delivery and assuring efficient arrival of the product or service is often overseen by the salesperson just as an insurance measure. After all, it is the salesperson that will bear the brunt of criticisms in this area. It has been estimated that a typical salesperson spends less than 20 per cent of his or her time selling and the rest of the time is taken up with planning, checking, double-checking and, of course, travelling.

TALKING POINT

Do you agree with what we have said about telephone selling never being capable of taking over from face-to-face selling? What are the advantages and disadvantages of the two methods?

Personal or direct selling is a key part of the marketing mix of almost all companies. Nearly every sale involves the company having personal contact with the customer in some way. A good personal relationship with the customer is the lynch-pin of continued success and the maintainence of this good relationship falls on the shoulders of the salesperson. The telephone is certainly having its effect on the personal selling area of operations, but in reality the telephone cannot ever replace face-to-face selling. It may well take over the responsibility for all the more straightforward tasks, such as taking routine orders and cold calling.

TEST YOURSELF

1 What is direct marketing?

2 Where can you find direct response advertising?

3 What are the three main varieties of direct mail?

4 Note down at least six sources of names for direct mail lists.

5 How have mail order companies assured their long-term viability in their struggle against the retail chains?

6 What are the stages in telesales?

7 How can you make sure that your staff are able to do their job well in personal selling?

8 How important is personal selling in most companies' marketing mix?

9 What is cold-calling?

10 Is there a difference between personal selling and direct marketing?

A WORKING CASE STUDY

Mobile messages

We first met Poppies in the Chapter 5 assignment. Now we look at another aspect of this franchise operation. Both Poppies and Guinness see the advantages of promoting their names on vehicles. In the case of Poppies this is on their own vehicles. They have a clear image, with the logo and the standardised way of lettering their name. As a franchising operation, Poppies consists of a large number of independent businesses which share the same common image and offer the same range of services. Each of the franchise businesses values the impact of the Poppies image and agrees that many enquiries are stimulated by potential customers seeing the vans. The public nationwide perceives Poppies as a single company, when, in fact, as we have seen, it comprises a large number of small businesses.

Guinness advertising has been described as 'off-beat'. In other words, the message is not automatically apparent in itself. Guinness marketing works on the premise that people viewing their advertisements will recognise the style and the standard slogan 'Guinness Pure Genius'. The off-beat approach is well illustrated in the photograph, with the main slogan stating 'Train of thought' on the side of a London bus. (*See* p 208.)

In both cases the main objective is for the public to recognise the image and logo of the organisation, and then act as a result of seeing it and identifying it with the basic message. In the case of Poppies, this is the range of cleaning and allied services; and in the case of Guinness, the advertisement represents part of a continuous general awareness campaign to increase the public's knowledge of, and interest in, the product. Poppies and Guinness recognise the effectiveness of this form of direct marketing and have thought through its image creation and customer perceptions of it.

Activities and tasks

1 In a group, monitor a busy stretch of road for half-an-hour or so, each of you noting down any names of companies on the vehicles which pass by. After this, try to remember what the company's business was and write this alongside the name of the company. Compare with the others in your group your ability to remember the names and the messages. This should give you an indication of how effective the company has been in its intention to relay a direct message to you.

2 In the role of Marketing Manager, design a logo (company symbol) and short message for a local electrical retail and repair shop. Try to keep a tight control on the number of words and complexity of the message.

3 Compare Poppies' logo and image with that of the Automobile Association. It is a rather unfair comparison, but think about the way in which the message is constructed and the amount of detail included. What element of the logos sticks out in your mind?

FURTHER READING

Understanding Organisations, C Handy, Penguin
Elements of Marketing, A Morden, DPP
Marketing, B Levy, M + E, Pitman Publishing

14   Marketing organisations

ORGANISATIONAL STRUCTURES . . . .

In order to keep and win customers, an organisation must be able to put their marketing plans into operation efficiently. Many good ideas and opportunities are lost through inefficient organisational structures. The organisational structure must enable all parts of the organisation to function together and efficiently. The concept of organisational culture is related to staff motivation. It is particularly important that the staff are motivated to make sure they satisfy the needs of the customer.

In any organisation an employee must be able to work with their colleagues, but they must also relate to and have a working knowledge of the other parts of the organisation. Organisations are generally run by a Board of Directors, each Director having a specific function as head of one of the various areas of operation. It is therefore important that the practice of good communication begins at the top. It is the Directors' responsibility to make sure that all the departments and staff are working towards the same goals and objectives.

In a large organisation, each area of operation would have a manager, or several managers, who form part of the organisation's family tree. Each manager should know who to approach for various information and to fulfil specific tasks, depending on the area of expertise involved.

Marketing, because of its wide-ranging implications across all the organisation's activities, needs to interact with most of the other departments in the organisation. The basic responsibility for identifying and fulfilling the needs of customers falls to the Marketing Department. The rest of the organisation should therefore be able to respond efficiently and rapidly to the demands made by the

Like many companies, Cadbury's has a strong corporate image. Note the prominent inclusion of the Cadbury's logo and the variants of it, which depend on the colour and style of the packaging.

Marketing Department, otherwise the success of the organisation may be hampered. There are several ways of organising the Marketing function of a company, and we will look at these in turn.

THE TRADITIONAL STRUCTURE . . . .

The traditional structure of Marketing Departments is often found in single-product or single-market organisations. The simplicity of the structure suits the organisation's needs, where the effort has to be concentrated only in one clear direction. The structure is hierarchical; in other words, it is organised in tiers or layers, where the responsibility and authority lies with those in the higher tiers. The organisation's objectives and strategies are filtered down through the tiers to those whose responsibility will be to action them. The Board of Directors will determine these overall strategic objectives; and the Marketing Department, in co-operation with the Sales Department, may then interpret these objectives and pass them on to their Sales Managers.

Corporate plans

Marketing

Sub-function plans
e.g. sales, advertising

The planning hierarchy.

Typical departmental structures will include a person at Director level, although the major responsibilities will be handled by a member of the middle-management of the company. That person in turn, whether Advertising and Promotions Manager, or Customer Services Manager, etc, may well have a number of junior managers whose responsibilities are limited to specific parts of the marketing effort.

Many organisations have smaller operations, where the responsibility for actioning decisions may fall on one or two individuals. In this case it is often the practice to seek the assistance of outside agencies whose expertise is required for specific tasks.

Where there is a Customer Services Department, this will find itself responsible for all the various aspects of assuring that the company gives good service. Swift product delivery, answering queries or complaints, training service staff and maintenance of good customer relations may all fall within the remit of this department.

The key to understanding the traditional structure is knowing where everyone fits into the jigsaw. It has clear advantages when the organisation's aims and objectives are simple, and when they have a simple product range. However, in multi-product situations, the organisation may experience difficulties in clearly defining responsibility for tasks. There is a very great danger that whole product ranges or features of the organisation's goals are neglected, or perhaps ignored entirely. It is for this reason that more complex organisations must resort to more complex forms of structure.

THE PRODUCT STRUCTURE . . . .

The product structure is most commonly found in organisations manufacturing consumer goods. One of the key features is that they have a wide range of products, each of which may well have its own Brand Manager. An interesting side feature to this is that a Brand Manager is responsible both for promoting his or her own product range, and for ensuring that its relative position in the company is maintained or improved. Many companies actively encourage this internal competition and find that greater rewards are won using this policy.

If each Brand Manager's attention is focused on one product, it will ensure that the particular product range gets its fair share of resources. The Brand Manager will bring in expertise as necessary in various areas and will chase the progress of sales promotions, press releases, sponsorships and product literature in an efficient and systematic way.

Working with the Brand Manager is a sales team, whose knowledge of the product range helps in keeping close contact with the retailer and other distributors. Highly motivated staff, armed with knowledge of the product, will be able to produce much

Product-orientated organisational structure.

better results and see that any action taken by the organisation is clearly passed on to those who require it.

Although this structure has its advantages, there may be a tendency to confuse the customer rather than inform them. Where different sales forces are operating in the same area, there may be conflict, resulting in confusion in the minds of the customer. In encouraging the competitive nature of the sales forces, too much time and effort may be given to promoting certain products, which simply detracts from the organisation's other products. This lack of co-ordination can easily damage the organisation's reputation and, for this reason, some companies have moved to a market structure.

TALKING POINT

How independent do you think a Brand Manager should be? Do you think that a Brand Manager will know what is best for his or her range of products?

THE MARKET STRUCTURE . . . .

This form of structure is often found where companies are selling the same product to a diverse range of customers. It is therefore very common in the business-to-business market. A market-orientated organisational structure stresses the need for staff, both in Sales and Marketing, to have a deeper knowledge of the product and the market that they serve.

The logical extension of this is the Key Account Management Structure, where a specific marketing programme is constructed to meet a single customer's needs. The larger the customer, the more demanding they may be in terms of technical assistance and back-up. The market-based structure allows the organisation to identify and channel resources and effort towards gaining new business or breaking into new markets. An important feature of this is that an organisation adopting this strategy will see the gaining of new accounts as a specialised activity which is very different from servicing existing customers. Market research has a strong role here, as does promotional activity.

Both the product and market structures work well for certain organisations, but they have very basic weaknesses:

1 They both rely heavily on resources in terms of manpower and time. This obviously increases the overheads that an organisation has to bear.
2 The main responsibility for the relative health of the product in a market falls to the Product (or Brand) Manager, but this does not necessarily accord with the overall strategy and thrust of the organisation's main objectives.

TALKING POINT

How important are the weaknesses in product and market structures? Do they mean that these kinds of organisational structure are useless?

3 Co-operation is often difficult. The Marketing Department may find it impossible to work well with the organisation's other areas of activity. It is for this reason that many organisations, having gone through both product and market structures, have moved on to what is known as the matrix structure.

THE MATRIX STRUCTURE . . . .

The matrix structure tries to be flexible, as well as enhancing communications within the organisation. The structure is quite hard to explain, but relies on the following features:

1 Brand Managers are still responsible for particular product ranges.
2 General marketing, which includes both advertising and marketing research, is provided on an organisation-wide basis.
3 The Brand Manager then feeds information into the organisation's centralised marketing services, and vice versa.

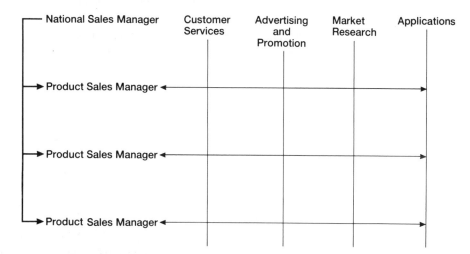

Matrix structure of an organisation.

Matrix structures can become extremely complex, as they endeavour to take advantage of the best features of the product and marketing structures. Product Managers are responsible to a Group Product Manager, who in turn reports to the Director of Marketing. Long-term planning is carried out at this Director level, but liaison is first sought with the Product Manager, Advertising Manager and Promotions Manager. The sales staff themselves fulfil the short-term selling responsibilities and tend to be organised along geographical lines. In this way, the sales staff acquire knowledge of the customers' needs in one area of the country and feed back their requirements to the organisation. The negative aspects of customers having to deal with different sales forces are eliminated, and greater and more efficient assistance can be called upon from the group's marketing organisation. The whole system again relies on people knowing who has responsibility for the various tasks, and on being able to define their own roles clearly.

THE ORGANISATIONAL CULTURE . . . .

Culture is an amalgam of knowledge, ideas, habits and values:

1 The values which people hold will lead them to do certain things in certain circumstances; in other words, to know what is right and what is wrong.

2 We are expected to behave in particular ways in given circumstances. These are known as 'norms', and are a series of unwritten rules which guide us in different situations.

3 Adopting a particular position is known as having a 'role'. This again means that we are expected to have a clear pattern of responses in given circumstances.

4 The beliefs that people hold relate to their opinions about things. In this you may include people's deeply-held attitudes and feelings on certain issues, e.g. those who feel that humans exploit animals unnecessarily may be vegetarians.

5 Because we adopt different roles in different circumstances, there is the question of role conflict. In some situations we may be a parent, but in others we may be a son or daughter. Conflict arises when our roles are incompatible and we cannot justify our actions and fulfil the demands of both those roles.

6 Finally there is the question of status. This is a socio-economic phenomenon. Some levels of status inevitably have more prestige attached to them than others, for example a Manager or Director, and it is this status that often determines our relations with others, particularly in a work environment.

If this organisational culture is so complex, how do we cope with the demands that it makes on us? Many companies spend a lot of time and effort in trying to cultivate a positive culture within their organisation. They may run training programmes, social facilities or incentives to encourage what they see as the correct attitudes. A common set of culturally-accepted rules must be beneficial to the company and its performance.

TALKING POINT AND ACTIVITY

Can we re-educate ourselves and change our basic values and opinions in the workplace? Find out how foreign companies, particularly the Japanese, endeavour to change the cultural outlook of their workforce to their own outlook.

If the primary goals and objectives of marketing, and indeed of the organisation itself, are to satisfy the wants and desires of its customers, then its organisational culture should strive towards this. To be customer-orientated is the key, and to be able to communicate internally as well as externally makes this goal far easier to fulfil.

TEST YOURSELF

1 What should a company's organisational structure ensure?

2 What is a traditional structure?

3 What is done by a Customer Service Department?

4 What is a Brand Manager?

5 What are the advantages of a product-orientated organisational structure?

6 Why do some companies prefer the market structure?

7 What is a 'key account'?

8 List the major features of a matrix structure.

9 Define the following:

a values
b roles
c role conflict

10 Is the matrix structure an organisational method which can be used for all companies?

A WORKING CASE STUDY

MY Games catalogue

The production of catalogues is a very common task and, although perhaps not one of the most exciting of marketing tools, it forms a cornerstone of many organisations' marketing strategy.

MY Games is a well-established company producing games and sports equipment, which it sells through its catalogue by mail order and also through retail outlets. Wherever possible, a purchaser is provided with a catalogue to stimulate further sales. The company specialises in traditional indoor sports, such as darts, snooker and bar billiards. The catalogue reflects the traditional nature of the products.

MY Games is a typical example of a company needing a good but definitely 'no nonsense' presentation of their product. There are numerous other examples to be found, all of which follow a similar format. The production of the catalogue, its look and its format, are a mirror-image of the organisation. Smooth and effective; interesting, perhaps exciting, product ranges; but, above all, reliable. Organisations try very hard to establish a reputation through their marketing and advertising activities, often to be let down by their poor organisational structure. MY Games has got the balance right and profited well from its foresight and planning as well as its ability to be flexible in all areas.

Activities and tasks

1   In the role of the Managing Director of MY Games, draw up your ideal organisational structure, taking the following into consideration:

a   The organisation has to cater for regular mail orders from the trade as well as having to work to obtain business from new outlets across the UK , and indeed all over the world.

b   Many of the products are imported from abroad, either as a finished item or part of a product that MY repackages in the UK.

c   The company has a very wide range of products that relate mainly to the leisure market.

d   MY Games is involved mostly in 'below the line' advertising, although it may directly promote products to the general public as support for its stockists.

2   Devise a simple customer order form that would have space to ask relevant information for various parts of the MY Games organisation as you have laid it out for task 1.

FURTHER READING

The Affluent Society, J Galbraith, Boston University Press

15 Keeping the dream alive!

WHAT IS CONSUMERISM? . . . .

Consumerism has been defined as a social movement which seeks to enhance the rights and powers of customers in relation to the seller. In other words, it recognises the need for consumers to be protected from unscrupulous businesses. The definition has been widened recently to include protection from non-business organisations such as the Government or Local Authorities.

RIGHTS . . . .

In the past, when businesses were small and customers were supplied on an individual basis, usually by local shopkeepers who they knew well, the need for protection was not that great. Buying products in an undeveloped world is much simpler. Quality and price are the two major considerations when buying and these are the responsibility of the purchaser. After all, the customer will simply not buy the product if it is inferior in quality or too expensive. Now many rights are protected by law. Traditionally buyers' rights include the following:

1 The buyer has the ultimate choice of whether to buy or not.
2 The buyer should be able to assume that what they are buying is at least safe for the use intended by the seller.
3 The buyer should be able to expect that the product is what the seller claims it to be, and that it fulfils the function stated.
4 The buyer should be made aware of any important aspects of the product, particularly in the case of food, which should show what ingredients are included.
5 The buyer should be protected from unscrupulous businesses or marketing practices.
6 The buyer should play a role in any changes in the product and influence organisations in adapting and making their product environmentally safer.

TALKING POINT

Can you think of any other rights a buyer should demand? Perhaps you can think of some that are specific to a particular product or service?

Just as buyers have rights, sellers have rights too. They are the following:

1 A seller should be allowed to sell anything he or she wishes, providing it is safe or at least a warning is attached to the product as a safeguard.
2 The price level is entirely a matter for the seller.

TALKING POINT

Whose rights should take precedence, the buyer's or the seller's?

3 The seller may use promotional means or incentives to induce the buyer to make a purchase.
4 Within a range of regulations, the seller may use any means available to promote the product. The major limitation to this, and quite rightly so, is that any statements made must not be untrue or misleading.

THE GROWTH OF CONSUMERISM . . . .

After Europe and America, in particular, had at least partly recovered from the Second World War, consumerism gathered pace, demanding immediate and radical changes. There are many reasons why this happened:

1 Greater equality and democracy in Europe led to the freedom for people to voice their protests. As education became more widespread, greater knowledge led to greater demands.
2 Rises in consumerism strangely follow periods of inflation. As prices rise and the customers' purchasing power falls, customers feel poorer and demand more from anything they do buy.
3 Improvements in communication have meant that most people are much more knowledgeable about the world. Bad news, in particular, travels fast and businesses which display weakness in any way can become victims.
4 People are now far more health and safety conscious. Many products which were traditionally used are now spurned, as the customer becomes aware of their health and safety problems. Cigarettes especially have suffered, with various advertising bans in the media. Artificial ingredients are now under fire as people become aware of the inherent dangers of additives.
5 The alcohol problem in the UK has been getting worse. This is a good example of a social problem. Crime, too, can be linked to alcoholism, and alcohol has been found at least partially responsible for up to half the murders in this country, two-thirds of the suicides and serious injuries, and even a fifth of occurrences of child abuse. Although Britain is well down the world league, we do consume massive

Standard corporate logos and image are in evidence here from Isuzu. Much more is inferred by the background to the vehicle. What do you think it says about the potential customer?

quantities of alcohol each year. Marketing has been blamed for encouraging young people, in particular, to consume ever-increasing amounts of drink.

6 Companies which misrepresent their products are on the decline. Any that do so will find themselves the subject of mass complaints from the public. Featured heavily in the media are misleading advertising or labelling, or products which fail to live up to the expectations of the consumer or, indeed, the claims that were made by the seller. Mail order especially has often been criticised in this respect. People have sent money and then received in return at best an unsuitable product or at worst nothing at all.

Advertising is seen as a major culprit and it has been argued that advertising is often deceptive. Either the wrong impression is given, or the full story is not relayed. Factual inaccuracies are illegal; omission is not. In many cases, the question of truth is left to the advertiser's ethical standards.

7 Pollution has been a subject of widespread concern for the past few decades. Petrol, industrial waste, and acid rain have all been singled out as major problems. Commentators argue that society is misdirecting itself, putting profit before the long-term future.

WHERE IS IT LEADING US? . . . .

Whether consumerism actually exists in any coherent form is debatable; what is not is the emergence of very well-organised pressure groups. These groups exert enormous pressure on both the government and the business community. Businesses have responded more readily to the demands of ecological groups than have successive Governments. Good retailers, such as Safeway, Sainsbury's and Tesco, all now have approved products readily available. Their ranges go from CFC-free aerosols to organically-grown vegetables. Some have not yet responded to the challenge to change to any great degree. Marks & Spencer, for example, whose product quality is not in question, rely heavily on intensive farming methods and the use of chemicals to produce their goods. They did market a range of organic foods but withdrew them due to low sales.

The Government, meanwhile, responded well to consumer pressure by setting up a number of official bodies, including the Advertising Standards Authority. However, it seriously lags behind in developing a cohesive environmental strategy that is acceptable to the pressure groups. Understandably, the process of changing or creating legislation is a long one. Pressure groups, meanwhile, are eager for change to take place and continually agitate to gain their objectives, much to the dismay of the Government.

Organisations are interested in promoting and selling their products and, not surprisingly, seek to resist changes that will prevent them from achieving their objectives. Organisations are not like ostriches; they cannot afford to hide their heads in the sand! They adapt of their own volition before legislation overtakes them and forces them to do what they do not wish to do. This social conscience is appreciated by both the general public and the pressure groups, and organisations are perceived as taking consumerist initiatives.

TALKING POINT

Is profit incompatible with social concern?

Demonstrating concern for their customers has been given a much higher priority by organisations, as customer satisfaction reaps great benefits. Improved safety standards in consumer durables, such as cars, and even house building, are good examples of this. Some areas of business can be considered self-regulating, where the industry itself lays down codes of conduct and good practice. In the PR field, organisations work hard to show their social concern and their active commitment to ecologically-sound business practice. The objective is to increase the public's understanding of the organisation and to rate it highly as a concerned organisation.

TEST YOURSELF

1 Define consumerism.

2 List four traditional buyer's rights.

3 List three traditional seller's rights.

4 Give three examples of why consumerism has become more important.

5 How can pressure groups force changes?

6 What is the ASA?

7 What role do Governments play in change?

8 What measures should be taken against organisations that deliberately mislead customers?

9 Can companies selling alcohol really be held responsible for the effects of their products?

10 What do you think is a consumerist initiative as far as a company is concerned?

A WORKING CASE STUDY

The Citizens Advice Bureau

During the Second World War, the government needed to give information to the general public. The newly created Ministry of Information produced a series of films to be shown in the cinemas, and printed leaflets and advertisements. In many towns and cities, a Citizens Advice Bureau was set up, usually with a voluntary staff, to give information and free advice. Today the CAB gives advice to anyone with a legal, financial or other problem.

The idea of having to 'market' government information had been largely ignored. When television first became popular, a series of Public Information films was run by the BBC, but apart from these there was really very little attempt to market this kind of information.

The 1980s saw a great increase in efforts to make information more accessible. For example, some readers may remember what tax return forms used to look like before they were redesigned!

Reproduced here is an excellent example of how information, in this case consumer legislation, can be presented in a simple and concise manner for the layman. This is part of a booklet *How to put things right*, available from Citizens Advice Bureaux, prepared by the government's Office of Fair Trading and the Central Office of Information. The wording is straightforward and the use of graphics not only serves to illustrate the text, but also helps the whole subject to appear less intimidating.

Activities and tasks Asking you to design a whole pamphlet of this kind is probably too long a task. However, you could visit your local post office and have a look at some of the forms and leaflets there (they nearly always have plenty to choose from). Pick out one that you feel could be made a bit more user-friendly and try redesigning and rewording it. Remember, though, that it still has to get the message over as well as looking attractive!

FURTHER READING

The Affluent Society, J Galbraith, Boston University Press

16 The green aspect – social marketing

SOCIAL MARKETING – A DEFINITION .

Social marketing has so far defied any attempt at a universally-acceptable definition. This is mainly because the boundaries of social marketing have yet to be agreed. Marketing should act in conjunction with the public interest by attempting to serve the needs and demands of society, as well as making a profit for the company involved, of course. We will try to be brave now and to define social marketing anyway.

Social marketing takes account of the consumer's needs for wider satisfaction beyond just product satisfaction. In other words, consumers place a value on their quality of life as well as the quality of their possessions. In its wider context, social marketing refers to the study of markets and marketing in general within the social system as a whole. There are two good examples of the former definition, both of which are related to our case study at the end of this chapter.

First is the question of people's need for cosmetic products. Alongside this is the consumer's horror of the use and abuse of animals in the development of these products. This has provided an excellent niche for companies, such as The Body Shop, supplying 'cruelty-free products'.

Secondly, the thornier issue of cigarette smoking, and the growing demand for total abolition, against the availability of 'less dangerous' brands. In this case, too, animals have suffered terribly, particularly dogs, to allay smokers' fears and give birth to the lower tar cigarette. It is clear therefore that many people are now placing a higher importance on social and humanitarian values and this directly relates to their choice and subsequent purchase of products.

TALKING POINT AND
ACTIVITY

Identify organisations, other than
those mentioned, that have
responded to the calls for change.

Let us now turn our attention to the wider issues, since the above examples can be considered as micro or social concerns. Marketing's major success, in what is known as the post-industrial age, has been in providing for our material needs. A direct consequence of this has been ecological disaster, widespread pollution, congestion in our cities and mountains of waste. We cannot blame marketing alone for these phenomena, but it must shoulder some of the responsibilities and seek to find new products, and indeed production methods, which help to minimise, or preferably to eliminate, harmful effects.

Another series of roughs, this time associated with the launch of a new product. The company perceived that its new range needed to project an image closely associated with traditional craftsmanship. Also deemed important was the 'Green' theme.

It is interesting to note the similarity in many of the designs.

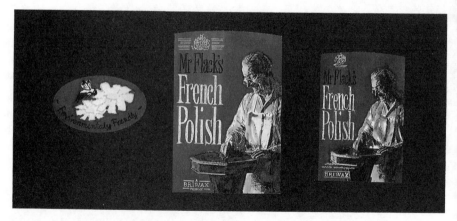

Visuals of final pack design.

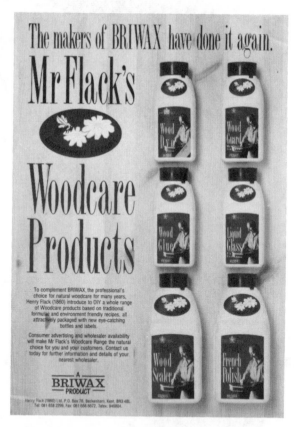

A mailer showing all of the range with its new image.

SETTING THE BOUNDARIES . . . .

If the principal task of marketing is to satisfy the needs of customers in an efficient and profitable way, then this must be attempted in a socially-responsible manner. What exactly is social responsibility? Is it enough to produce 'safe' products? Is honest advertising sufficient? Or does a commitment to reduce pollution suffice? All these questions are elements of social responsibility.

Many commentators now see marketing as having a social responsibility to influence customers' values. This goes far further than simple economic considerations. In markets where there is a clear link between the product and inevitable social effects, e.g. the car's links with pollution and congestion, the organisation must be prepared to satisfy the customer, while at the same time making sure that satisfaction does not get in the way of social cost. If an organisation is able to get this balance right, then its image is greatly enhanced.

Many organisations involve themselves in welfare issues, such as poverty and education. They can be powerful movers in social attitudes and change. The cynical viewpoint when looking at the motives of these organisations would see their efforts as mere image building. Despite this, companies have begun to mobilise their expertise to develop social roles.

We must return to the question of boundaries, and who should make such decisions. The answer should lie in assessing an organisation's willingness and ability to move social attitudes. By successfully incorporating a social angle in their overall marketing policy, an organisation can be seen to relate to social issues just as well as any elected representative could do.

TALKING POINT

Do you think that organisations would be prepared to reduce their profits in exchange for the consumer viewing them as 'socially aware'?

Having noted all of this, and appreciated the efforts of certain organisations in this field, we must not walk away with the idea that they are not interested in simple profit. What it does mean is that profit is no longer the only objective, although long-term profits may depend on showing environmental concern and developing environment friendly products. Profit is the key to the company's continued success, and even the most enlightened and aware company cannot conceive of being involved in social issues without the funds that profit provides.

HOW DOES THE GOVERNMENT FIT IN? . . . . .

It is debatable whether legislation emanates from the Government or from pressure from consumers, or indeed from organised pressure groups. In any case, the issues that have been raised regarding social concerns have required legislative solutions. It is in the organisation's interests to be a prime mover in social change rather than simply reacting to the demands that legislation brings. Adopting a considerate attitude to social issues is increasingly not an option but a question of necessity, as the legislation already exists. Organisations must endeavour to become socially-orientated as a result of their own efforts rather than as a result of law. A complication is that Governments do not last very long, so it is in the organisation's interests to adopt a longer-term view. There are many examples of organisations ignoring their social responsibilities where the Government has then forced them to recognise these commitments. Acting first has been seen time and time again to be beneficial.

TALKING POINT

Surely the Government has the responsibility in the long run to force legislation on the business community? What stops it?

The role of the Government in long-term social development is unclear. Pollution, for example, will probably remain with us whatever the political complexion of the Government may be. On the other hand, if an organisation rethinks its production, packaging and distribution, it can have a marked effect on pollution. Some of these 'safety measures' may mean higher costs in the high street shops, but may not necessarily mean a reduction in sales. This, of course, assumes that the organisation has had sufficient foresight to educate potential customers as to the beneficial nature of their purchases, against the additional cost.

NON-PROFIT-MAKING ORGANISATIONS . . . . .

Many of the features of marketing that we have so far considered assume that the organisation is interested primarily in making a profit. There are literally thousands of organisations which are commonly known as 'non-profit making'. They range from organisations like Oxfam, through local councils, to The Methodist Church. None of these are commercial profit-making organisations. However, many of the marketing techniques which profit-making organisations employ are of value to these organisations.

The accepted definition of a non-profit-making organisation is that it is not primarily concerned with economic goals such as profit. However, these organisations do involve themselves in profit-making activities to fund their wider objectives. It is perhaps more accurate to describe these organisations as 'non-loss-making'. This, too, is not entirely accurate, as many of them engage in very forceful and effective profit-making activities.

There is no typical structure to a non-profit-making organisation. Indeed, many are in the private sector and enjoy a charity status which exempts them from most tax concerns. The only thing a charity has to do is to be non-profit-making, but the wider definition of non-profit-making organisations encompasses those that are not charities, and range in size from the equivalent of a sole trader to a huge multi-national organisation.

HOW DO THEY DIFFER FROM COMMERCIAL ORGANISATIONS? . . . .

The management of a typical non-profit-making organisation has, by its very definition, to be different from a profit-making one. Here are some of the key differences:

1 They have less clear or precise objectives. In the case of a commercial company, success is measured in profit. In a non-profit-making organisation, the objective may be to stop all animal experiments in the UK, or to feed anyone in the world who is suffering starvation. Success is measured in terms of degree; in other words, the organisation must approach its goal gradually. This may make the management of the organisation very difficult, as there will inevitably be differences of opinion about the direction and pace of effort.

2 Attracting resources is a perennial problem for these organisations. Some may be publicly-funded but may need to find additional resources. Others rely wholly on charitable donations. In this instance there is considerable competition, coupled with the danger that those who donate this money cannot see any tangible return, i.e. they do not get anything back for the money they have paid out.

3 These organisations must satisfy a seemingly bewildering range of aspirations, opinions and priorities. The organisation faces the danger of being pulled in too many directions at the same time.

4 Measuring levels of attainment is very difficult, even if the organisation's objectives are clear.

5 Political pressure may be a constant consideration and, in certain circumstances, will affect the organisation's resources, its objectives and, in some cases, even threaten its existence. A good example of this is the Greater London Council, which conducted a long-running battle with the government that ended in its closure.

TEST YOURSELF

1 What is social marketing?

2 What is social responsibility as far as companies are concerned?

3 How does social responsibility relate to company image?

4 How does government policy relate to social issues?

5 Define a non-profit-making organisation.

6 List at least ten examples of non-profit-making organisations.

7 List three differences between non-profit-making and profit-making organisations.

8 How should a company respond to pressure for change?

9 Why do non-profit-making organisations exist?

10 A non-profit-making organisation is just a charity. True or false? State your reasons.

A WORKING CASE STUDY

BUAV European campaign

On p 233 is a press release from the British Union for the Abolition of Vivisection. This was issued to the media a few days before the launching of their European campaign which aimed to gain a ban on testing cosmetics on animals:

News from BUAV

campaigning to end animal experiments

**British Union for the Abolition of Vivisection, 16a Crane Grove, London N7 8LB.
Telephone 071-607 9533. Fax 071- 700 0252.**

**CAMPAIGNERS CALL FOR END TO
COSMETIC TESTS IN EUROPE**

Leading European animal societies join forces for the first time today
(17/7/90) to launch a hard-hitting international campaign to ban cosmetic
and toiletry tests on animals throughout the European Community.

Campaign co-ordinators, the British Union for the Abolition of Vivisection
(BUAV), have gained the support of top European animal societies, including
the International Fund for Animal Welfare (IFAW) and groups from Holland and
West Germany. Other groups are expected to join the campaign soon.

The groups will distribute hundreds of thousands of striking campaign
leaflets, posters and postcards especially designed by Spitting Image
caricaturist, David Stoten. A petition calling on the European Parliament
and Commission to ban cosmetic and toiletry tests will aim to attract over
2 million signatures. Euro-wide advertising, publicity events and political
lobbying will also play a major role in what is expected to be the largest
animal rights campaign to date in the European Community.

BUAV National Campaigns Organiser, Steve McIvor, states:
> 'Europe has become the new arena for the campaign to ban
> cosmetic tests on animals. Now is the time for the
> European Community to take action. Public opinion demands
> that these crude, cruel tests should be stopped immediately.'

The Campaign coincides with the new European Commission proposals to update
the 1976 Cosmetics Directive - regulating the safety of cosmetic products -
which are due to be published soon. Intensive lobbying of MEPs and the
Commission has apparently prevented proposals for increased animal testing
being included. However, the amended Directive will still permit tens of
thousands of animals to suffer in eye, skin and poisoning tests. The new
proposals are expected to go before the European Parliament in the autumn.

ENDS

The press release.

This caption accompanied the photograph sent out by *BUAV* to the media:

European cosmetic testing campaign

The ugly face of the beauty business is reflected in the shocking image for a campaign aimed at banning cosmetic and toiletry tests on animals within the European Community, which is launched today by the British Union for the Abolition of Vivisection (BUAV) in co-operation with top European animal societies.

Designed by Spitting Image caricaturist David Stoten, the 'research rabbit' displays the pain and misery of thousands of animals used to test such products as soap, shampoo and lipstick every year. It will appear in leaflets, posters, postcards and European-wide advertising.

Activities and tasks

1 In the role of an editor of a national newspaper, rewrite the press release in this case study into a news item.

2 In the role of a cosmetic manufacturer that does not undertake animal experiments to develop its products, write a press release in response to the one in this case study, stating your position and that the comments made in it do not refer to you.

3 How would the BUAV measure the effectiveness of its campaign, short of realising its ultimate objective in the banning of all cosmetic experiments on animals?

FURTHER READING

Organisational Buying Behaviour, Hill and Hillier, Macmillan

17   Industry to industry

WHAT IS INDUSTRIAL MARKETING? .

The basic principles of selling are the same, no matter what the market or what the product to be sold. These principles do not change to any great degree, even if the consumer is now another company or the product is not a consumer product but an industrial one. Organisations which supply raw materials or basic components to other organisations have tended to lag behind the mainstream consumer product manufacturers in adopting marketing concepts. There are three main factors which are now changing this:

1   Increased competition, even in the industrial markets.
2   The rapid pace of economic change.
3   The vast amounts of money involved in large-scale industrial businesses.

The pace of change is quickening in the markets in which the industrial product manufacturers operate. In the past, an organisation that did not plan ahead in a very detailed way could not only still survive but positively flourish. Today, this is not the case. Management decisions are crucial, and central to the long-term well-being of the company. Organisations which do not have a clear idea of where they are going will tend to concentrate on sorting out the immediate problems and not consider their long-term prospects and profitability. Skilful though they may be, the management is wasted and depleted by the demands of making day-to-day decisions.

An organisation can only consider itself successful if it has satisfied the needs of the customer and shown a profit in doing so. In short, the organisation needs to capitalise on what it does well and utilise all of its strengths to achieve its aims. The job of the Marketing Manager is to organise the talent of staff and assets within the organisation and mobilise them to work towards its objectives. These talents and assets should include the following:

- Financial strengths
- Product knowledge
- Research and development skills
- Sales ability
- Marketing ability

The sort of products sold on the industrial market are somewhat different from those sold on the consumer market. They tend to be more technical and, for this reason among others, manufacturers tend to be product-orientated rather than sales-orientated. It is probably this reason alone which has caused these organisations to have been extremely slow in adopting any notion of a market-orientated approach in their business philosophy.

CORPORATE PLANNING . . . .

As with any other market, the industrial market is subject to constant change. Organisations tend to find they are always striving for short-term aims as they respond to changing markets as quickly as possible. This does not help the creation of long-term plans. Industries have been forced to organise their planning and look to the future in a far more considered way.

So what is corporate planning? It has been defined as the planning (don't say!) of the development of all the resources of the business in a fully co-ordinated way. There is more. Corporate planning endeavours to commit itself to achieving a plan which embraces all of the organisation's activities. The basic objectives of the organisation are worked out in relation to what it sees as the marketing opportunities which are available to it. Resources are also a key feature, and marketing opportunities are directly related to the ability of the organisation to exploit them.

The organisation's knowledge and awareness of the market and any environmental considerations should be continuously updated. Any factors which may affect the organisation and its chances to exploit the market must be examined. The mistake should not be made of just considering the immediate users of the product. Thought must be given to the future of the 'end-user' market. Who is going to use the finished product made from our raw materials in years to come? Future consumption will very largely control the future fortunes of the industrial producer. What might future consumption be? Working back from the anticipated volume, trends and growth in the consumer (end user) market, the organisation can assess how possible changes will influence these figures. It can then anticipate the patterns of 'demand' and the health of its market as an industrial producer. Let's look at this process in some more detail:

1 Making a market assessment Taking account of your competitors and their probable future plans. What sort of products and services do they offer? What is their market share? What are the probable future trends? You should look at their marketing skills and consider whether or not they are likely to be successful in the future, based on what they are able to do now. Can they innovate? Marketing research can play a vital role here and it is likely that an assessment can be made of the competitor's future product or market position as a result of this research.

2 **Examining your own resources** This is often neglected by organisations, but it is a very essential part of the preparation of a marketing plan. A regular review, at least yearly, should be made, particularly to see if any assets are declining in value. This examination should include:

- The age of management personnel
- The age of plant (buildings, etc) and machinery
- The stage of the life-cycle that the principal products have reached

TALKING POINT

How important is the morale of staff in a business that has no real contact with the consumer?

When looking at the resources of each of the major parts of the organisation, you should pay particular attention to the following major areas:

a The volume and pattern of the sales of your main products and the profit margin of each one.

b Sales by area, both at home and abroad.

c Sales achieved among specific types of customer or specific outlets.

d The image of the organisation in the eyes of its customers.

e The degree of liaison between the various departments, particularly Sales and Production.

f The level of morale among junior and middle management.

3 **Setting your objectives** These will obviously vary a great deal from business to business. The idea of identifying your basic objectives is to establish your general strategy. Your objectives should include at least some of the following points:

a *Turnover objectives* How great a percentage increase do you want for the sales to rise over the inflation rate?

b *Profitability objectives* Identifying what profit you want to show from one particular market or indeed from any one particular customer.

c *Market share objectives* To achieve and maintain a particular share of the UK market and perhaps to achieve and maintain a particular share of the export market.

TALKING POINT

How easy is it for an organisation to keep to its corporate plan?

We have seen, then, that the main purpose of corporate planning is to try to look at the relative strengths and weaknesses of the organisation from an objective viewpoint and to decide exactly how these qualities or problems can be best mobilised to ensure the profitability of the organisation on a long-term basis.

WE'RE LAUNCHING
A NEW DELIVERY SERVICE
FOR SHEET MATERIALS.

As from the **19th September 1988,**

Mallinson Denny (Southern) Limited will

be introducing a new **24 Hour Delivery**

Service into your area for **Sheet**

Materials. Details of this service will

be with you soon or if you just can't wait

please contact **Graham Robinson**

on **0474-564477.**

Mallinson Denny (Southern) Limited
Canal Basin, Gravesend, Kent, DA12 2SQ.
Tel: 0474-564477 Telex: 96161 (MDGSN G)

A typical example of an industry-to-industry mailshot. There is a constant search for new angles to make a company's message stand out from the rest. In reality this search is seldom successful. This company has decided to use a cartoon to catch the reader's eye. Judge for yourself how successful it has been.

INDUSTRIAL MARKETING MIX . . . .

We have seen that marketing strategy basically comprises three main areas:

1 The setting of the targets through which the organisation intends to achieve its objectives.
2 The period of time over which these objectives are proposed to be met.
3 The resources that are available and those that will be used to achieve these objectives.

The fundamental goal is profitability and gradual growth of the organisation in line with its growing profitability. This, of course, can be achieved by a number of different methods, including:

1 The research and development of new ideas which can become profitable products and services.
2 The purchase of other organisations in allied areas that may complement your organisation in some way.
3 A merger with another organisation that relates in some way to the market interests of your organisation.
4 Sub-contracting or licensing the production of products from other organisations to increase your product range with the minimum of investment and delay.

TALKING POINT

How can an organisation best deal with a short fall in any one of its resources?

Profits are the key to continued, or indeed any, growth. The organisation needs to take a serious look at its resources, as these will, in turn, generate the profits it desires. These resources include:

• Finance
• Plant
• Manpower
• Organisational ability
• Recognition of marketing possibilities

A satisfactory marketing mix is dependent upon the recognition of the market's needs. It also requires the recognition of the organisation's objectives, and the planning of a strategic marketing philosophy which incorporates the various methods of obtaining these objectives. How best to serve the particular segments of the market must depend on the needs of that market. Any decision should be based on the ability of the organisation to apply its efforts to meeting the needs of each of its market segments. The development of its marketing plan should involve a clear definition of the problems, including:

1 The collection of the facts
2 The analysis of the data
3 The selection of the appropriate marketing mix
4 Choosing the appropriate solutions

TALKING POINT AND
ACTIVITY

Try to put the elements of the
marketing mix in order of priority.

External factors may affect the marketing plan. Socio-economic influences can affect the markets of the users of the organisation's products. Government regulations, including restrictions on business, can also have an impact on the long-term plans of the organisation. External factors that we have looked at elsewhere include seasonal changes, changes in market demand, changes in technology, product obsolescence and the competition. In addition to these external considerations are a number of internal ones. The elements that make up the marketing mix can be very diverse. The main ones are:

- Market research
- Product quality, pricing, development and range
- Sales force, aids and promotion
- After-sales service
- Advertising
- Stock levels
- Credit
- PR
- Packaging
- Sampling

STRATEGY AND GROWTH . . . .

The progress of an organisation is generally assessed in terms of its growth in sales and profits. If it sets out its objectives, the organisation can then try to deploy its resources in the best way to bring about this progress. If progress is not forthcoming, the organisation should be able to redeploy its resources to better effect. Diversification may well be the key to achieving growth. We will look at this in some detail shortly.

There are three main methods of expanding the organisation's activities:

1 Specialisation is the adaptation of the organisation's existing range of products to meet the special needs of consumers. The idea is to cater for additional markets. Growth is expected by getting into new markets with what you already offer, rather than trying to launch new products.

2 The organisation may diversify by acquiring other businesses. The purchasing organisation will not just buy in new products or lines, but acquire the accompanying staff and expertise of the purchased business.

3 New products can be acquired by developing them yourself, by buying them in from other organisations, or by licensing the product from another business. For a far more detailed look at the development and place of new products in the business operations of an organisation, see Chapter 7.

TALKING POINT AND ACTIVITY

Try to identify the diversification possibilities for a producer and importer of tea.

DIVERSIFYING . . . .

We have touched on diversification already, but let's look at it in a little more detail. There are three main reasons for diversification:

- To replace inadequate investment
- To complement an existing product range
- To be a 'hedge' against future saturation of the market

Diversification can be carried out in a number of different ways:

1 **Unrelated diversification** Limited usually to financing the management of newly-acquired businesses or product ranges (so not related to the existing businesses or products).
2 **Related diversification** Utilising the organisation's existing expertise, production and general development skills.
3 **Vertical diversification** The organisation uses its resources to acquire businesses that supply or distribute to the retailers which sell the product to the consumer.

Each and every business must count the cost of diversification, since this cannot be done without an effect on the organisation as a whole. Appraisal of the likely effects must first be made, based on the following objectives:

a *Qualitative objectives* Looking at the type of business to be purchased and which markets are involved.
b *Quantitative objectives* What is the size of the operation? How good are the sales? What are the profits? Can we improve these if we purchase the business?

The different methods of carrying out diversification have inherent advantages and disadvantages (doesn't everything?):

1 When a company wants to use its research and development resources to create a new product, it will have maximum control over it. The company can make sure that the new product fits perfectly into the product range, that its staff are fully utilised and that it keeps the lion's share of the profits that are generated. If the product is a failure, however, then the effects may be disastrous in all these areas.
2 Bringing in specialists is the alternative to doing it yourself, but only at the research and development stage. Otherwise the benefits are the same. Existing R and D staff may not be too keen on having these 'upstart outsiders' brought in and morale may take a tumble! The plan could backfire if the outsiders do not prove to be all they were cracked up to be, and then you'll hear, 'We told you so!'.

TALKING POINT

Which do you think is the better strategy – acquiring licences or acquiring businesses?

3 Acquiring licenses to produce products from overseas has a big advantage, as the product is already tested and shown to work. The downside is that profits generated have to be shared with the creator of the product through royalty payments. The biggest danger is that you may well end up relying too heavily on the licensor and neglect your own R and D.

4 If an organisation can acquire another business, then it automatically gets its hands on all the assets of the acquired business. Businesses that have useful assets and a good management structure tend to be highly priced. Alternatively, you may end up acquiring lots of assets and manpower that you do not want.

MARKET RESEARCH . . . .

The industrial Marketing Manager is usually at least one step further removed from the end-user market than the Marketing Manager in a consumer-orientated company. In this sense, the industrial Marketing Manager will be much more in need of good market research.

So what is industrial market research? It tries to provide information that helps the organisation understand the markets in which it operates and may operate in the future. This type of market research is perhaps better described as market intelligence. The information should be collected on a rolling basis and look forward to what the market may be like in the future.

The field research is different from consumer research. Sampling has to be modified as a clear picture of the market is not so easy as with the consumer viewpoint.

Sampling can be on a much smaller scale, because of the size of the markets involved in industrial marketing. Interviewing skills need to be better, as the respondents will be specialists and far more sophisticated than their consumer counterparts.

Smaller businesses tend to lag behind in realising that market research is important. Research budgets are invariably small, as they seem to think they can get all the necessary information from their sales force. Despite the size of the marketing budgets and the fact that the costs of industrial marketing are usually much smaller, many businesses are unwilling to spend anything at all on market research. They find it hard to recognise that their sales force may not be sufficiently objective in their research.

Outside consultants, if employed, will open up many new possibilities in the thinking of a company in the industrial field. Senior management in many medium and small companies is blissfully unaware of the possibilities of research. Marketing research can highlight the shortcomings of the company's marketing effort and show how the problems can be rectified with surprisingly little effort.

DISTRIBUTION . . . .

Having established there is a market for your products it may sound obvious that a company needs to ensure that its products are available. After all, if they are not, how can the customer buy them? Two words accurately define distribution – availability and accessibility. Even the most elementary analysis of a company's operation should identify that these are principal concerns, yet it is a failing of a great many companies that they have not ensured that availability is good. Customers are lazy, and if your product is not available and accessible easily, they will not seek you out; they will buy elsewhere. As often as not, the customer will buy what is available, and not necessarily what is best or ideal. They may also have deadlines to meet and cannot wait until your product is available.

Distribution can be a complex problem and it depends on the effectiveness of the network a company has set up to ensure their product is on the shelves when the customer shops. Middlemen are used extensively, but there is a cost to be paid for these middlemen handling any stage of your distribution. In order for them to distribute your product, they need to be given a cut of your profits. It would seem logical for manufacturers to undertake distribution themselves and keep all the profit, but most manufacturers find they need to use middlemen, or even that it is better to do so.

TALKING POINT

Do the advantages of using a middleman outweigh the loss that a manufacturer suffers in terms of profit margin from cost to retail price?

WHAT THE MIDDLEMAN DOES . . . . .

The main role of middlemen is to make the product more available and more accessible. They do this in the following ways:

1 They buy in bulk from the manufacturer and sell in smaller quantities to the customer.
2 They help relieve the manufacturer's storage problems by storing the product themselves.
3 They assist in reducing delivery times to customers by holding a buffer-stock for the manufacturer.
4 They are able to deliver smaller quantities of products in a more flexible way than manufacturers could ever do.
5 They can promote the manufacturer's products on a local basis with great efficiency.
6 They can offer credit to their customers which does not affect the manufacturer's cash flow.
7 They may have some flexibility in setting the price according to local market demands.
8 They can offer useful after-sales services on a local basis.
9 They can offer a personal touch in direct sales, which manufacturers, with their broader base, cannot achieve.

GETTING THE PRODUCT TO THE CUSTOMER .

Good distribution gives the customer a good impression of an organisation. Efficient distribution can be costly, but it is the job of the Distribution Manager to ensure that the right goods are delivered to the right place at the right time, and undamaged. Here are some considerations in maintaining effective distribution:

1 Being reliable – long delays are extremely irritating. It is a good tactic to offer slightly longer delivery times but be able to guarantee them, rather than promising short delivery times and seldom being able to achieve them.

2 There is no point in getting the goods to the customer on time if they are not in a fit state. Strict controls over packaging, handling and transportation are key features in making sure that the product is delivered undamaged.

3 Should the product be defective, prompt replacement is vital to the image of the organisation.

4 The customer is equally concerned that the product continues to function as required. If it fails in some way, not caused by the customer, then the customer quite rightly demands that the product be repaired or replaced. There is also legislation regarding this.

5 Discounts can be given for large orders. Sometimes, particularly with trade customers, such as shops, orders must be of not less than a specified size, to make distribution worth while.

6 Distribution Managers must consider balancing minimum order size with the possibility of losing custom and goodwill. If they have set too high a minimum order level, their customers will find demand is not large enough to keep that level of stock, and that goods must be stored a long time in limited shelf space, and they will not order the item at all. However, if this means distributing smaller amounts, turnover may be insufficient to make it possible to carry on distributing the product.

TALKING POINT

Minimum order levels often prevent smaller retailers from stocking product lines, as they cannot afford, justify or expect to be able to sell that many of a product. Is setting a minimum order level good policy, as its advantages are that costs are cut by only servicing the larger customer?

Channels of distribution

Manufacturers must consider how many middlemen are required between themselves and the customer. Just what kind of distribution network is suitable will largely depend on the product. The number of levels or tiers varies. The manufacturer may supply direct, in which case there are no tiers, or there may be as many as three or more. The most common is one tier, where large retail chains buy direct from the manufacturer and then sell on to the customer. Two-tier distribution channels are still common where small retailers lack the buying power to buy direct from the manufacturer and are forced to purchase via a wholesaler. Most manufacturers do not stick to one type of channel; they may well use a combination of several. The type of network that a manufacturer chooses depends on three main considerations:

Manufacturer ⟶ End user

Manufacturer ⟶ Retailer ⟶ End user

Manufacturer ⟶ Wholesaler ⟶ Retailer ⟶ End user

Manufacturer ⟶ Agent ⟶ Wholesaler ⟶ Retailer ⟶ End user

Distribution channels.

1 **Intensive distribution**   This strategy aims to get the product into as many outlets as possible in order to maximise availability and accessibility, eg convenience or impulse-buy products would require great availability and accessibility – after all, you can buy a can of Coca-Cola almost anywhere.

2 **Exclusive distribution**   This is the opposite of intensive distribution. Accessibility and availability are deliberately restricted in order to make the product appear exclusive. Outlets are chosen carefully, as their image and ability to handle the product is a key consideration in whether they are allowed to stock it, e.g. it would be unusual to find a solid gold Dunhill cigarette lighter in your corner shop tobacconist!

3 **Selective distribution**   As with most things, there is always a compromise. Manufacturers may wish to have intensive distribution but, by the nature of the products they are selling, this may not be possible. There is little point in convincing a local newsagent to stock the latest Nicam stereo television. The manufacturer may wish to have intensive distribution in all relevant outlets, but would consider it futile to extend distribution beyond this.

TALKING POINT AND ACTIVITY

Which is the most appropriate distribution network for the following, and why?
a   baked beans
b   milk
c   exotic fruit and vegetables

Managing the network

The manufacturer should try to avoid any conflicts which may affect the channels of distribution. Each member of the network is interested in a smooth distribution which maximises profits and lessens expenses. Competing distributors will come into conflict. Healthy competition between outlets should be encouraged, but, if price-cutting becomes a tool of competition, this will have a detrimental effect on the manufacturer's brand image, and this should be avoided.

Manufacturers should try to manage their distributors with a strong policy on pricing and the level of discounts available (and how these may be passed on to the customer). At the same time, they should offer enough freedom to motivate the outlet to stock their brand. The manufacturer must offer good profit margins, display and sales promotional material, and joint advertising.

TALKING POINT

Do you think that retailers should have this strong position and dictate their requirements to the manufacturer?

In the UK, in particular, retailers are very strong. In some respects, they even control the manufacturers. Big retail chains demand much more say in the types of product that are available, delivery times, quantity levels, packaging and price. Manufacturers would be foolish to ignore them. Own brand labels can be seen as a retailer's reaction to poor performance by manufacturers, and these have cut deeply into manufacturers' profits. Some manufacturers who produce own-label products for retailers are virtually sub-contractors, and only the larger manufacturers have been able to combat this trend.

TEST YOURSELF

1 What are the factors that bring about changes in the industrial market?

2 What sections of the organisation must the Marketing Manager mobilise to achieve the organisation's objectives?

3 What should an organisation consider when looking at its own resources?

4 What is a market share?

5 What is corporate planning?

6 What is a marketing mix?

7 What external socio-economic factors influence an organisation?

8 What is diversification?

9 What is unrelated diversification?

10 Why can sampling size be smaller in industrial marketing than consumer marketing?

11 Define distribution.

12 List five functions of a middleman.

13 List three considerations in maintaining effective distribution.

14 What is a two-tier channel of distribution?

15 What is intensive distribution?

16 What is exclusive distribution?

17 What is selective distribution?

18 What should members of a distribution network ensure?

19 What must a manufacturer offer in distribution terms to encourage outlets to stock its products?

20 What effect did the distribution of 'own-label' products have on manufacturers?

Hay Pollock

Hay Pollock is a large enterprise dealing with subcontracted transportation, from courier services to international group haulage, an area where there is extremely stiff competition. Shown here is a reproduction of the company's new mailshot folder, along with the original 'ideas' sketches and the brief given to the artist.

Since competition is so fierce, the product needed not only to be slick and professional but also to have the ability to grab the attention of the customer very quickly.

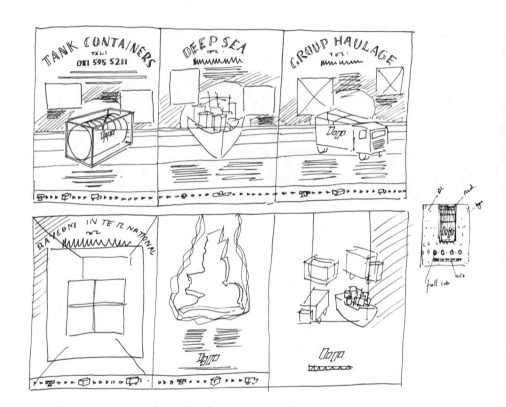

The first thumbnail sketch.

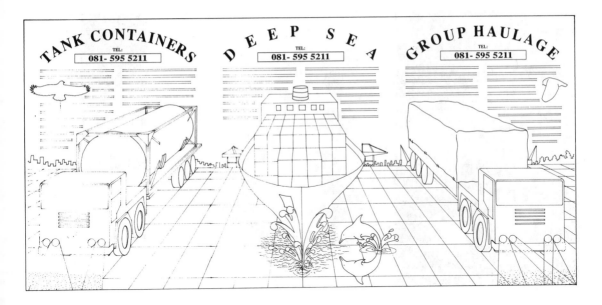

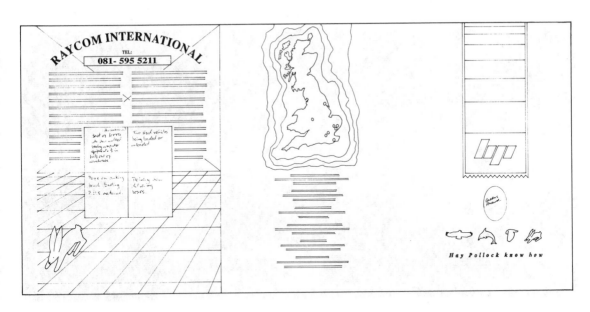

The idea expanded...

... and the finished mailshot.

Activities and tasks

1   This exercise is a little different from the others in the book. Study the artwork illustrated here and see if you can spot the motifs that have been used to represent:

   a The three main areas of the company's activities.
   b The nationwide coverage offered by the company.
   c The high-tech resources available to the company.
   d Finally, try to decide why there is a recurring use of fish and birds.

2   *Do not* read this task until you have completed task 1!

   Among the aspects that the folder needed to get across were the different branches of the company's activities (the ship, container and lorry motifs); its nationwide coverage (the map of the UK); and, more subtlely, the company's high-tech resources (alluded to by the grid theme throughout the main illustrations). The message was finally carried by the recurring motifs of dolphin, eagle and owl to represent the company's three main areas of activity.

   Refer to the Reflex Reds and Blues case study in Chapter 8, and plan a simple distribution chart that can cater for both home and overseas sales.

3   How is the language, image and approach different to a consumer-based brochure? In the role of the Marketing Manager of the company, devise a similar brochure that would cater for personal haulage for the consumer.

FURTHER READING

International Marketing, L Walsh, M + E, Pitman Publishing
Managing Export Distribution, G Davies, Heinemann

18   Overseas marketing

CONSTRAINTS OUTSIDE THE DOMESTIC MARKET . . . .

You could argue that the basic principles of marketing are universal and apply, no matter what the circumstances. Unfortunately life is not that simple. Let's look at the main considerations that have an impact on export marketing:

1   **The product**   A great many companies rely on home sales alone. Therefore it is not surprising that they tend to develop their products with the home market in mind. Few Sales Managers with export responsibilities have the necessary power within the company to exert themselves and put forward their need for export-specific products. As a result, the product range that they offer is probably not ideal for the market, and so they are at a disadvantage in trying to sell it.

2   **The markets**   Profitable sales very much depend upon the company's knowledge of the country to which it intends to export. It must understand any cultural differences that may affect the trade and how the business culture of the country differs from its own country's traditions and methods. There are many pitfalls for the unwary.

TALKING POINT

What kind of reputation does the UK have? Would you try to 'buy British'?

3   **The reputation of the country of origin**   Most people, given the choice, would buy products made in their own country. Many products start with a disadvantage simply by being foreign in the eyes of the consumer. Traditional and very rigid prejudices aid this view of the product. Products, when offered overseas, benefit or suffer from their national reputation. Japan, for example, is seen as producing

goods high in quality and reliability, whereas a Czech car would not enjoy the same reputation!

4 **Distance**   The speed of supply is vital, but it has to be reliable. Language may be an asset to communication in areas where there is a common language, but otherwise it may foster huge and avoidable delays. Companies need to establish a network of local representatives or agents to alleviate these problems of distance and language. Building an overseas business market may rely on this network above all.

MARKET RESEARCH . . . .

Making the assumption that companies know something of their own home market (which may be a massive assumption), they will know comparatively little of foreign markets. The process of finding out about these markets differs greatly from home market research. It is extremely dangerous to make any assumptions about overseas markets. Nor should a company select a potential market before really having a good look at it. Markets should be chosen based on a sound knowledge that they offer the best likelihood of business opportunities. Here are the basic questions that a company should ask before dispatching anything abroad on an organised basis:

1 What proportion of our output is available for the export market? This will determine the short-term importance of the export effort.
2 What financial back-up can we give our export effort? Consumer goods will need large advertising budgets; industrial products will need quite a lot less. A small budget is best spent in one market and not spread out over several.
3 What personnel do we have available? Does the company have access to sales people with the necessary language skills? If not, some markets should not be considered.
4 How do we set the price levels? Will some export markets expect prices far lower than is economically viable? If so, then these markets must be ruled out.

As you can see, the main task is to match the company's needs, strengths and objectives with the possibilities that the market offers. The research process need not be lengthy; neither need it be expensive. Embassies and High Commissions are very helpful, on the whole, and will assist if they can.

SCREENING THE MARKET . . . .

After eliminating a number of markets because they do not match the company's ability or willingness to exploit them, the next stage is to look at the country's official regulations. How will your products and your organisational systems match up to their requirements? These will include:

TALKING POINT

The changes in Europe in 1992 will have a massive impact for taxes and tariffs. What impact will these changes have in the long term?

- Taxes – may affect price differentials.
- Tariffs – preventing profitable competition.
- Quotas – limiting the numbers of imports.
- Exchange controls – preventing outflow of money.
- Patents and trademarks – protecting a home producer.
- Licensing – similar to quotas, permitting imports only when there is a shortage of the product in that country.

The next stage is to look at the market potential of the country. This involves looking at the political, economic and social situation in the country to try to get an idea of future trends. A calculation of the consumption figures will also help to predict sales growth.

Still keen to export? OK, then the next stage is to try to work out the market segmentation. Your company should have some idea of the general demand for its product. Now you must attempt to break up the market and, by quantifying it, identify the segment that will actually consume your product. Price, geographical distribution of consumers, the distribution network, consumer attitudes and product features should all be looked at here.

Are you still interested? Right, then next comes sales potential. The market segments may look very promising, but what about the opposition out there? You should try to figure out the strengths and weaknesses of the competition. By doing this, a company can then assess how much of its resources will have to be poured into that export market to make an impact. A rough sales forecast for the next five to ten years should be the ultimate goal.

With all the unpromising markets discarded, a deeper look is needed at some of the features that now have to be considered:

1 **Taste** Preferences vary greatly. Some coffee manufacturers offer no less than forty or more different versions of the same product worldwide.
2 **Colour** Believe it or not, in different countries different colours are positively preferred or avoided. The Australians have a preference for colours that match their flora! Moslems dislike yellow, as it is associated with Buddhists, Italians just love pale blue, and Thais will only put black dentures in their mouths as they chew tooth-blacking betel nuts!
3 **Size** The Americans just love huge packs of consumer goods that will last them a month, whereas people in the UK prefer their supplies to last them just a few days. In poorer countries, with the lower wage levels, they want to buy single items, such as one razor blade.
4 **Intended use** Variations of a product are required, to match what the consumer wants out of the product. Styling and design may have to change. In some countries, products are used more often and need to be more durable by comparison to other countries where they are used infrequently.
5 **Ergonomics** Linked to the height, shape and even average weight of the user. Fancy trying to sell a Volvo to a pygmy!

6 **The climate** This may directly affect the efficiency of a product. Ignoring the effects of baking hot weather on soft plastic kitchenware could be very messy!

7 **Training of staff** In the UK, machinery manufacturers have had to include a training programme to teach staff how to use the product. This back-up is an integral part of the overall sales package. This may not be the case in other countries. Equally, products may not sell if training in their use cannot be provided.

8 **Credit terms** In some countries, the trade customers may well have to sell a good deal of your product before they can afford to pay you. Otherwise, credit terms are either 30 days (optimistic) or even 180 days! Credit can be more important than the purchase price in certain countries. This leads to further complications, as a company may have to increase prices to accommodate an extended credit facility. However, the company can use this to their advantage by offering longer credit terms than a competitor.

9 **Repair and maintenance** Just what does happen when your printing press breaks down in The Gambia? Promises of speedy help and repair are difficult. You cannot assume that sub-contractors in the country are able to undertake the task.

TALKING POINT

Try to identify the tastes and colours preferred by most people in the UK.

RESEARCHING FROM THE UK . . . . .

We do not intend to go into all the sources in minute detail, but here are the main places to look for help and information:

1 **The Department of Trade and Industry** The DTI has worked very hard to help UK businesses set up trade links overseas, and they have details of the following readily to hand:

a Tariffs
b Licensing regulations
c Quota restrictions
d Labelling laws
e Health implications
f Local tastes and trading methods
g Strength of local competition
h News of market opportunities
i Computerised intelligence to subscribers

The DTI also runs an extensive library which holds all the official statistics compiled by foreign countries, together with foreign telephone directories, foreign business catalogues and semi-official surveys of various countries.

2 **Banks** These hold a vast range of information in their overseas information services. This includes market profiles, import and exchange regulations, status and credit reports on countries, and a host of other information.

3 **Chambers of Commerce**   Some are good, some bad. They have packaging and shipping regulations and other details.

4 **Foreign Embassies**   They will help with useful lists of customers, agents and media details.

5 **The Confederation of British Industry**   Produces a bulletin with useful general information.

6 **Libraries**   There are plenty of commercial libraries with a variety of material.

7 **Trade Associations**   Reliable information on packaging and documentation.

8 **Press**   Foreign newspapers with detailed readership breakdowns.

9 **Forwarding Agents**   These advise on packaging and documentation, as well as details on shipping costs and methods.

10 **Foreign Advertising Agencies**   Provide statistics and details of advertising opportunities.

11 **The Market Research Society**   Provides extensive field surveys of various countries.

12 **The International Trade Centre**   This helps underdeveloped countries to establish trade links. It holds information on promising markets.

TALKING POINT AND ACTIVITY

Who would you go to first for information on overseas marketing opportunities? Try to research the prospects in general for a country of your choice.

DISTRIBUTION OVERSEAS . . . .

The two main problems of distributing to overseas countries are:

- Transporting the goods to the market.
- Ensuring sales and distribution in the country.

Most organisations have no real strategy in trying to achieve overseas sales. However, many have been able to gain trade links through various means. Some of the following problems indicate the reasons why a few organisations do not tend to bother with export markets:

1 Inevitably, someone, somewhere wants what you have got to sell and may write to you or telephone to place an order. A single order may not be economically viable to service.

2 If the seller has no direct link with the buyer, demand can only be predicted by guesswork, which sometimes pays off.

3 If you cannot forecast sales, how can you organise your production?

4 If the seller cannot influence the ultimate end user, then the only marketing tactic may be price.

The way around these problems is to engage the services of someone in the market itself. There are two different sorts of agent that you can use:

The commission agent – who has a local sales force and receives payments purely on results.

The distribution agent – who is either a stockist or a wholesaler. These agents stock your goods and get their money from marking up the price of your products as they sell them on to the retailer or end user.

Alternatively, you could try selling direct to the market itself, either by regularly visiting the country on sales trips or by setting up your own local sales offices. The latter is only really feasible when you have got the volume of sales up to a reasonable level. Usually this means it is undertaken after a local agent has broken the ground for you. Agents do not like to be used and then dropped in this way, and this will cause ill-feeling.

TALKING POINT

Which option offers the best overall prospects for building up an export market?

SELLING OVERSEAS . . . .

Overseas representatives are often considered to have landed a great job. True, in some respects, but very much not so in others. The job requires a wide knowledge and a greater ability than the average UK sales representative to make on-the-spot decisions. Negotiations have to be carried out largely in isolation, as consultation with the UK office would be a lengthy and expensive process. Delegation of authority and power are the key features of having an effective overseas sales force. Overseas representatives must have a good working knowledge of the language, and know the cultural values and traditions of their customers. They need to be the eternal diplomat.

OVERSEAS ADVERTISING . . . .

Each country's range of potentially-useful advertising media is different. Each offers a range of problems as well as prospects. Here is a brief look at the different sorts of media:

1 **Television**   Many countries do not have commercial TV. Colour TV is by no means available worldwide.
2 **Radio**   Commercial radio is much more established overseas than in the UK, and good advertising possibilities are to be had.
3 **The press**   Many countries do not have national daily newspapers; many have a religious rather than socio-economic readership. Standards of reproduction are very variable, and there are often very few specialist papers and magazines or any magazines aimed at women.
4 **Cinema**   Impact must be visual to get over the translation problems.
5 **Outdoor advertising**   This can be most effective if you can link the product with a particular image, particularly in countries with a high level of illiteracy.

Using the same advertising copy as in the home market is a big problem. Literal translations just may not work, so a completely different approach is often needed. Most companies resort to image or visual impact as their main thrust to get the message across. Marlborough cigarettes, for example, feature an American cowboy. For their African market, they have simply substituted a black man for a white man. In all other respects, the advertisement is exactly the same.

If the company has the capacity to brief an agency well in the overseas country, the agency will be able to get the message across to its consumers just as well as the best companies in the UK.

PRICING POLICY . . . .

This is a complex and thorny problem. In the UK, prices are quoted as either with or without delivery costs included, the former being known as 'ex-works'. This is how prices are quoted to the overseas market:

1 **Ex-works**   Customers are left to work out how much on top of the quoted price it will cost them to get the product to their business for onward distribution. This is a standard way of quoting price and can be considered rather lazy, as the customer has to work out whether the deal is advantageous after the transport costs have been added on.
2 **Free On Board (FOB)**   This includes the costs of getting the product to the ship or plane, but not the costs of transportation onward from there.
3 **Cost Insurance and Freight (CIF)**   Covers the costs of transporting the product to the point of entry in the country of destination.
4 **Cost and Freight**   Leaves the customer to organise the insurance.
5 **Free Border**   Takes the product as far as the border of the country.
6 **Customer Works**   All costs for taking the product directly to where the customer wants it.

The most common forms are the free border and the CIF quote. In all cases, though, great care must be exercised in working out the costs as these can be very high and they can mean the difference between profit and loss.

1 How does overseas marketing differ from marketing to the home market?

2 What are the internal constraints that are placed on overseas operations by a company?

3 List three official regulations that may affect overseas sales.

4 What is the most common credit term?

5 What does the CBI offer to the company wanting to sell overseas?

6 What is a commission agent?

7 List the qualities needed in an overseas sales representative.

8 What is the problem with overseas TV advertising?

9 What are the key features that should typify overseas advertising campaigns?

10 What is CIF?

A WORKING CASE STUDY

European Precision Mouldings

European Precision Mouldings is a small company in the plastic injection moulding business. It has recently reorganised itself to attract foreign business, and add to its successful UK business base.

European Precision Mouldings

ENGINEERS IN PLASTIC

Dear

European Precision Mouldings have been engineers in the plastics industry for nearly 20 years and as you know have always taken the attitude that SERVICE, and we use the capitals intentionally, is a major factor in the actual production process. It is therefore with some pleasure that we can inform you of a new addition to our Board.

Mr Stephen Webb joins us as a Director in the truest sense of the word, with responsibilities encompassing the company's entire range of activities.

Stephen has an extremely impressive track record in the world of plastic component production. Amongst some of his more recent achievements is overseeing the installation of one of the few 'Two Colour' Moulding production lines in the UK and laying the plans for an almost fully automated Product Marking System utilising 'Pad Print Technology'.

With a wealth of experience, of which the above mentioned constitute just a fraction, we feel confident that Stephen's appointment can only improve our already well-respected service. In addition we also feel that the new ideas and philosophies he brings with him will be of considerable interest to new customers as well. To this end he will be contacting you in the near future to discuss the ways in which we may be of assistance to you.

We trust that you will find his ability to put complex engineering concepts into concise and accurate terms refreshingly different. This ability, perhaps above all others, is his most impressive feature, a feature made all the more attractive in a world of ever growing complications.

We trust you will afford him the courtesy of an appointment at your earliest convenience.

Yours sincerely

John Smylie
Managing Director

PROPRIETORS: ENGINEERS PROTOTYPE MOULDINGS LTD
DIRECTORS: J. SMYLIE D. DRUMMOND S. WEBB N. PAXMAN
REGISTERED IN ENGLAND No. 430725
REGISTERED OFFICE: CAUSEWAY HOUSE, 1 DANE STREET, BISHOPS STORTFORD, HERTS CM23 3BT

E.P.M. LTD
HIGH WYCH
SAWBRIDGEWORTH
HERTS CM21 0JS
TEL. 0279-600428
FAX. 0279-723846

Press release.

Business card.

European Precision Mouldings

ENGINEERS IN PLASTIC

velope.

PROPRIETORS: ENGINEERS PROTOTYPE MOULDINGS LTD
DIRECTORS: J. SMYLIE D. DRUMMOND S. WEBB N. PAXMAN
REGISTERED IN ENGLAND No. 430725
REGISTERED OFFICE: CAUSEWAY HOUSE, 1 DANE STREET, BISHOPS STORTFORD, HERTS CM23 3BT

E.P.M. LTD
HIGH WYCH
SAWBRIDGEWORTH
HERTS CM21 0JS
TEL. 0279-600428
FAX. 0279-723846

Letterhead.

European Precision Mouldings

ENGINEERS IN PLASTIC

THE PROBLEM WITH PLASTICS

European Precision Mouldings have been engineers in the plastics industry for nearly 20 years and have always taken the attitude that **SERVICE**, and we use the capitals intentionally, is a major factor in the actual production process. As such, we not only **DESIGN** and **BUILD** the **TOOLS**, but **MANUFACTURE** the components In House, **SOURCE MATERIALS** to **YOUR SPECIFICATION** and **PRODUCT MARK** in a variety of formats, etc, etc.

INJECTION MOULD TOOL:-
DESIGNERS.
MANUFACTURERS.
PROTOTYPE AND
PRODUCTION RUNS
UNDERTAKEN.

In short, we will aid you, the customer, right from the pre-design stages to the product's final installation.

How much, or little, of this expertise you use is up to you. Many businesses can provide a comprehensive list of services but, as you will no doubt appreciate, in our case it would be quite impossible, since our service is tailored to each individual client's requirements. As such our list would closely resemble a Trade Directory, in thickness if nothing else!

SO WHERE DO WE COME IN?

The manufacture of plastic components can often seem a maze of problems, indeed even the people who work in it have been known to refer to the business as 'The Dark Art of...' So where does that leave you..............................

E.P.M. LTD
HIGH WYCH
SAWBRIDGEWORTH
HERTS CM21 0JS
TEL. 0279-600428
FAX. 0279-723846

PROPRIETORS: ENGINEERS PROTOTYPE MOULDINGS LTD
DIRECTORS: J. SMYLIE D. DRUMMOND S. WEBB N. PAXMAN
REGISTERED IN ENGLAND No. 430725
REGISTERED OFFICE: CAUSEWAY HOUSE, 1 DANE STREET, BISHOPS STORTFORD, HERTS CM23 3BT

Mailshot.

Activities and tasks

1 What is the approach made by EPM and what image is the company trying to put across?

2 Research the limitations that EPM would find in exporting to an EC country of your choice.

3 Where would EPM find information to help them assess the possibilities of a West African country?

4 Design a similar Corporate image to sell waterproof clothing to countries in central Africa.

Glossary of useful terms

Above the line Media advertising, usually aimed at the public.

ACORN A Classification Of Residential Neighbourhoods – classifies people by their housing and assumes similarities.

Added value Associating a product with high quality and good customer service. Making it appear better than the competition.

Advertising One of the techniques of informing the public of your product or service.

After-sales service Making sure that the product performs well after purchase.

Below the line Sales promotions/POS, brochures/mailshots, etc.

BRAD British Rate And Data – a publication giving a listing of media costs.

Brand image The public view of the product.

Brand name The name given to a product to differentiate it from other products.

Branding Giving a product an identity of its own.

Cash cows Products which have reached the mature stage in their product life cycle, bringing in revenue for very little cost.

Competition Defined by the experts as an organisation which produces products that are similar to something that you produce.

Competitors Any rival organisation that may take sales away from you.

Consumer The 'end-user' of the product or service. This may be the manufacturer using your product in their production process, or the customer buying from a retailer.

Consumer market A section of the community who buy products for themselves.

Consumer marketing Marketing aimed specifically at the consumer.

Consumer products Products aimed specifically at the consumer.

Consumer research Research looking into the habits/attitudes/opinions of the consumer.

Consumerism The collective power of the consumer in influencing those who provide the goods and services.

Costing The act of working out mathematically the costs of a product.

Delphi method   A panel of experts who are kept apart from each other in order not to be influenced by one another. Used in developing marketing analysis.

Demography   The study of population growth, decline and movement.

Design   The act of creating an image for a product, service or advertising campaign.

Direct mail   Making a sales approach to the customer through the post.

Direct response   The attempt to make a customer act immediately.

Discretionary income   Money that people have left after all essential spending has been done.

Disposable income   Money that people have left after tax and National Insurance payments.

Distribution   The process of getting a product or service to the customer, often measured in terms of availability and accessibility.

Dogs   Products which have reached the decline period of their life cycle.

Durables   Tangible goods that are expected to last some time, like furniture or large electrical goods.

EPOS   Electronic Point of Sales – a computerised system that reads the bar code on a product and prints out price and name on a till receipt, and assists reorders.

Exhibitions   Demonstrations of the goods or service direct to the public or the business/retail trade. Not always a selling situation.

Field research   Collecting 'first-hand' information from the consumer market.

Fixed costs   Costs which remain static whatever the level of production or sales.

Franchising   Usually a relationship set up where the franchisor provides merchandise/management help and promotional help in return for the franchisee agreeing to buy just from the franchisor and passing across a percentage of the sales.

GDP   Gross Domestic Product – total of people's earnings within a country.

Generic   A particular product type. Tea is a generic product, but PG Tips is not – it is a brand.

GNP   Gross National Product – total of country's earnings.

Hard sell   Pressurised selling direct to the consumer.

Image   The design created for a product or service, and the message given to the consumer about a product or organisation.

Industrial marketing   Marketing directed specifically at the business or industrial sector.

Inflation   A financial situation where costs and prices rise and money value decreases, which erodes the purchasing power of businesses and customers alike.

Loss leader   A product offered at a loss-making price, for example to attract customers to a shop.

Marginal costing   Policy that attempts to cover the variable costs together with a contribution to the overheads.

Market   A group of individuals or organisations who are potential buyers.

Market leader   The pre-eminent product or service in a market.

Market research   Usually refers to research about customers, competitors and markets, etc.

Market segmentation   The process of breaking down markets into groups that might usefully be targeted.

Marketing   Supplying customers with what they want, when and where they want it, at a price that both satisfies them and provides a profit.

Marketing mix   Combining marketing methods to achieve profitable exploration of the market.

Marketing research   The use of scientific methods to collect information about customers, competitors and markets, etc.

Merchandising   Part of sales promotion aimed at generating the customer's interest in a product or service.

Middlemen   People or organisations which handle distribution of the manufacturer's goods or services to the customer.

Motivation   The generation of, or the existence of, the desire to do something.

Non-durables   Tangible goods that are often used up quickly, like food for example.

Organisational market   A market where the customer is a business organisation, or a manufacturer using the product in the production of other products (eg raw materials).

Panels   Groups of consumers who record their purchases.

Perceived quality   A customer has a tendency to associate a high price with high quality. The quality may not necessarily be inherent, but the manufacturer still charges a high price.

PEST   Political, Economic, Social and Technological factors which make up the external environment that can influence an organisation.

Point of sale (POS)   Displays, posters, racks, signs, etc, by or near the product in a shop.

Positioning   The way a product or service is seen in relation to competing products in the same market segment.

Postal surveys   Mailing or distributing door-to-door of written questionnaires for potential customers to complete, and perhaps a sample of the product for them to try.

Price   The value that the seller attaches to a product or service.

Price competition   Price setting in relation to the price charged by competitors; also known as competition-orientated pricing.

Pricing   The price structure of a product or range, which takes into consideration its cost, the organisation's objectives, demand, perceived quality, the competition, distribution, legislation and regulations, etc.

Primary sources   New data.

Problem children   Products which fail to get past their launch stage in the product life cycle.

Product   Broadly, anything that is offered to a market that might satisfy a need. A product does not have to be a physical thing – it could be a service or an idea.

Product life cycle   A product's beginnings (or launch), growth, maturity and decline in popularity and sales.

Product line   A group of products which are closely related, as they are intended for a similar end use, such as Heinz soups.

Product mix   The total range of products which an organisation offers.

Profit margins   The difference between total costs and selling price of a product or service.

Profitability   The successful marrying of a good pricing policy with the costs and market situation, to give a profit to the organisation on sales of the product.

Public Relations (PR)   Activities meant to influence favourably the public's perception of an organisation.

Purchasing power   Either the disposable income or the discretionary income of the customer.

Questionnaires   A series of questions, written or orally delivered, which the respondent is invited to answer.

Research and development (R&D)   In an organisation this department is the supposed source of new ideas and suggestions on product innovation, and testing of new products where applicable.

Sales forecasts   The process of predicting sales, profits and turnover.

Sales promotion   Short-term incentives to encourage purchases.

Sampling   Investigating a representative sample of the market.

Scheduling   The planning of a media campaign by setting out the details in a timetable format.

Screening   The process of reducing a large number of product ideas to a manageably smaller number.

Secondary sources   Previously collected data.

Segmentation   The process of breaking down markets into groups with some common traits that might usefully be targeted.

Service   An intangible activity that is usually a professional skill, such as hairdressing or advertising.

Stars   Products which have successfully reached their growth stage.

Targeting   The policy of matching the organisation and its products with a market segment or segments that exhibit need for the product.

Telephone surveys   Short and to-the-point interviews over the telephone that aim to research into consumer attitudes, opinions and behaviour.

Telesales   Selling products by telephone.

Test marketing   A limited launch of a product, to test response.

Trademark   A symbol, word or picture which is associated with a particular product or a product range, and may be registered to give it legal protection.

USP   Unique selling proposition – something which makes the product unique or sufficiently different from other products.

Variable costs   Costs which vary with the value of goods made and sold.

Index